Experiencing the Gospel

Evangelical Missiological Society Monograph Series

Anthony Casey, Allen Yeh, Mark Kreitzer, and Edward L. Smither
SERIES EDITORS

———————————

A Project of the Evangelical Missiological Society
www.emsweb.org

Experiencing the Gospel

An Examination of Muslim Conversion
to Christianity in Cambodia

Thomas W. Seckler

PICKWICK *Publications* · Eugene, Oregon

EXPERIENCING THE GOSPEL
An Examination of Muslim Conversion to Christianity in Cambodia

Evangelical Missiological Society Monograph Series 5

Copyright © 2020 Thomas W. Seckler. All rights reserved. Except for brief quotations in critical publications or reviews, no part of this book may be reproduced in any manner without prior written permission from the publisher. Write: Permissions, Wipf and Stock Publishers, 199 W. 8th Ave., Suite 3, Eugene, OR 97401.

Pickwick Publications
An Imprint of Wipf and Stock Publishers
199 W. 8th Ave., Suite 3
Eugene, OR 97401

www.wipfandstock.com

PAPERBACK ISBN: 978-1-7252-5351-3
HARDCOVER ISBN: 978-1-7252-5352-0
EBOOK ISBN: 978-1-7252-5353-7

Cataloguing-in-Publication data:

Names: Seckler, Thomas W., author.

Title: Experiencing the gospel : an examination of Muslim conversion to Christianity in Cambodia. / by Thomas W. Seckler.

Description: Eugene, OR: Pickwick Publications, 2020. | Evangelical Missiological Society Monograph Series 5. | Includes bibliographical references and index.

Identifiers: ISBN 978-1-7252-5351-3 (paperback) | ISBN 978-1-7252-5352-0 (hardcover) | ISBN 978-1-7252-5353-7 (ebook)

Subjects: LCSH: Christian converts from Islam—Cambodia | Conversion—Christianity

Classification: BV2625 S43 2020 (print) | BV2625 (ebook)

Manufactured in the U.S.A.   05/12/20

To the precious ladies in my life. In order of appearance, they are my mother Jean, wife Debbie, and daughters Jessica and Sarah. Their encouragement and support have buoyed me during my studies. They are all wonderful.

Contents

List of Illustrations and Tables | x
Acknowledgments | xi
List of Abbreviations | xii

1. Research Focus | 1
    Research Concern   2
    Significance of the Research   2
    Definitions   3
    Research Context   5
    Assumptions   9
    Research Focus   9
    Research Questions   10
    Limitations   10
    Delimitations   11

2. Literature Review | 12
    Conversion in General   12
    Communication and Contextualization of the Christian Message   15
    Interaction with the Message   17
    Previous Studies on Muslim Conversion to Christianity   20

3. Methodology | 25
    Overview and Frame of Research   25
    Impact of Researcher   26
    Interviews   28
    Supplementary Data   33
    Data-Gathering and Analysis Procedures   34

CONTENTS

4. Communication and Contextualization of the Christian Message | 36
From Whom Did Cambodian BMBs Hear the Message? 36
What was Communicated? 40
What Methods Were Used in Communication? 45
How Was the Message Contextualized? 48
- Contextualization through Choice of Language 51
- Contextualization through Use of Experience-Near Terms and Concepts 54
- Contextualization through Communication within the Framework of Understanding of the Listener 60
- Materials Demonstrating Contextualization 68

How Do BMBs Communicate the Christian Message to Others? 72
Conclusion 85

5. Prominent Themes and Factors in the Conversion Process | 87
Primary Themes 89
- Sin and Cleansing 89
- Heaven and Judgment 91
- Jesus 93
  - Jesus Is 94
  - Jesus Did 94
  - Jesus Does 96
- The Bible 103

Secondary Themes 105
- Witness of Others 105
- Dreams 107
- Love 111
- A Sense of God's Leading 113

Discussion 117
Conclusion 127

CONTENTS

6. Personal Experience of the Christian Message | 128
    How Was the Message Personally Meaningful?   129
        The Message Addressed Life's Questions and Desires   129
        The Message Connected to Someone in a Personal Way   131
        God's Perceived Actions were Meaningful   136
        The Method of Communication was Meaningful   139
        The Messenger of Communication was Meaningful   143
    Discussion   144
    How do Cambodian BMBs Describe their Journeys to Belief in Jesus?   149
    How do Cambodian BMBs Describe their Current Beliefs and Lives with Jesus?   159
    Conclusion   164

7. Summary, Missiological Implications, and Recommendations | 166
    Summary   166
    Missiological Implications   168
    Recommendations   171
    Conclusion   175

Appendix A: Interview Questions | 179
Appendix B: Cloth Illustrated with Bible Stories | 181
Bibliography | 183
Author Index | 189
Interviewee Index | 191

Illustrations

1. Primary Locations of Western Cham in Cambodia | 9
2. Map of Cambodian Provinces | 31
3. Primary and Secondary Factors Affecting Individuals in Conversion | 116
4. Factors Contributing to the Message Being Viewed as Personally Meaningful | 148
5. Cloth Illustrated with Bible Stories | 181

Tables

1. Statistical Information about Muslims in Cambodia | 8
2. Woodberry's Findings of What God is Using in Individual Conversions | 21
3. Home Locations of Interviewees by Province or City | 30
4. Primary and Secondary Factors in Conversion | 115

Acknowledgments

WHILE PRIMARILY MY OWN work, this monograph is formed and supported by the work of many others. I want to thank my professors at Trinity Evangelical Divinity School. Their combined instruction has molded, challenged, and inspired me. I particularly want to thank Dr. Robert Priest and Dr. Craig Ott. Their expertise in areas related to this dissertation has been invaluable, and their support and direction have instilled confidence.

Forty Cambodian followers of Christ courageously met with me and agreed to be interviewed. They willingly shared their stories, thoughts, experiences, and at times emotions. What they communicated provides the basis for this study. Thank you.

I want to thank four Cambodian staff members, Tevy, Rony, Mael, and Nael, who worked several months to transcribe and translate the recorded interviews. They carried out this tedious and demanding task with optimism and perseverance.

My wife, Debbie, has not only been steadfast in her support and encouragement but also assisted in numerous ways including editing the manuscript. Thank you for being my wife, and for being at my side during this entire process.

Finally, I would like to thank the Almighty God, who has loved me, accepted and adopted me, and has allowed me the privilege to both serve him and to study. This work is because of him and for him.

Abbreviations

BMB	Believer in Christ from a Muslim Background
CD	Compact Disk
MBB	Muslim Background Believer
MFC	Muslim Follower of Christ
NGO	Non-Governmental Organization
RQ	Research Question

1

Research Focus

RELIGIOUS CONVERSION IS BOTH complicated and fascinating. It often introduces marked changes into one's life, relationships, and perspectives. It is thus not surprising that scholars such as psychologist William James or anthropologist Joel Robbins have devoted attention to this topic. Missiologists have also expressed interest in religious conversion, partially because a better understanding of it can lead to the clearer communication of the gospel message to others.

Context can significantly impact both the openness of individuals or groups to convert to another religion and also the frequency of conversions. Followers of Islam have historically been among the least likely to convert to Christianity. Various social factors doubtless help account for the pattern, including both the inconceivability that one would leave the fold of Islam and the strong social sanctions that often follow when one does, ranging from criticism to outright persecution. And yet in recent decades, in a wide variety of regions of the world, there have been dramatically increasing numbers of those from Muslim backgrounds who have become followers of Christ.[1] While some quality studies have been completed on the subject of people from a Muslim background converting to Christ,[2] more research is needed on this topic. Previous studies have often focused on general factors that attracted individuals to Jesus or influenced their conversion. One's interaction with the message itself has not been studied as deeply, including how the gospel message was experienced as personally meaningful. This more narrow focus is one of the objectives of this Cambodian study. Most research conducted by others has occurred

---

1. Miller and Johnstone, "Believers in Christ"; Garrison, *Wind in the House of Islam*.

2. E.g., Bultema, "Muslims Coming to Christ"; Gaudeul, *Called from Islam to Christ*; Greenham, "Study of Palestinian Muslim Conversions"; Greenlee, "Christian Conversion from Islam"; Hoskins, "Conversion Narratives"; Woodberry et al., "Why Muslims Follow Jesus."

in locations where Islam is the majority religion and/or among majority ethnic groups in those locations (for example, studies in North Africa and the Middle East). While those studies are valuable, few have been conducted on Muslims in areas where they are the minority religion or are a minority ethnic group. The Cambodian context provides an opportunity to study religious conversion among individuals whose ethnic group and background religion are both a minority in that country. Cambodia is also located in Southeast Asia, where few studies have been completed about Muslim conversion to Christianity, but where significant populations of Muslims exist. Some previous studies have utilized primarily a quantitative approach with the use of surveys.[3] Information gained from this method is helpful, but the qualitative approach used in this Cambodian study offers the opportunity to gather rich data about the manner in which Muslim-background individuals have interacted with the gospel message.

Research Concern

Cambodia is one context where conversion is occurring among those who have traditionally followed Islam. The majority of Muslims in Cambodia identify with the Cham ethnic group. Cambodian Muslims (Cham and otherwise) are a minority among the majority Buddhist-background inhabitants, and they have deep historical roots in Islam. However, in recent years there have been a small but growing number of Cambodian Muslims who self-identify as followers of *Isa* (Jesus) or as Christians. The conversion of Muslim background people to Christianity in Cambodia has previously not been studied.

Significance of the Research

On the social scientific level, this study is significant in that it increases understanding about religious conversion, specifically about conversion from Islam to Christianity. More narrowly, this research seeks to understand one of the most fundamental aspects of religious conversion, the impact of the religious message itself in the lives of humans. One's conscience, will, intellect, and emotions may all be involved in this complex process, as well as external actors such as other humans. Interaction with

---

3. E.g., Woodberry et al., "Why Muslims Follow Jesus."

a religious message and conversion is often powerful and life-changing. It needs to be more fully understood.[4] A focus of this study is thus that of messaging. First, how is the religious message communicated? Second, how is the message understood by individuals and how do they perceive it as personally meaningful and compelling—in short, how is the message experienced by those who receive it?

The above insights have missiological implications. Clarity on these issues impacts both how people present a religious message and how people understand and assist individuals or groups who have converted. It also informs the process of contextualization; specifically the communication of a message in a manner which is naturally understandable and resonates with one's lived experience. These findings can benefit both those working in a Muslim context and those working in areas where other belief systems are prevalent. This research also reveals additional insights about Muslim conversion to Christianity in general, including which factors or experiences are influential in the process of deciding to follow Jesus. The findings in this study add to the body of knowledge about reasons for Muslim conversion to Christianity as discovered by other scholars.

Definitions

I will define three phrases: Christian conversion, Christian message, and Believer in Christ from a Muslim background (BMB). In addition, I will delineate between the terms "Cham" and "Muslim."

Christian Conversion

Although there are many good definitions of religious conversion in general, for this study a more specific description of Christian conversion is helpful. John Stott clarifies that in the Bible the term conversion usually describes turning, either a change in direction or a return to a former place.

---

4. Regarding the need for research, see Skreslet, who in reviewing doctoral dissertations from 1992 to 2001 revealed that only 3 out of over 900 were based on the topic categorized as "Conversion, and Islam" ("Doctoral Dissertations," 126). In the article reviewing the subsequent decade, Priest and DeGeorge noted that only approximately three percent of dissertations focused on "World A" countries, defined as those "where less than 50% of the people have been evangelized" ("Doctoral Dissertations on Mission," 200). Cambodia can be considered a World A country.

The essence and primary components of conversion are thus seen in his following quote: "Since the turn from idols and sin is usually called 'repentance,' and the turn to God and Christ 'faith,' we reach the interesting biblical equation that 'repentance + faith = conversion.'" Furthermore, Stott clearly delineates between conversion, which features the human response, and regeneration, which is wholly God's act of providing a new birth "from above."[5] As a human response, conversion can be studied empirically, whereas God's work of regeneration cannot. Stott's discussion and "equation" above provides a framework for this study.

Christian Message

For this research, the Christian message (or gospel message) is defined as follows: *The Christian message is the good news about who Christ is and what he has done for sinful humanity, including the historical facts, the personal demands, and the implications for life. This message contains truth about the human condition and also about God, Jesus Christ, the Holy Spirit, and their combined work. It invites a response and potentially impacts one's life.* There are multiple facets to the Christian message, and Cambodians in this study focused on various aspects of the message at various times. The terms "Christian message," "gospel," and "gospel message" will be used interchangeably in this document.

A Believer in Christ from a Muslim Background (BMB)

Across the globe, there are individuals originating from Muslim contexts who have decided to follow Christ. They are genuine believers, living under Christ's authority and for his glory. These people have been commonly referred to as Muslim background believers (MBBs). Miller and Johnstone prefer the use of the term BMBs (believers in Christ from a Muslim background), as this emphasizes the current beliefs of the individual rather than their previous affiliation.[6] I agree and am choosing to use this term as well, instead of the more common "MBB." Some BMBs (BMB when singular) in the world continue to identify as Muslims, and may be referred to as Muslim followers of Christ (MFCs), which is explained by Higgins, Jameson

---

5. Stott, *Christian Mission*, 168-69.
6. Miller and Johnstone, "Believers in Christ," 13.

and Talman as "These followers of Christ from Muslim backgrounds consider themselves and are seen by their friends, family, and communities as Muslims."[7] Others, however, choose not to identify themselves as Muslim. In Cambodia, I am unaware of any followers of Christ from a Muslim background who continue to identify as Muslim. I thus choose to use the singular term BMB in this study, instead of MFC as well.

"Cham" vs. "Muslim"

The use of "Cham" vs. "Muslim" should be delineated for this project. The Muslim population in Cambodia as of 2016 is 371,000.[8] The majority of these identify with the Cham ethnic group who descended from the ancient Champa kingdom. Collins distinguishes three major groups of Cham in Cambodia, the traditional *Jahed* or *Imam San*, the large group of *Chang Wang*, and the *Chvea*, who speak the Khmer language but not the Cham language, and who do not necessarily identify as Cham.[9] This study includes respondents from all three of the above groups. Each of the groups clearly identifies as Muslim, but only two strongly view themselves as Cham. Thus for this document, the broader term "Muslim" will be used instead of "Cham."

Research Context

It is important to understand the context for this study. Muslims in Cambodia are a minority in this Buddhist-majority nation. Their population of 371,000 is approximately 2.5 percent of the Cambodian population, which totaled 14,676,591 in 2013.[10] The vast majority of Cambodians are members of the Khmer ethnic group, which is traditionally Buddhist.[11] Most Muslims

---

7. Higgins et al., "Myths and Misunderstandings," 41.
8. Department of Non-Buddhist Religion, "Statistical Chart."
9. Collins, "Muslims of Cambodia," 60–62, 66, 77.
10. National Institute of Statistics, "Population Survey 2013 Final Report," vi. "General Population Census of Cambodia 2008," 19, projected a 2017 population figure of 15,848,495.
11. The Cambodian National Institute of Statistics identifies 97 percent of Cambodians as having the Khmer language as their mother tongue (14,244,330 out of a total of 14,671,591), and 98 percent of Cambodians as following the Buddhist religion (14,367,081 out of a total of 14,671,081) (National Institute of Statistics, "Inter-Censal Population Survey 2013," 10, 22).

in Cambodia claim ancestry from the ancient Champa Kingdom in Vietnam. Collins describes four separate migrations from Vietnam to present-day Cambodia between the years of 1471 and 1835 as a result of conflict with the Vietnamese and other peoples.[12] Further details about the major groups of Cham in Cambodia are described as follows. The first group, the traditional *Jahed*, cling to their ancient religious practices and identify themselves as those who worship only one time per week. This group is also referred to as the *Imam San*, and constitutes ten percent or less of all Cambodian Muslims.[13] They are fluent in the Cham language, value the ancient Cham script, and are skilled in reading it, unlike the other two groups.[14] The second group is the *Chvea*, who practice Islam regularly but do not speak the Cham language. Rather, they speak only Khmer.[15] The term "Chvea" is the Khmer word used for Java, which points to the likely ancestry from Muslims who came from the Malay-Indonesia area. Thus they are not likely direct descendants of the Champa kingdom, though they do strongly adhere to Islam. In Cambodia, they sometimes refer to themselves as "Khmer Islam," pointing to their identity as Cambodians but with a separate religion of Islam.[16] The third group is the *Cham* or *Chang Wang*. They comprise the majority of Cham people, generally practice Islam in a more orthodox way, and value their close ties with Malaysia.[17] The final two groups pray five times per day as Muslims around the world are accustomed to. The first group of the *Jahed*, by contrast, prays only once per week, mid-day on Fridays, according to instructions given by a previous influential religious teacher, Imam San. Thus one clear demarcation between Cham groups identified by themselves is that some formally pray five times per day and others only one time per week.[18] Another demarcation lies between the two

---

12. Collins, "Muslims of Cambodia," 21–33. The Cham living in Cambodia are known as the Western Cham ethnic group, Grimes, *Ethnologue*, 1:394. A remnant of Champa descendants still exist in Vietnam. They have a unique language and culture and are known ethnically as the Eastern Cham. For the remainder of this document, the Western Cham in Cambodia will be referred to simply as the "Cham."

13. Collins, "Muslims of Cambodia," 60, 62, 66; Eng, "From the Khmer Rouge to Hambali," 48.

14. Trankell and Ovesen, "Muslim Minorities," 23; Maunati and Sari, "Construction of Cham Identity," 108.

15. Collins, "Muslims of Cambodia," 77.

16. Trankell and Ovesen, "Muslim Minorities," 22.

17. Collins, "Muslims of Cambodia," 61–62.

18. Maunati and Sari, "Construction of Cham Identity," 124, 113.

groups who are descendants from the Champa kingdom (the *Jahed* and the *Cham/Chang Wang*) versus the *Chvea* whose ancestors originated in the Malay-Indonesia area. The majority of those interviewed in this study identified as "Cham,"[19] and three individuals identified themselves as "Khmer Islam." Khmer Islam interviewees, who are fluent in Khmer but not Cham, were interviewed in the Khmer language. The majority of other interviews were conducted in the Cham language.

Setudeh-Nejad clearly states that the Cham people, although a minority group, exhibit a "strong cultural identity."[20] Other scholars, however, note that this identity is not simply one entity but is "fluid and contested".[21] In his dissertation, Eng identifies two core and three peripheral identities of contemporary Cham. The core identities are being Muslim and "descendants from Champa whose indigenous language is Cham." The secondary identities are sectarian, economic, and political.[22] In his writings, Collins concludes that two key challenges for the Cham are, "how to preserve their distinct identity as a minority, and how to secure their livelihood in a changing economy".[23] This is not surprising, especially with the attention that Muslims in Cambodia have recently received, particularly from the Islamic world. Pereiro writes,

> Since . . . 1993, the Cambodian Muslim community has undergone a rapid transformation from being an Islamic minority on the periphery of the Muslim world to being the object of intense proselytization by foreign Islamic organizations, charities and development organizations. This has led to a period of religious as well as political ferment in which Cambodian Muslims are reassessing their relationships to other Muslim communities in the country, fellow Muslims outside of the country, and an officially Buddhist state.[24]

Although they are a minority population and often live in rural areas, Cambodian Muslims are not religiously isolated. They are being influenced

---

19. "Cham" here refers to those who consider themselves descendants from the Champa kingdom and includes individuals from both the *Jahed* and the *Cham/Chang Wang* groups.
20. Setudeh-Nejad, "Cham Muslims of Southeast Asia," 451.
21. Maunati and Sari, "Construction of Cham Identity," 108.
22. Eng, "From the Khmer Rouge to Hambali," ii.
23. Collins, "Muslims of Cambodia," 97.
24. Pereiro, "Historical Imagination," i.

in many ways, including by various Non-Governmental Organizations (NGOs) or conservative Islamic movements such as the Tablīghī Jamāʿat (known in Cambodia as Daʿwah Tabligh).[25] Christian NGOs have also worked among Muslims in Cambodia, and some Muslims have chosen to embrace Christianity. Though few in number, there are remarkably more BMBs in Cambodia now than in the year 2000, when it was estimated there were less than ten Christian believers.[26]

The Cambodian Ministry of Cults and Religion provides the following statistical information regarding Muslims in Cambodia:[27]

Table 1. Statistical Information about Muslims in Cambodia

Subject	Total Number
Muslims in Cambodia	371,132
Mosques	487
Prayer Centers (smaller than mosques)	576
Muslim Schools	363

Over 90 percent of Muslims in Cambodia follow the Sunni branch of Islam. Of the four main divisions existing within Sunni Islam, nearly all Cambodian Muslims are associated with the Shafi'i branch.[28] Geographically, Muslims in Cambodia can be found in nearly all provinces, but they are concentrated in central Cambodia, often along the major rivers, as traditionally many are involved in the fishing industry. Figure 1 provides visual information about the location of Cham Muslims in Cambodia.[29]

---

25. Collins, "Muslims of Cambodia," 94–95; Bruckmayr, "Cham Muslims of Cambodia," 11.

26. After conducting this research, I estimate there are 300–400 Cambodian BMBs, although any figure is hard to confirm. Miller and Johnstone use a figure of 1,100 ("Believers in Christ"). The estimate in the year 2000 was informal and was done by the author and others.

27. Department of Non-Buddhist Religion, "Statistical Chart."

28. Eng, "From the Khmer Rouge to Hambali," 43, 48, 49.

29. Joshua Project and Bethany World Prayer Center, "Cham in Cambodia."

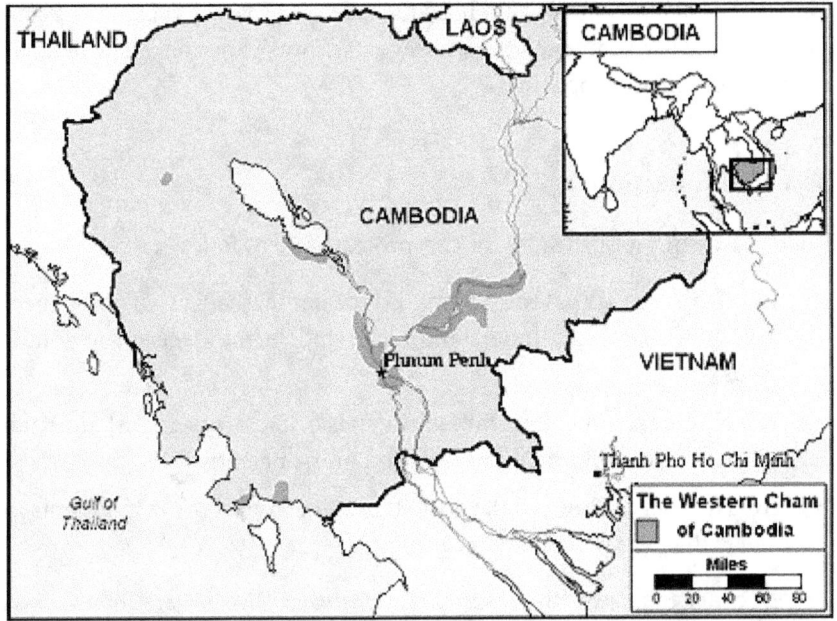

Figure 1. Primary Locations of Western Cham in Cambodia

Assumptions

This research is based on three assumptions. First, the Christian message is meaningful to many people. It may challenge, assist, or convict them, but it is important to them. Second, people are able to communicate about their interaction with the message and how it is meaningful to them. Although they may be talking about previous events, they are able to reflect on them and on their importance in their lives. Third, the manner in which the message is communicated can influence both how well it is comprehended and how it is perceived by those hearing it, including its personal relevance and desirability.

Research Focus

This study examined and analyzed the conversions of forty Cambodian Muslims to Christianity, with particular focus on (1) examining the role of contextual adjustments made to make the Christian message more understandable and compelling, (2) identifying core themes or factors that converts report as central in their own conversions, and (3) exploring and analyzing the ways in which the message itself was experienced as personally meaningful and appealing.

Research Questions

The research questions (RQs) for this project were as follows:

1. RQ Number 1: What role, if any, did the contextualization of the message play in clearly understanding it, and in the decision to follow Jesus?
2. RQ Number 2: What prominent themes or factors were instrumental in the conversion process as revealed in the narratives?
3. RQ Number 3: How did the gospel message impact the respondents in a way that was personally meaningful?

In order to answer these research questions, BMBs were interviewed and were encouraged to share their personal story about deciding to believe in and follow Jesus. This invitation to share their personal story was the initial topic in all interviews. Follow-up questions were asked based on what the interviewee shared. In addition, questions were asked about such topics as how they received the message, what interested them in it, why it was important to them, and how they communicate it to others in a way which is clearly understood. Discussion around these and other questions revealed answers to the research questions.[30] Chapter 4 of this document addresses RQ number one above, whereas chapters 5 and 6 focus on RQ's number two and three respectively.

Limitations

The scope of this study is limited to believers in Christ from a Muslim background in Cambodia. Although the *Chang Wang* group represents the largest number of Cham, it appears that a larger proportion from the *Imam San* group has become followers of Christ. One limitation is that there are not many BMBs in Cambodia (approximately three to four hundred total). Second, the BMBs are living in various locations around the country, many of which are remote. Although I was able to travel to many

---

30. A complete list of interview questions is found in Appendix 1.

locations, it was not possible to visit all the locations where BMBs reside. Third, some BMBs are not interested in being interviewed. Reasons for this may include their unfamiliarity with me as a foreigner, their perception that they are not knowledgeable or clever in speech, or their fear of being widely known as a follower of Christ. Muslim conversion to Christianity is understandably a sensitive topic in Cambodia. In addition, the atrocities experienced during the reign of Pol Pot and the Khmer Rouge (1975–1978), when at times children and others spied on individuals and provided information about them to the authorities, have led to many Cambodians not easily trusting others.[31] Thus they are sometimes reluctant in providing personal information.

Delimitations

There are four delimitations in this study. First, only individuals eighteen years old or older were interviewed. Second, only those individuals who fit the criteria as someone who identified as a follower of Christ were interviewed. This excluded current followers of Islam, and also Muslims who were sympathetic to Christianity. In addition, the respondents all lived within the borders of Cambodia.[32] The third delimitation is that only forty individuals were interviewed. Although there are many more BMBs in Cambodia, it is felt that forty people constitute an adequate sample size to allow rich information to be gathered. Fourth, this research focused on the interaction of a person with the biblical message. It is understood that many other factors may be involved in the process of conversion. Some of these were revealed in the course of this study and were investigated. Findings related to these factors are reported in chapter 5. The focus of this study, however, was primarily on the phenomenon about how one interacts with, experiences, and is personally impacted by the gospel message.

---

31. Ross, *Cambodia*, 57; McKenzie-Pollock, "Cambodian Families," 291, 293, 297.

32. There is a small population of (Western) Cham people living in the neighboring country of Vietnam. It is unclear, however, if any are BMBs.

2

Literature Review

THIS REVIEW OF PREVIOUS research is organized along four major topics: conversion in general, the communication and contextualization of the Christian message, the reception of and interaction with the message, and previous studies of Muslim conversion to Christianity.

Conversion in General

Many authors highlight the aspect of "turning" or "change" as essential to the definition of conversion, especially conversion to Christianity.[1] David Kling identifies the New Testament Greek terms *epistrephein* (meaning to turn back or return), and *metanoia* (meaning to think again or repent) as central to the Christian understanding of conversion.[2] An encounter with Christ is fundamental to Gordon Smith's understanding of Christian conversion, and the act of converting—deciding to believe in and follow Jesus—is seen as a response to that encounter.[3] Paul Hiebert writes of bounded and centered sets and suggests the concept of *direction* is helpful in understanding conversion, whether people are moving toward God or away from him.[4]

Andrew Walls identifies two broad understandings of conversion, that of it being an "external act of religious change," or "critical internal religious change in persons."[5] Arthur Nock delineates between "adhesion," where one accepts new worship forms as supplements to their current practice, but not as a new replacement of their old life, and "conversion,"

---

1. Walls, "Converts or Proselytes?" 2, 6; Peace, "Conflicting Understandings of Conversion," 8.
2. Kling, "Conversion to Christianity," 598.
3. Smith, *Beginning Well*, 16.
4. Hiebert, *Anthropological Reflections*, 124–26.
5. Walls, "Converts or Proselytes?" 2.

LITERATURE REVIEW

which involves a radical reorientation of the inner soul of a person, with an understanding that "the old was wrong and the new is right."[6] For some, religious conversion is primarily an external act; for others, it is a profound internal reorientation. It is understood that for certain individuals, conversion is mere external change or religious "switching."[7] This study, however, is concerned with conversion experienced as personal internal change, which often includes different beliefs and understandings than previously held. Moreover, in many Islamic contexts, conversion to Christianity comes with risks and is therefore done only after much consideration. I characterize the vast majority of interviewees involved in this study as experiencing conversions of significant internal religious change.

Lewis Rambo has written, "Conversion is a process of religious change that takes place in a dynamic force field of people, events, ideologies, institutions, expectations, and orientations."[8] This definition emphasizes the myriad factors impacting conversion, many of them external to the individual. Many scholars have sought to identify and understand these factors, ranging from the influence of others in their sphere of relationships,[9] personal psychological characteristics and motivations,[10] individual crisis,[11] biographical events,[12] desire for perceived benefits,[13] etc. These factors are important, and the study of them is valuable. This study, however, focuses primarily on the impact of the religious message itself in influencing conversion.

Some scholars such as Ines Jindra have pointed to the importance of the religious message itself in conversion. In her study of conversion in the United States, she concluded that "religious belief" theory, which is tied to the content of the message, was better in explaining her data than network theory, which focuses on the influence of social relationships. One of her main conclusions is thus that religious content matters, especially, for instance, when one is seeking to change their lives from a problematic

---

6. Nock, *Conversion*, 7.

7. Streib discusses six potential deconversion pathways. One of them is "religious switching," in which the change is made to a "quite similar system of religious beliefs and rituals" ("Deconversion," 272).

8. Rambo, *Understanding Religious Conversion*, 5.

9. Lofland and Stark, "Becoming a World-Saver"; Stark and Finke, *Acts of Faith*.

10. James, *Varieties of Religious Experience Study*; Starbuck, *Psychology of Religion*.

11. Rambo, "Psychology of Conversion," 165; Smith, *Beginning Well*, 47–48.

12. Lofland and Stark, "Becoming a World-Saver," 870, 874; Jindra, *New Model of Religious Conversion*, 89, 96.

13. Stark and Finke, *Acts of Faith*, 117; Woodberry, "Conversion in Islam," 38.

trajectory to something better. Jindra challenges scholars to honestly consider the content of the religious message when interpreting the conversion of others, instead of only looking at factors such as crisis experiences and education.[14] Other researchers such as Hefner and Robbins have also noted the importance of the religious message and doctrine itself as important in the conversion process.[15] This Cambodian study seeks to study conversion in a way that retains a central focus on conversion as a response to specific religious messages and meanings.

Traditionally conversion was often seen as a point-in-time encounter. William James, for example, often studied individuals who had remarkable conversion experiences, many which were of a crisis nature. For him, the sudden or crisis essence of a religious event contributed to its definition as a conversion.[16] Radical discontinuity is reflected in these experiences. Contemporary scholars such as Robbins and VanKlinken have also emphasized rupture as part of the experience of conversion to Christ, where significant changes occur in the lives of the converts.[17] Others have drawn attention to conversion as a process, which occurs over time and may involve a series of decisions, usually gradual and even spanning a lifetime.[18] Discontinuity may still be evident, but it may occur over time, punctuated by key experiences.

Some researchers have sought to identify common waypoints of these processes. Tippett's schematization describing group conversion, for example, utilizes periods of time punctuated with intense points of realization or encounter (a period of awareness followed by a point of realization, then a period of decision followed by a point of encounter, then a period of incorporation).[19] Hibbert utilizes Tippett's model and, in applying it to Muslim and Hindu cultures, advocates the addition of another stage, that of identity negotiation.[20] Rambo proposes a sequential seven stage model of conversion consisting of the following elements: context, crisis, quest,

14. Jindra, *New Model of Conversion*, 17, 21, 156, 186; Jindra, "How Religious Content Matters," 275.

15. Hefner, "World Building," 12; Robbins, *Becoming Sinners*, 101.

16. James, *Varieties of Religious Experience Study*, 112.

17. Robbins, *Becoming Sinners*; Robbins, "Globalization"; Van Klinken, "Men in the Remaking."

18. Rambo, "Psychology of Conversion," 165; Smith, *Beginning Well*, 31; Hibbert, "Negotiating Identity," 62; Richardson and Stewart, "Conversion Process Models," 24–25.

19. Tippett, "Conversion as a Dynamic Process," 207.

20. Hibbert, "Negotiating Identity."

encounter, interaction, commitment, and consequences.[21] These stages do describe human decisions, but they do not necessarily reveal information about how people were responding to their perceptions of a deity such as God or messages about the deity. Moreover, the perspective that religious conversion is often fundamentally focused on God is not clearly evident in Rambo's model. The above models and schematizations broadly cover all possible phases of conversion. While helpful, the models do not clarify what message or messages are being considered, nor what conversion means to those involved. Those questions are best answered through personal discussions with converts. Individual conversion experiences often do not exhibit each of the phases described above, but they usually do include some type of process, whether short or long.

Communication and Contextualization of the Christian Message

Scott Moreau, Gary Corwin, and Gary McGee provide the following description of contextualization, "The core idea is that of taking the gospel to a new context and finding appropriate ways to communicate it so that it is understandable to the people in that context. Contextualization refers to more than just theology; it also includes developing church life and ministry that are biblically faithful and culturally appropriate."[22] They highlight that the message is to be communicated in an appropriate way in order for it to be readily understood among those in that specific context. In discussing contextualization, Paul Hiebert writes, "While it is true that the gospel is divine revelation and therefore, in one sense, unchanging, it must be communicated in terms of their language, culture, and worldview for humans to understand it."[23]

Clear communication often involves the use of language and terms which are readily understandable. Robert Priest's research among the Aguaruna-Jívaro ethnic group in Peru revealed that the vocabulary used in both discovering and describing their sin was not imported from the outside but rather already existed in their own culture as ordinary words commonly used. He utilized the term "experience-near" to describe

---

21. Rambo, *Understanding Religious Conversion*, 165–69.
22. Moreau et al., *Introducing World Missions*, 16.
23. Hiebert, "Worldview Transformation," 28.

this.[24] The "experience-near" concept can be applied not only to terms used but also broadened to include worldview perspectives, beliefs, and topics which are familiar. That is, communicating a message in a manner which acknowledges the perspectives and beliefs of the listener can make it more understandable and personally applicable. This approach reinforces Hiebert's statement above about the importance of communicating the gospel message in "terms of their language, culture, and worldview." As will be noted later, the experience-near terminology is also applicable to the perspectives many Cambodian BMBs have developed about God. Their words revealed that they experienced him as near, personal, and involved in their lives, which contains parallels with experience-near language that is intimate and familiar.

The use of familiar and easy-to-understand metaphors and illustrations aids in clear communication. Craig Ott describes the importance of metaphor in both communicating meaning and impacting emotions and the affect. He identifies four biblical metaphors describing the gospel: law, relationship, cleansing, and deliverance. Ott notes that each of these metaphors communicates biblical truth, but that they may resonate differently in different cultures. Utilizing the appropriate metaphor for a specific context is thus important for proper communication and may powerfully influence understanding and emotions.[25] The use of metaphor is an example of how the biblical message is communicated and potentially speaks to an individual or group.

Sometimes the message is communicated well through stories. Jack Colgate notes the effect chronological Bible storying and point-of-need Bible storying have had in communicating the gospel to Muslims in a manner which is understandable and relevant.[26] All of the above communication methods can assist in clarifying the message and making it personal.

---

24. Priest, "I Discovered My Sin!," 96–97; Priest, "'Experience-Near Theologizing,'" 190–91.

25. Ott, "Power of Biblical Metaphors," 360–62, 370.

26. Chronological Bible storying is described as "a method of presenting scriptural truth through telling a series of Bible stories that maintain the chronological flow of Scripture," whereas point-of-need Bible storying is when "a single bible story is told to address a particular need" (Colgate, "Bible Storying," 221–22).

Interaction with the Message

Many scholars have written about how people interact with the Christian message and perceive it as personally meaningful. One aspect of interaction is a feeling that the message addresses one personally. As defined earlier, the human act of conversion includes both repentance and belief (or faith) in Jesus. Implied in the above is an understanding of one's personal sin, as well as a conviction that belief in Jesus is important in one's life. Priest's research among the Aguaruna-Jívaro revealed that the topic of personal sin was a significant one for many in their conversion to Christianity.[27] The Aguarunan language contains a term for God (*Apajui*). It also contains multiple words describing various types of wrongdoing and evil, which were understood and attributed primarily to others, not to self. A sense of personal sin was not generally prevalent before hearing the Christian message. Many who later converted, however, spoke of a realization that they were *personally* guilty of wrongdoing, some actions that were already disapproved by their own culture and others which were not. This personal realization was often tied to hearing the "word of God" (discourse understood as coming from *Apajui*) and can be described as seeing or discovering oneself as a sinner. This word of God was not just a bad word, but also a good word that spoke of a good path which was appealing. Hearing about both the good and the bad contributed to this personal realization of sin. Individuals came to view some previous actions as sinful, and some feared punishment from God, which was connected in part to both their previous fears of retaliation by human enemies when a homicide occurred and from the realization that God sees all and is able to punish. A more prominent theme in conversion, however, was the opportunity to have a personal relationship with God and walk with him.[28] The Christian message connected to the lived realities of people in a powerful way.

Priest also introduces two concepts which affect how one receives a message about personal sin, and which also may decrease one's internal resistance.[29] The first is the communication of the message in story form, which allows one to imagine themselves in the narrative. The second is the hearing of sin described in the lives of others. As previously noted, the use

---

27. Priest, "I Discovered My Sin!," 95–97, 100–101.
28. Priest, "I Discovered My Sin!," 100, 103, 105.
29. Priest, "Tell Me," 5.

of story can assist in the clear communication of the gospel message.[30] This method can contribute to the message being viewed as personal, including understanding individual sin.

Peter Stromberg uses the term "impression point" to illustrate a meaningful experience where an individual gains a new and profound understanding of oneself. He describes it as "a symbolic phenomenon in which a new understanding of self, a new understanding of a symbol system, and a feeling of commitment are all generated at once."[31] What was previously unclear becomes crystallized. Stromberg applies the concept of impression point to religious conversion, using St. Augustine's conversion as an example. He argues that the passage that Augustine read during his profound experience, Rom 13:13, directly connects with Augustine's circumstances and is an instance where "the Word and experience merge."[32] Stromberg identifies an example of a life-changing experience in which symbol, intellect, and emotions interact powerfully. Stromberg and Priest describe meaningful experiences individuals have regarding the gospel message and a sense of personal sin. Others, such as James, have documented various examples of individuals wrestling with a message, acknowledging a connection between it and their own lives, feeling convicted by personal wrongdoing before God, and later embracing the message.[33]

Joel Robbins researched Christian conversion among the isolated Urapmin ethnic group in Papua New Guinea. Robbins observed that the gospel message impacted the Urapmin profoundly and that the conversion process appeared to have two stages.[34] The first, portrayed as utilitarian, was for the potential benefits that could be obtained, including regaining status in the context of humiliation. The second stage, which occurred later and was termed intellectualist, was one in which the message helped give meaning about the people and the rapidly changing world around them. It may be debated whether or not the first stage was a one of sincere conversion to God and a message about him. In this second stage, however, God was central, and information from him about humans and the world in which they live was meaningful. One way the

---

30. Colgate, "Bible Storying."
31. Stromberg, "Impression Point," 61.
32. Stromberg, "Impression Point," 60.
33. James, *Varieties of Religious Experience Study*, 90–92, 109.
34. Robbins, *Becoming Sinners*, 14, 15, 35, 87, 114–15.

gospel message is seen as personally important is when it answers questions being considered and addresses felt needs.

Conscience is another factor involved in an individual's interaction with a religious message. Priest states that conscience is naturally occurring inside every human being. Although it is given by God, it is not supernatural in itself. That is, it does not require a supernatural agency in order to function.[35] This does not mean, however, that supernatural agency is not involved in conversion. In discussing the response of King David in the Bible after being confronted for sinful behavior by Nathan (2 Sam 12:1–14), Priest observes that there are two elements involved, a message proclaimed from the outside, and the inner conscience of David. He notes that David's conscience affirmed the truth of this external message about himself. Priest thus writes that in the proclamation of the Christian message, there is often an appeal to the conscience of the individual, and that this conscience can "bear witness" to the truth of the message about the person. Furthermore, the Holy Spirit is involved, working through both the communicated message, which is external to the person, and also the internal conscience of that person to foster a sense of conviction of sin.[36] Other authors have emphasized the role of the Holy Spirit as one interacts with the biblical message about sin, self, and salvation through Christ.[37] In Harding's study of fundamental Christianity in the United States, she noted the clear perception by many that the Holy Spirit was at work during the conversion process.[38] David Wells writes, "Without the convincing work of the Holy Spirit, conversion would not be desirable."[39] John Stott argues that it is only the Holy Spirit who can open the eyes and bring light to the darkness of people.[40] The above discussion highlights the role of the supernatural in conversion. The focus of this study is the manner in which humans choose to follow Jesus. People are making decisions, and some indicate that their perception about God's involvement is part of the decision process. They communicate that God's leading and/or the activities of their conscience contribute towards the message impacting them personally.

35. Priest, "Missionary Elenctics," 291, 294.
36. Priest, "Missionary Elenctics," 292.
37. E.g., Engel, "Road to Conversion," 187, 192.
38. Harding, Book of Jerry Falwell, 36, 60.
39. Wells, Turning to God, 21.
40. Stott, Christian Mission, 186.

Previous Studies on Muslim Conversion to Christianity

Previous research has yielded valuable insights. Woodberry, Shubin, and Marks examined surveys of seven hundred fifty Muslims who had committed to following Christ.[41] The respondents originated from thirty nations and represented fifty ethnic groups. The researchers identified three prominent factors influencing conversion: "seeing a lived faith," "the message is the medium," and "subconscious influences." That article was written after an original one in 2001, in which data for one hundred twenty of the respondents were analyzed. In the 2001 article, six categories of findings are revealed,[42] and the theme of love was emphasized, with the authors stating that, for the largest number of individuals in their study, love was the most compelling reason for turning to Jesus. Love was categorized in two ways: love demonstrated to people by followers of Christ, and love coming directly from God and revealed in the Bible. In a different publication, Woodberry discusses findings from six hundred fifty people who had completed his questionnaire.[43] Under the topic, "What God is Using in Individual Conversions," he lists two categories and prioritizes items which influenced conversion under each category. The first category is "Influence of Experience," and the second is titled "Spiritual Needs Better Answered by Faith in Christ."[44] The following table summarizes his findings.

---

41. The authors note that the survey was an "extensive questionnaire" on the fundamental question about their decision to follow Christ. The respondents originated from all major Muslim regions in the world. In the survey, "The participants ranked the relative importance of different influences and whether they occurred before, at the time of, or after their decision to follow Christ." The authors note that this survey "does not claim scientific precision," but that it does offer a glimpse of the key ways in which God's Spirit is affecting Muslim hearts (Woodberry et al., "Why Muslims Follow Jesus," 82).

42. The six categories of findings are (1) a sure salvation, (2) Jesus, (3) A holy book: the power of the Bible, (4) I have had a dream, (5) The greatest of these is love, and (6) and I have called you friends: relationship with God (Woodberry and Shubin, "Muslims Tell," 2–6).

43. Woodberry, "Global Perspective," 14–17.

44. Data from the same survey appears to be used for three articles written at different times: Woodberry and Shubin, "Muslims Tell"; Woodberry, "Global Perspective"; Woodberry et al., "Why Muslims Follow Jesus." Each article refers to the number of surveys which contributed to the findings for that article. Different categories of findings are indicated in each article, but the difference in categories between articles is not explained.

Table 2. Woodberry's Findings of What God is Using in Individual Conversions

Rank of Importance of Item for Each Category	Influence of Experience	Spiritual Needs Better Answered by Faith in Christ
1	Lifestyle of Christians	Inner peace
2	Answered prayer	Assurance of forgiveness
3	Miracles and the power of God in specific situations	Assurance of salvation (tied for third)
4	Healing	Love of God (tied for third)
5	Dissatisfaction with the form of Islam or individual Muslims they had experienced	Guidance to spiritual truth in the Bible
6	Dreams and visions	A desire for fellowship in spiritual matters
7		Free from fear
8		Free from loneliness
9		Deliverance from demonization

Jean-Marie Gaudeul conducted qualitative analysis on the conversion narratives of one hundred seventy Muslims who turned to Christ, primarily in Africa.[45] His research revealed the following five themes about motivations for conversion: "Jesus is so attractive," a Muslim "thirst for truth," a sense by some Muslims that they are "without family" and that "God's community" provides a new family, "the need for forgiveness," and "a thirst for God" and a relationship with him. Duane Miller prefers the categories given by Gaudeul to those of Woodberry and Shubin, though he suggests the addition of a category described by Woodberry that could be labeled as "visions, dreams, and miracles."[46]

Miller also conducted his own research as part of his PhD work, asking ministers who are experienced in ministry to Muslims to respond in writing to two questions, one of them focusing on the factors they perceive have contributed to the upsurge in Muslims making a commitment to Jesus. These ministers lived in various locations and included both nationals

---

45. Gaudeul, *Called from Islam to Christ*.
46. Miller, "Living Among the Breakage," 72–73.

and foreign-born individuals. Miller acknowledges that the findings are not representative or comprehensive. They do, however, contain helpful information for the present study. The thirty responses revealed three broad types of factors, the first being transcendental factors such as increased prayer, recognition of God's timing, dreams, visions, and miracles. Second, factors related to missionary strategies and methods were noted, such as the use of Bible storying. The third category was that of factors related to communications and globalization, such as the exposure one has via satellite TV or as one lives in a different country.[47] Significantly, he observes that these factors appear to work together synergistically, where the final impact is more than simply the sum of the individual parts.[48] In his article with Patrick Johnstone, Miller adds an additional fourth factor to the above, that of political and social upheaval in Muslim areas, which may contribute to Muslims questioning their beliefs.[49]

Regarding more regional studies, James Bultema studied the conversion of Muslims in Turkey to Christianity as part of his doctoral research. He interviewed thirty individuals with the purpose of answering the questions, "What were the factors that brought these believers to Christ?" and "What are the commonalities among those factors?" In his analysis, Bultema provides three categories describing the reasons people turned to Christ: "Word," referring to the impact of God's word, "Witness," describing what is communicated to others by Christ-followers, and "Worship," tied to the experiences people have had with local congregations.[50] For his PhD research, Ant Greenham examined Palestinian Muslim conversions to Christ by interviewing eleven men and eleven women with the purpose "to hear in the convert's own words why he or she became a believer."[51] Following the interviews, he utilized a comprehensive questionnaire as another instrument in order to verify his results and gain additional information.[52]

---

47. Miller, "Living Among the Breakage," 89–90, 94–114.
48. Miller, "Living Among the Breakage," 115.
49. Miller and Johnstone, "Believers in Christ," 12.
50. Bultema, "Muslims Coming to Christ."
51. Greenham, "Study of Palestinian Muslim Conversions," 117–18.
52. Greenham's questionnaire includes statements and responses according to a Likert scale (e.g., strongly agree, agree, minimally agree, minimally disagree, etc.). Examples of statements to be considered are as follows: I was living in a Muslim community when I came to Christ. I have been baptized. I am an active member of a local church. I used to pray five times per day. Reading the Bible led to my conversion. I trusted Jesus because he gives assurance of eternal life. I was influenced by a death or serious illness (Greenham,

In his analysis, he notes that each person was impacted by not one but several conversion factors, which had varying degrees of significance. He also identifies five categories which have greater prominence (reading the Bible, role of believers, truth of Jesus's message, God's miraculous involvement, and the person of Jesus), and seven which have lesser prominence (assurance of salvation, political instability, rejection of Islam, Christian media, personal crisis, community, and God's honor).[53]

As part of his research on Muslim conversion to Christianity in Kyrgyzstan, David Radford conducted 49 in-depth interviews and utilized 427 quantitative surveys. His focus was on religious identity and social change, and he explored four factors which impacted the process of conversion: dreams/visions, convicting words of someone, major problems/crises, and deliverance from spirits. He groups these into categories of "experiential factors," (deliverance from spirits, dreams, etc.), and "relational factors," (words or changed lives of others). He observes that a single factor was not prominent, but the factors seem to work together as they influenced the process of conversion.[54]

Daniel Hoskins's PhD research involved interviewing thirty-six individuals in central Asia in order to understand what their conversion narratives reveal about the influence of their context and also about their perspectives regarding their own conversion. His emphasis on the importance of the cultural and historical context in conversion is helpful.[55] The context of the Muslims in Cambodia, existing as a minority people and receiving religious input from outsiders, may influence how they perceive themselves and the message. Hoskins also highlights the impact language has on the conversion narratives and notes that the narratives are often expressed in one or more themes or "languages." He discovered that three "languages" were commonly communicated in the narratives, the language of joining, the language of rejecting, and the language of believing.[56]

For his PhD dissertation, David Greenlee interviewed single, male, adult, urban converts from Islam to Christianity in Morocco in order to identify social, cultural, communication, and supernatural factors in their process of conversion. He describes a theory of congruence that he feels

---

"Muslim Conversions to Christ," 277–83).

53. Greenham, "Study of Palestinian Muslim Conversions," 171, 153–69.
54. Radford, *Religious Identity and Social Change*, 24, 80–82.
55. Hoskins, "Conversion Narratives in Context," 26–27, iii.
56. Hoskins, "Conversion Narratives in Context," 167.

helps explain conversion among these young men. Greenlee explains congruence simply as the similarity between the old and new, and the ease at which a transition is made between previous belief in Islam and a new belief in Christianity. Some concepts in Islam and Christianity are congruent, such as Christ's virgin birth and miracles. Other concepts, such as Christ being the Son of God, are clearly incongruent. Furthermore, he states that congruence may also include the sense that felt needs of the non-believer can be met by Christianity and the Christian community. He observes that individuals who were not content with aspects of Moroccan society were often attracted to the foreign nature of Christian belief. However, for others content with Moroccan society, it was important that the Christian witness had a Moroccan "flavor." Greenlee concludes by identifying two principles about congruence in conversion and church growth.[57] These principles will be reviewed later during the specific discussion about congruence. Greenlee's theory of congruence, as well as the findings of researchers above, have connections with the present Cambodian study.

The above research is helpful and provides background categories about factors or motivations influencing conversion that can be compared to my findings. However, the studies are also broad, often seeking to identify and weigh general categories. They do not focus on the specific interaction one has with the gospel message, including how the message was personally meaningful and compelling. This is a specific focus of my project.

---

57. Greenlee, "Christian Conversion from Islam," 208–9, 211.

3

Methodology

Overview and Frame of Research

THIS RESEARCH UTILIZES A qualitative approach, which is defined by Joseph Maxwell as having the purpose to help us better understand "(1) the meanings and perspectives of the people you study—seeing the world from their point of view, rather than simply from your own; (2) how these perspectives are shaped by, and shape, their physical, social, and cultural contexts; and (3) the specific processes that are involved in maintaining or altering these phenomenon and relationships." Maxwell emphasizes the importance of viewing the world from the perspective of the person or group being studied. He also adds that qualitative research is characterized by an approach which is open-ended, which focuses on textual or visual information rather than numerical data, and which has a purpose of gaining a particular understanding about a topic, instead of making generalizations.[1] Earl Babbie writes that field research is usually qualitative. Furthermore, conducting qualitative field research allows one to gain a more comprehensive perspective and understanding of a particular phenomenon.[2]

A qualitative approach is most suited for this study. There are a variety of factors influencing conversion of BMBs in general and also impacting how an individual or group grapples with the religious message. Not all of these are known for the population being studied. A qualitative study utilizing in-depth interviews, therefore, is more appropriate for this project, as it allows for the gathering of rich data on these topics, and in a manner which is natural for those interviewed.

The use of a phenomenological approach also frames this research. At its foundation, phenomenology is "a philosophy of knowledge that

---

1. Maxwell, *Qualitative Research Design*, viii.
2. Babbie, *Practice of Social Research*, 282.

emphasizes direct observation of phenomena".[3] Although I am not directly observing religious conversion taking place, I am seeking to understand the phenomenon from the perspective of the participants themselves, as they experienced it, with the assumption that the "important reality" lies in their perceptions about their experiences. Kvale and Brinkmann characterize this type of inquiry as components of the phenomenological approach.[4] Rambo emphasizes the need to study the conversion experience of different individuals in order to understand the issues they face, advocating a phenomenological approach.[5] Rambo and Reh describe the essence of phenomenology as going "beyond bare facts to the level of facts-as-perceived," with the purpose being to "discover and describe what a person actually experienced." This approach, when practiced well, "renders human experience with richness and depth."[6] Radford is an example of a researcher who utilizes a phenomenological approach to research conversion among Muslims. He explains, "My approach was largely phenomenological in that I sought to understand the processes, context and meanings with reference to Kyrgyz conversion from the subjects' (Kyrgyz Christians) point of view."[7] While this Cambodian study differs from the one conducted by Radford, both are characterized by desiring to gain understanding about the phenomenon of conversion by looking deeply at the lived experiences and perspectives of those who have converted.

Impact of Researcher

I am a Christian. My wife and I were Christian missionaries in Cambodia for seventeen years. This position is a strength for this research as it allows me to better understand the perspectives of respondents and to speak naturally about the topic of belief in Jesus. It can also contribute to individuals feeling comfortable speaking with me because we share similar beliefs. Because I am a Christian, researcher bias is a concern. Maxwell identifies researcher bias as a threat to validity.[8] One potential bias is that I may have preconceived ideas about how and why people decide to follow

---

3. Bernard, *Research Methods*, 23.
4. Kvale and Brinkmann, *Interviews*, 26.
5. Rambo, "Conversion Studies," 436.
6. Rambo and Reh, "Phenomenology of Conversion," 230, 256.
7. Radford, *Religious Identity and Social Change*, 24.
8. Maxwell, *Qualitative Research Design*, 124.

Christ, including the dynamics of how the biblical message speaks to them. It was important for me to realize this, and to deliberately be open-minded in the responses I received, including rigorously evaluating my conclusions as I analyzed data.

My length of experience in Cambodia provides a foundation for gathering rich data. I have lived among the people, participating in their day-to-day lives. I have a history of seven years working specifically with Muslims in Cambodia, a background that provides insights and allows increased validity to this study. In addition, I am fluent in both the national Khmer language and the Cham language, which is the mother tongue of most interviewees. Longevity in Cambodia has contributed to a deeper understanding of the cultures present and to greater skills in communication.

Another topic that relates to my identity as a white western missionary is that of reactivity by respondents.[9] Because of my work in Cambodia, I had previously met approximately twenty-five percent of those interviewed. This contact was potentially both a benefit and a detriment to collecting information. Because individuals knew me, they may have felt more open and relaxed as they spoke. However, their previous interaction with me may have brought preconceived notions about me or about the information I was seeking. Those who have met me have primarily experienced me as a Christian teacher or missionary, and also at times as one who assisted them in various ways, such as with medical needs. In addition, they likely saw me as having more power than they, due to factors such as my identity as a foreigner, my relative wealth, my higher education, and my previous practice of providing assistance. Because I am a white westerner, they may have felt reluctant to discuss certain topics with me, such as ones relating to personal experiences or beliefs that they feel I may not support or understand. These factors may have contributed to interviewees—whether they personally knew me or not—seeking to answer the questions as they think I would desire, including the "Christian" answers they may have assumed I would have expected. This potential reactivity was addressed in four ways. First, at the beginning of the interview, I explained that I was no longer working with my previous organization but was simply conducting research as a student. Second, I explained that I was not looking for a "right or wrong" answer, but rather the answer they had, one based on their individual thoughts and experiences.[10] This approach follows Bernard's advice in beginning interviews,

---

9. Maxwell, *Qualitative Research Design*, 124–25.

10. Before conducting interviews, I met with a prominent BMB in order to check

"First of all, assure people of anonymity and confidentiality. Explain that you simply want to know what *they* think, and what *their* [italics in original] observations are."[11] Third, at the conclusion of all interviews, I met with a prominent BMB to discuss findings. Our interaction included a discussion about reactivity. His comments helped clarify what I had experienced during interviews. Fourth, as I analyzed data, I considered the possibility of reactivity and made adjustments, deemphasizing certain content when it appeared to be influenced by participant reactivity.

Interviews

I conducted interviews in Cambodia for five months, July-November 2017. Semistructured qualitative questions were used to interview forty adult BMBs.[12] As the purpose was to interview BMBs, a primary selection criterion was for interviewees to agree with the statement, "I am a person who follows Christ *(Isa)*."[13] In his study in Kyrgyzstan, Radford discusses the importance of people self-reporting that they are a convert, meaning they acknowledge they have "made a change from one religious or non-religious position to a new religious position." It is understood they may still be in a process of converting or learning the implications of conversion.[14] After determining that the interviewees met the selection criteria in the Cambodian study, I asked them how long they have been following Jesus. The average length of time they note they had been following Christ was seven years (median was five years).

Purposeful sampling was used to identify people who met the interview criteria. Respondents were identified both through personal contacts

---

the interview questions for understandability and cultural appropriateness. He provided a phrase in the Cham language that exactly captures the concept of not seeking a "right or wrong" answer. This phrase was used in the explanation to interviewees before each interview began. Furthermore, an illustration was given to them in order to more clearly convey the desire that they communicate their thoughts and feelings, instead of what they perceive I might want to hear.

11. Bernard, *Research Methods*, 215.
12. Merriam, *Qualitative Research*, 88.
13. It is understood that worldwide some BMBs continue to identify as Muslim and some do not. The criteria stated above avoids this issue and focuses on the most important aspect—that of being a follower of Christ—which I believe all BMBs would acknowledge.
14. Radford, *Religious Identity and Social Change*, 6.

METHODOLOGY

I have among BMBs in Cambodia and through the contacts my colleagues and acquaintances know.[15] A snowball approach (or network sampling) was also used to identify potential respondents, with those interviewed being asked if they could refer me to others they knew who would be willing to be interviewed.[16]

Efforts were made to interview a diversity of people, according to their gender, age, grouping, and location. As "men and women experience religion differently",[17] it was desired to interview a balanced representation of males and females. The selection method used led to more potential male contacts than females. However, sixteen females were interviewed (representing forty percent of the total number), along with twenty-four males (sixty percent of all interviews).[18] The age of interviewees ranged from eighteen years of age to sixty-seven, with a mean age of forty-one, and a median age of forty-three.[19] As previously noted, Cambodian Muslims are members of different groups, with the majority associating with the *Chang Wang* and much smaller portions with the *Imam San* and *Chvea*. For this study, twenty-one interviewees (fifty-two percent of total) identified themselves as belonging to the *Chang Wang* group, sixteen interviewees (forty percent of total) with the *Imam San* group, and three (eight percent of total) with the *Chvea* group (or *Khmer Islam*).

Cambodian Muslims live in diverse locations, and interviews were conducted in a wide variety of locations. Three interviews were conducted in the capital city of Phnom Penh, with the majority of interviews occurring in small towns or rural areas after traveling to those locations.[20] Individuals from eleven different provinces plus the city of Phnom Penh were interviewed. The home locations of those interviewed are indicated in the following table, according to the location and the number of people

---

15. I will use the terms "interviewees" and "respondents" interchangeably in this document to refer to those who were interviewed.

16. Merriam, *Qualitative Research*, 78–79.

17. Cheong, "Socio-Religious Identity," 7.

18. Some data was received from an additional male as well. As he was not involved in a complete interview, he is not included in the above figure and other statistics. He is identified as the final male interviewee, Rady.

19. For females, the average age was thirty-seven and the median age was forty-three. For males, the average age was forty-three and the median age was forty-one.

20. Most of the interviews occurred where people were currently living. Some interviews, however, occurred in a different province from which the person was living.

interviewed living there. A map including the name of the provinces is provided in Figure 2.

Table 3. Home Location of Interviewees by Province or City

Name of Province or City	Number of Interviewees Residing There
Kampong Chhnang	11
Tbum Khmum	9
Kratie	5
Phnom Penh City	3
Battambang	2
Stung Treng	2
Kampot	2
Koh Kong	2
Kampong Cham	1
Kandal	1
Pursat	1
Rattankiri	1

METHODOLOGY

Figure 2. Map of Cambodian Provinces[21]

Although most respondents were not related, two couples and one set of sisters were interviewed.

Efforts were made to conduct the interviews in locations in which the respondents felt most comfortable and in which they felt free to communicate without restraint. Most interviews were conducted in the home of the respondent, but others occurred in neutral locations.[22] Because

21. CartoGIS Services, "Cambodia Colour Provinces."

22. The majority of respondents were interviewed alone. During several of the interviews, other family members or friends were present. This is natural as often conversations, even of a serious nature, take place in the presence of others. In instances where

some females may not have felt comfortable being interviewed by a male, they were asked if they desired someone else to be with them during the interview. My wife accompanied me when I interviewed females in order to be present if requested.

The interviews were conducted in the language preferred by the respondent. In most instances, the Cham language was used. In four cases, the interview was conducted in the Khmer language.

Confidentiality was important to both protect the identity of the respondent and to put them at ease. Before the formal interview took place, respondents were informed that their personal information would not be shared and that a generic code would be used to identify each individual (F1 for female number one, F2 for female number two, M1 for male number one, etc.)[23] At the beginning of each interview, ten to fifteen minutes were used to discuss the purpose and method of the interview, establish that the respondent met the selection criteria, discuss confidentiality, gather demographic information, and gain consent for the interview.[24] After this, the formal interview began and was recorded using a Sony digital recorder. The average recorded interview lasted forty-five minutes. Each interview began by asking the respondent to simply tell the story of their conversion. This open-ended approach was used because it avoided prompting the respondent to discuss specific topics. Follow-up questions were asked afterward about specific topics they mentioned, based on the initial response of the interviewee. Following a discussion about each individual's conversion narrative, questions were asked regarding their perceptions of the gospel message and their belief in Jesus. These questions focused on addressing RQs number two and three: which factors they reported as important in their conversion, and how the message was personally meaningful and relevant. After the above discussion, questions were asked related to the contextualization of the message (RQ number one), including how they received the message and how they communicated it to others. Thus, the pattern of

---

others were present, I asked the interviewee about whether or not they felt comfortable having that person/s there, and they gave their consent for the presence of the other/s. If they were not comfortable, a more private area was found in which the respondent could be interviewed alone.

23. This was the method utilized by Greenham, "Study of Palestinian Muslim Conversions," 117.

24. Demographic information collected from interviewees included their age, gender, the location of residence, length of time acknowledged having followed Jesus, and grouping which they identify with (*Imam San, Chang Wang, or Chvea/Khmer Islam*).

each individual interview was first an opportunity for the respondent to share their conversion narrative, then questions regarding their personal experience of the gospel message and choice to believe in and follow Jesus, followed by a discussion of how they received the message. At the conclusion of each interview, respondents were presented with a small gift as a token of appreciation for their time.[25]

Supplementary Data

In order to gain additional information and to triangulate data, three other methods of inquiry were used in addition to the primary interviews.[26] First, three contextualized resources were gathered and examined. The first of these is a Bible published in 2014. This Bible uses a popular Khmer language translation as its base and changes specific religious terms to be more appropriate for a Cambodian Muslim audience. The second resource was a tract written to communicate the gospel message to Cambodian Muslims. This tract, written by two cross-cultural workers,[27] was examined. I met with each of the workers involved in writing the tract, and a recorded interview was conducted with the main author in order to better understand the rationale and the design of the tract. The third contextualized resource was a large cloth printed with illustrations of Bible stories. This cloth was used by some individuals for teaching the gospel; they hung it on a wall and explained the stories. The second type of inquiry was participant observation which was used in two meetings.[28] The first meeting was held in a rural area to study and discuss Christian teachings. Both BMBs and non-BMBs were in attendance. The second was a training seminar for approximately

---

25. Bernard suggests paying those interviewed for their time spent at the current local rate. I felt that presenting a practical gift would be more appropriate in the Cambodian context. As gifts from other countries are valued in Cambodian culture, items were purchased in the United States and brought there. Males were given an aluminum flashlight and females were given Tupperware-style containers for storing food (*Research Methods*, 209).

26. Merriam describes triangulation as, "using multiple investigators, sources of data, or data collection methods to confirm emerging findings" (*Qualitative Research*, 229).

27. In this document I use the term "cross-cultural worker" to refer to a Christian NGO worker or missionary who is not from Cambodia.

28. Bloomberg and Volpe explain participant observation as occurring when the researcher is immersed in a setting and both participating and observing with the purpose to "experience reality as the research participants do" (*Completing Your Qualitative Dissertation*, 155).

ten BMBs, organized and led by another BMB. I observed and took notes during training sessions, including one in which the leader demonstrated how to communicate the gospel message using the large hanging cloth mentioned above. The third type of inquiry was the gathering of statistical data about Muslims in Cambodia. This was accomplished by visiting Cambodian government offices and a Muslim NGO.

Data-gathering and Analysis Procedures

All interviews were recorded on a Sony digital recorder. Four Cambodian university students were hired part-time to transcribe the interviews and translate key portions into English. The students were mother tongue speakers of the Cham language and were fluent in the Khmer and English languages. As there is no standardized way to write the Cham language that is understood by all Cambodian Cham, the transcription of the interviews was done using the International Phonetic Alphabet (IPA).[29] Most of the content of each interview was transcribed. Following that, significant portions were translated into English.

In order to protect the interview data, the Cambodian staff conducted all their work on designated computers provided by the researcher in an office location. As previously noted, interviewees were informed that their personal information would not be shared, and that a generic code would be used to identify each individual (F1 for female number 1, etc.). Cambodian staff knew the identity of the interviewees only by their given code. I was present in the office the majority of the time that transcription and translation work was conducted. As such, I was able to answer questions and check the quality of the work done. All transcription and translation occurred in Cambodia, and the task took approximate four months to complete.

As interviews were being conducted, I wrote personal memos in order to record details about the context of interviews, note reflections, and assist in analyzing data.[30] After the interviews were completed, I met with the prominent BMB who assisted me initially and discussed my research findings with him. He was able to confirm and clarify some of my discoveries.

---

29. The students were trained in phonetics by the researcher. A Cham dictionary exists in which the words are written using the IPA. This was an important resource.

30. Babbie, *Practice of Social Research*, 377, 379; Maxwell, *Qualitative Research Design*, 19–20; Merriam, *Qualitative Research*, 172.

METHODOLOGY

NVivo 11 software was used to code and assist in the analysis of data. Initial codes were chosen according to the topics associated with the research questions. Open coding was also utilized, with codes chosen based directly on the responses and terms used by those interviewed.[31]

---

31. Babbie, *Practice of Social Research,* 377.

4

Communication and Contextualization of the Christian Message

IN ORDER TO UNDERSTAND how a message is perceived as personal and real, one must examine the manner in which it is communicated. The first research question for this study concerns the role that the contextualization of the gospel message played in conversion. As previously noted, questions about this RQ were asked at the end of the actual interviews. However, the findings for this research question will be discussed first, based on the logic of presenting how individuals received the message before discussing their interactions with it. This chapter is organized around several important questions related to this topic: (1) Whom did the Cambodian BMBs hear the message from? (2) What was communicated? (3) What methods were used in communication? (4) How was the Christian message contextualized? and (5) How do BMBs communicate the Christian message to others?

From Whom did Cambodian BMBs Hear the Message?

Interviewees reported that they received the gospel message from a variety of people and organizations. These messengers may be categorized into four groups: Cross-cultural workers, Cambodian BMBs, Cambodian Khmer Christians (non-BMBs), and organizations. Many individuals spoke about cross-cultural workers as directly presenting the message or being involved in the facilitation of its spread. These cross-cultural workers (Christian missionaries or NGO workers) originated from countries outside of Cambodia. One particular person, who will be called Steven, was mentioned by over one-third of interviewees. Steven was involved in development work for an NGO, and he often coordinated his work and traveled with a Cambodian BMB, who will be referred to as Isak.[1] Omar, a community leader aged in his sixties living in central Cambodia, simply said, "Steven came to cure and to teach and we learned in groups." He pointed to Steven as the source of the message. Other cross-cultural workers were identified as well by interviewees. Chenda, a mother in her mid-twenties living in a remote village in western Cambodia, noted that she heard the message initially as a child in her former village. But she spoke much about how over a period of time a female cross-cultural worker, Mary, met with her, gave her a Bible, and explained it to her.

Some individuals interacted with more than one cross-cultural worker, at different times, and sometimes with different results. Imran, a fisherman in his late twenties, reported that he has now believed for four months and that he was exposed to a film about Jesus shown in his community when he was young.[2] Later, he met a cross-cultural worker who gave him a Bible in the Khmer language. Imran said he was clearly not interested at that time because he knew that "we are the religion of Allah." Furthermore, he was concerned about looking at the Bible too much, as it could cause him to be confused, lose his way, and go toward Jesus. Recently, however, he met with a different cross-cultural worker, Timothy. This person presented the message in such a way that "I understood that *Isa* (Jesus) is within Allah as well.[3] Because of that, I was quite interested."

---

1. The names "Steven" and "Isak" are pseudonyms. In order to protect the identity of individuals, all names used for interviewees and cross-cultural workers for the remainder of this document are pseudonyms. Furthermore, the approximate age of a respondent is used instead of their exact age.

2. Many words can be used to describe the decision or act of converting. Imran used the word "believe" when discussing his decision to request forgiveness and follow Jesus. In this book, the words "believe" and "follow" will most commonly be used because those are the terms which were often used by the respondents themselves. It is understood, however, that these terms at times include other concepts such as changing one's heart or repenting.

3. Interviewees consistently used the words *"Nabi Isa"* or *"Isa"* to refer to Jesus Christ when speaking the Cham language. These are the Islamic terms used for Jesus (*"Nabi Isa"* meaning the prophet Jesus and *"Isa"* referring simply to Jesus). When Khmer was spoken, as with Imran, the above terminology was still often used. Alternatively, the Khmer term *"Preah Yesu"* was sometimes used to refer to Jesus. Moreover, interviewees almost always used the Islamic term "Allah" when speaking about the God of the Bible. For the remainder of this document, I will commonly use the English translation "Jesus" instead of *Nabi Isa*, *Isa*, or *Preah Yesu*. In addition, I will use the English term "God" instead of Allah (or include both words paired together) when respondents are referring to the God of the Bible. When they are referring to the Muslim deity, I will use the word "Allah."

Previously, he saw the message of Jesus as being foreign to his beliefs. Upon encountering this new person, he saw that information about Jesus actually fit into his larger understanding of Allah (God) and his ways. This presentation of the message within the listener's existing framework of understanding will be discussed in greater depth later.

Interviewees also referred to the importance and frequency of hearing the message from Cambodian BMBs, who were usually from the same cultural background. At times, these BMBs were associated with cross-cultural workers, as with the case of Steven and Isak. Kari, aged in her forties and living in the same area as Omar, noted that Steven and Isak would arrive together, and both would speak. Frequently people would hear the message directly from a Cambodian BMB, often someone with whom they already had a relationship. Narin, in his late twenties, said he became a follower of Christ one month before our interview. He explained that he heard the message from his sister, his brother, and his landlord, all of whom lived in his community. Regarding his brother, he stated, "He tells other people to study with him. He teaches about Jesus. I also go to see him teaching." When asked whom he heard the message from, another man, Hamat, simply pointed to an individual nearby, giving his name and identifying him as the one who told him.

Cambodian followers of Christ from the Khmer ethnic group were also involved in telling the gospel message to Muslims. Srey Mum began her interview by stating she heard the "good news" from her husband, who is a Khmer Christian. She went through a process of comparing the religions of Islam and Christianity before choosing to follow Christ. At the same time, the belief that her husband loved her and thus did not want her to "walk in the wrong way" motivated her to seriously consider the message he spoke of. Borey is similar to Srey Mum in that he also was raised Muslim but has a Khmer spouse. Borey tells of meeting with an older Khmer church elder he knew while sitting in front of a hospital. In his words, the man told him, "Your wife is already believing in God. Why are you still not believing? Come here, I'll tell you. . . . You should follow your wife and believe." This man explained more, noting that there were many similarities between Christianity and Islam, and thus Borey can come and follow Jesus. This encounter was part of Borey's story, and it instigated a two to three month period of thought, after which the man again asked if he was going to follow Jesus or not. Although Borey later had significant interaction with a cross-cultural worker, his discussions with this Khmer Christian occurred prior to that and were instrumental in his conversion. Hassad, around thirty years old, stated that he has followed Christ for ten years. His first exposure to the Christian message came through a Khmer physician who also served in the local church. Communication was in the Khmer language. Hassad began attending the church meetings, and even later became involved in helping with the children. In this context, he noted, "The Lord started to show the path, little by little, that Jesus is truly God and came to save all humans on earth from sin." He explained that the context of this was among Khmer believers, using the Khmer language. He would later meet BMBs who would interact with him using the Cham language as they spoke about following Jesus.

A final source of the gospel message is that of organizations such as NGOs. Several individuals referred to a specific Christian medical clinic where they received treatment. Cross-cultural workers were often instrumental in referring these people to the clinic, and at times in assisting in paying for the expenses incurred. The clinic is staffed with both Khmer and expatriate professionals. Tahira, in her forties, discussed visiting the clinic for treatment. As she was there, she viewed publicly shown videos about Jesus, which interested her. She added that she was given a book at the clinic about Jesus, which she later read. Tahira also mentioned two cross-cultural workers by name living near her. They met with her periodically after she returned from the clinic and talked about the Bible.

Yasmin is a young lady who began following Jesus three months before being interviewed. Her story is a complex one and involves prolonged sickness. After being treated by several individuals without success, she was taken to the Christian clinic mentioned above. Yasmin tells of a lady there who explained to her about *Nabi Isa* (Jesus), and who invited her to follow him. Yasmin adds that this person did not force her. Moreover, she prayed with Yasmin and for her. Yasmin marks this as a significant event, one in which she felt she could begin following Jesus. Other experiences in her story occurred before and after these. They reveal much about her path to belief and will be discussed later. As previously noted, the cross-cultural worker Steven was employed by an NGO. Several interviewees referred to that NGO and its medical work when discussing how they were exposed to the message. This NGO is another example of individuals hearing the Christian message through an organization.

It is clear from above that many and varied "messengers" were involved in the lives of respondents. In summary, it is observed that people often heard the gospel message from more than one person. Furthermore, individuals were exposed to the message from a variety of sources, including not only BMBs and cross-cultural workers, but also other Cambodian Christians or organizations. Their discovery of Christian teaching was often multi-faceted and influenced by many actors.

What Was Communicated?

Examining what topics were communicated provides further insight into the conversion experiences of those interviewed. As interviewees responded to the question "What did the people tell you?" four primary topics emerged. First, stories—particularly from the Old Testament—were shared. Second, Jesus was focused upon, including what he did and its implications for life. Third, people were instructed to do good deeds. Finally, they were challenged to believe in and follow Jesus. Additional detail about these responses is given below.

Stories were told as a way to explain the gospel message. Sagy's home, like many in rural Cambodia, is placed on wooden or concrete piles seven to twelve feet above the ground. This architecture provides a shady area under the structure of the home, which is routinely used as a rest or work area during hot tropical days. Sagy and I sat, legs crossed, underneath his home on a flat wooden platform. As he reflected on the message he received, he mentioned that the person told stories about the great flood, about the prophet Abraham, and the related concept of sacrifice. Pes is another older gentleman also living in a rural village. He recounted that the cross-cultural worker Steven explained the story of Adam. He added that previously another cross-cultural worker had provided him with a Bible and pictures, but had not explained the meaning, so he did not understand. Steven, however, discussed and clarified the creation story and the life of Adam as part of his presentation of the Christian message.

Not surprisingly, topics surrounding the person of Jesus were the most prominent ones communicated. More specifically, interviewees mentioned discussions about Jesus's identity, his actions, and their implications for life. Nida is in her mid-twenties and has followed Christ for three to four years. She recalled that Bill, a cross-cultural worker, explained that "Jesus was truly God," and that he "came to this earth to help us escape from sin, to be our Lord." The discussion of Jesus's identity was important, and it was closely tied to his works. Rahman, approximately thirty years old, told of a

Cambodian BMB who spoke to him about two topics. The first, "salvation," included an explanation that Jesus tolerated the cross to accept sin. The second was a Bible story about the person of Lazarus, a friend of Jesus. He explained that although Lazarus had already died, Jesus simply spoke the words to call him back from the dead. Jesus's work and actions were an important component of the presentation of the gospel message. Malik, who has followed Jesus for seven years, noted that he had listened to Steven several times over a long period of time and that Steven emphasized Jesus was the one who helps to save and release humans from sin.

The implications of Jesus's work in human lives were frequently focused on by those who were communicating the Christian message. Sofia, approximately thirty years old, has been a Jesus follower for three years. An older BMB relative initially shared the gospel message with her in the Cham language, but she noted that she was not interested and did not believe it at that time. Later, as a university student, she listened to others who encouraged her to believe in Jesus because he would help her and because she would be able to live in happiness with him. They explained that if she followed Jesus, after death she would also go stay with him in heaven. Sofia provided further details about what the BMB relative told her and her family. In her words, he said, "Believe in Jesus! [Then] nothing will come and trouble us, and Satan cannot trouble us as well. Please believe in Jesus because it's easy for us after we die. If we believe in Muhammad, he cannot help/save us. Only Jesus can save us." Much is contained in these few words. In the above quote, we see a strong encouragement to believe, with an explanation that Jesus is the one who can truly help. In addition, his personal help is outlined, including both protection from the attacks of Satan in this life as well as comfort in the afterlife. As will be seen later, Sofia discussed personal experiences of being bothered by spiritual forces and later relief from them which she ascribed to Jesus. Although she was not initially interested in this message from her relative, it is possible that the offer of protection from spiritual forces was personally significant and remembered by her.

Other interviewees provided information that both correlated and contrasted with that of Sofia. Hamat spoke strongly about heaven. He related the words of the BMB who simply told him, "If you follow Jesus, you will go to heaven." Similarly, Imran, previously introduced, reflected on how Timothy, a cross-cultural worker, spoke to him. Timothy explained about the story of Jesus and about "the right way, the right way to heaven."

Although additional topics were also discussed, the theme of heaven again emerged in the presentation of the gospel message.

Some of the words heard by Razaa, however, contrast with the generally encouraging messages above. Razaa was given a message of difficulty and obstacles in following Jesus. He summarized the words spoken to him by a pastor,

> If you believe in Jesus Christ and you have only happiness, you don't need to believe. It means that there will be persecution if you really believe. If you believe and then you have persecution by others, and they cause you to feel upset, then it means your faith is genuine. Jesus himself was persecuted. This is a true story. My pastor told me, "When you follow Jesus Christ, do not think you will have happiness all the time."

A third topic interviewees reported as being communicated to them was the instruction to do good deeds. Shaza lives in a central Cambodian village in which several other BMBs reside. She is in her forties and conveyed that one cross-cultural worker, Kevin, told them to do good deeds, to follow Jesus, to love their neighbors, and to love each other. Malik, living nearby and also referring to Kevin, recalled him teaching that "Jesus is the one who commands us to not do wrong deeds." Najee, around fifty years old and living far from the previous individuals, mentioned different people who asked them to do good deeds and to believe in Jesus. This reminder to do good deeds fits with the common understanding in Cambodia of reward and punishment resulting from good and bad deeds. Doing good deeds is valued, and both Buddhist and Islamic leaders refer to this practice.[4]

A final significant topic communicated was the encouragement to believe in and follow Jesus. Examples of this have already been seen above, often connected to reasons to believe. Abdul is in his fifties and has followed Jesus for four years. Talking about when Steven and Isak came and taught together, he recalled them emphasizing both that Jesus is good and that it is good to follow him. Although most Muslims speak highly of Jesus as a prophet, they do not honor him to the extent that Christians do. It is thus understandable that in this context people would emphasize that Jesus is good. The words of Steven, Isak, and others often included an invitation to deliberately believe in or follow Jesus. The above summarizes

---

4. A saying known by virtually all Cambodians is literally translated as "Do good, receive good; do bad, receive bad." In both Cambodian Buddhism and Islam, doing good deeds is often tied to receiving spiritual merit.

the key content of what was conveyed as people presented the Christian message to others.

There are two topics related to the above subject which warrant discussion. The first concerns the fact that individuals are remembering and reflecting on previous events, which for some occurred many years ago. The information they are providing is not occurring in real time. As such, people make their own decisions, both consciously and subconsciously, about what is recalled or reported. Snow and Machalek use the term "biographical reconstruction" to describe the process where a convert interprets their past in light of the conversion experience, often instilling new meanings to previous events.[5] They refer to James's observation that often at the time of conversion, there is a separation between the old and the new, where the past is dismantled and reconstituted with the new.[6] Thus reconstruction can occur from the time of conversion onward. Lofland and Skonovd discuss three levels of social reality in the study of conversion accounts. The first level, "raw reality," is that of the conversion experience itself. The second level refers to the accounts given about the conversion experience. The third level is that of the analysis of the event and the accounts. The authors are making the point that there may be a difference between the actual event and the recounting of it and that the analysis of conversion is a step further removed.[7] James Beckford, studying the conversion accounts of Jehovah's Witnesses, concluded that the actual conversion accounts cannot be trusted as objective as they have been influenced by the convert's understanding of the guidelines of the Watchtower Society, which governs the movement.[8] While these are legitimate concerns, there is also value in examining conversion from the perspective of the converts themselves. Other scholars are more optimistic than Beckford and say that much can be gained from the approach of examining conversion narratives.[9]

In his study of Muslim conversion to Christianity in Kyrgyzstan, Radford outlines three objections to the trustworthiness of conversion narratives. First, the accounts of the converts may be developed according to the style and expectations of the specific religious group that was joined.

---

5. Snow and Machalek, "Convert as a Social Type," 266–68.
6. James, *Varieties of Religious Experience*, 177.
7. Lofland and Skonovd, "Conversion Motifs," 375.
8. Beckford, "Accounting for Conversion."
9. Rambo and Reh, "Phenomenology of Conversion," 257; Stromberg, "Role of Language," 130; Hindmarsh, "Religious Conversion as Narrative," 350.

Second, the accounts of the converts may change over time, with different interpretations revealed at different times. Third, the accounts of the converts may not be entirely accurate, as over time people's ability to remember may be flawed.[10] In spite of these real challenges, Radford still sees much value in examining conversion narratives from the perspective of the actors themselves, "Although there are problematic issues relating to conversion narratives, such as biographical reconstruction, it is important to consider conversion from the convert's viewpoint when analyzing the content and the form in which it is communicated."[11]

For this Cambodian study, interviewees were often asked to reflect on past events. There was a gap in time, short or long, between what occurred and the description of it. In response to the question, "What did people say to you when they told about the Christian message?" some people bluntly said that they did not remember. Others recalled the event and words with more detail, although somewhat fuzzy on certain specifics. Still others, however, displayed a sense of clarity in their account, which needs to be taken seriously. The material provided in the interviews reveals information about both the original communicators and about the interviewees themselves. Insight is provided about what the communicators said and how content was organized. This opens a window into people's minds, values, and approaches to communication. The recollections of the respondents are also a lens to gain a better understanding of what was important to them at the time. Often what was remembered were those topics or events which were personally meaningful. One example of this is the words of Razaa, who clearly remembered the pastor explaining that one was not to simply expect happiness as a result of following Jesus.

A second topic related to "what was communicated" is that of contextualization. Contextualization of the gospel message will specifically be examined later, both how the message was contextualized to interviewees, and how they currently seek to communicate it to others. However, evidence of contextualization is already apparent in the data above, including such methods as selecting and telling Bible stories which are understandable to those listening. Furthermore, topics such as heaven and the protection from spiritual forces are important to many Muslim Cambodians, as is the value of acting good and doing good deeds. These topics dovetail with the values and concerns of many of the recipients, and the communication of the message

10. Radford, *Religious Identity and Social Change*, 42.
11. Radford, *Religious Identity and Social Change*, 49.

using these terms and concepts is an example of contextualization. Other windows to contextualization are found in the following section.

What Methods Were Used in Communication?

Interviewees reported several practical methods used by others to communicate the Christian message. The most common method was simply that of speaking, which may have ranged from personal dialogue to teaching to answering questions or explaining. Many of the details associated with this manner of communication will be discussed later in the section on contextualization. Four other prominent practical methods of communication will be reviewed here: use of the Bible, studying in groups, use of diagrams, and the use of multimedia tools.

For a large portion of interviewees, their early exposure to Christianity came with exposure to the Christian Bible. Six individuals specifically talked about being given a Bible to read. Although he did not understand it initially, Pes above spoke about being given a Bible by a cross-cultural worker. Aisah is a middle-aged mother whose son is a young adult. She was given a Bible by her son. She recounts how he, referring to his mother's struggles with spirits and sickness, handed her a Bible with the following words, "Mom, you have been sick too much, so please read this Bible, so that you can get better and have victory over Satan. If you read and finish this book, you can feel free from the sickness." Another female, Fatimah, recalls the visits of Isak and Steven, noting that they gave Bibles to her and to others. In addition, they talked about stories from the Bible. This practice reinforces the approach identified in the earlier section, where Old Testament Bible stories were communicated when explaining the Christian message. Although it is unclear whether or not the method was technically that of Chronological Bible storying,[12] stories were often told, both from the Old and New Testaments. Many individuals interviewed routinely referred to a story from the Bible during their conversation. Additionally, many respondents commonly began the interview by recalling Bible stories they knew or were taught.

The study of the message in groups was also referred to as a method used. Aminah is a small business owner in a rural community. She remarked

---

12. Colgate describes Chronological Bible storying as "a method of presenting scriptural truth through telling a series of Bible stories that maintain the chronological flow of Scripture" ("Bible Storying," 221–22).

that several individuals would gather and study the Bible that Kevin gave them. Omar recalls both the method and content of communication used by Isak and Steven with the following words,

> They called each group in order to explain. They explained that from before until now, all people have sinned. Before we heard news about Jesus, we all had sin. And regarding that sin, whoever does not receive this news about Jesus, they have to suffer/hang for their own sin . . . It means we have to solve that problem by ourselves. Our mistake has to be solved by ourselves. But after we have Jesus and the news that he came to sacrifice for everyone to save us from our sin, we follow him and escape from sin.

Isak and Steven organized people into groups, which met together for teaching. A theme taught was that of personal sin, and of possible release from the consequences through a commitment to Jesus and a belief in his sacrifice for human sin. This content was contrasted with the message that individuals who do not receive or believe this news about Jesus will have to be responsible for solving their own problems concerning sin. Although not highlighted earlier, this topic of personal sin was prominent in the communication of the Christian message. It will be seen later that this particular subject was also on the minds of many as they pondered the message.

The third method of communication was the use of diagrams, pictures, and other books. As previously mentioned, Tahira received a book while being treated at a Christian medical clinic. The book contained pictures as well. The community in which Kari lives was visited by Steven and Isak several times. She stated that Steven gave them a book. That book was not the Bible per se, but it did contain illustrations. Kari adds that Steven also gave them another object, a compact disk (CD) to listen to, which relates to the following topic.

The use of media is a final often-mentioned method used to assist in communicating the Christian message. One category of this is that of audio recordings. Kari refers to an audio CD given to her. Isak, approximately fifty years old, recalls listening to an audio cassette tape many years ago. The cassette introduced the terms "the King Father and the King Son," which intrigued him. Based on this, he later asked Steven for an explanation. The instrumental discussion these two men had will be detailed in the upcoming contextualization section. As earlier noted, Narin heard the gospel message from his brother and other relatives in his home community. He also reported listening to a Cambodian Christian radio station as a source of information. The broadcast was in the national Khmer language, but he was still interested in the content. Whether hearing the message in Cham or Khmer, he understood that Jesus was the focus.

MP3 audio recordings were also employed in gospel communication. Minat, in her thirties, lives in the same general area as Narin. She said she was given a set of MP3 recordings in the Cham language by Kevin, which was stored on her cell phone. As she is not literate, she added that these recordings were all that she could access. Minat was quite pleased with the recordings, as evidenced by her not only energetically saying, "[I] like to listen" but also by her asking her relative to bring her phone to her during the interview and then proceeding to play several recording for me. For her, the MP3 recordings on her phone were more convenient than listening to a cassette recorder, which cannot be carried with her. It is apparent that another female, Najee, who has followed Christ for three years, benefits from the recordings. She said she listened to the recordings every night, even though she was not able to easily remember what people said. She was able to just listen. Najee added that she listens with her children late into the night as she lies down. In her words, "I . . . listen continually. I want to remember and store [that information], so I can talk about it next time." Najee noted that she wanted to be prepared to explain to others if they asked her about these things. Like many of those interviewed, she said that she was not clever or knowledgeable. She did appreciate the MP3 recordings she was given. Besides being used for initial communication of the gospel, these recordings have also been used for the teaching and encouragement of those who have already decided to follow Jesus.

The most common category of media described by interviewees was that of film. Several types of films and videos were referred to, some of them quite old and others recently produced. One specific film about the life of Jesus was completed in the Cham language approximately a decade ago.[13] Most of the other films and videos about Christianity use the Khmer language. Tewi is middle-aged and, like nearly all those interviewed, resides in a village in which most inhabitants are Muslim. She recalled an event approximately twenty-five years ago when cross-cultural workers visited that village and publicly showed a film about Jesus. This event had a powerful impact on her, revealed in her statement, "Before they came here to play the movie, I did not

---

13. Two interviewees spoke with pride about the role they had in the film. Their voices were recorded and used for specific characters in the movie, titled *Jesus* and produced by Krish and Sykes.

yet believe. But after they played it, I started to believe." Tewi added that the cross-cultural workers did explain the message, but they did not ask if anyone wanted to believe or force people to follow Jesus. She stated that believing was an individual decision based on whether or not they were personally interested. Tewi and others pointed to the theme that there is freedom to choose to follow—or not to follow—Jesus. Tewi was also exposed later to other films and videos about Jesus. Both she and her sister Tahira referred to watching a DVD at the Christian medical clinic they visited.

Imran, previously introduced as one who has followed Christ for four months, also recalls exposure to a movie as a youth. A film was shown near his village, which is located far from that of Tewi. He remembered the images of Jesus being beaten and hung on a cross, and also that those screening the film connected it with Christianity. Imran simply reported that he watched this movie, and, similar to his earlier response to the Bible he received, displayed no specific interest in it. Nowadays, Imran has other movies and video clips which he watches, stored digitally on his phone. He remarked that he watches them with interest so that he can understand much. He has watched them several times on his phone but has yet to watch the complete film. The stated reason for this incomplete viewing is (in a sign of the times) because his young child bothers him to use the phone to watch cartoons. Many other interviewees reported viewing movies or video clips about Jesus or Bible teachings. These movies had a powerful impact on individuals such as Sara, as will be examined later. The use of films is one of several methods used to communicate the Christian message.

How Was the Message Contextualized?

In order to communicate the message clearly, modifications and adjustments were made in language and delivery. Some of these choices were deliberately decided; others occurred naturally and almost without thought. Moreau et al. describes contextualization as communicating the gospel in a new context in a way that is understandable.[14] Paul Hiebert notes that although the gospel itself is in a sense unchanging, it needs to be communicated according to the culture, language, and worldview of the listener in order for it to be clearly understood.[15] Similarly, in writing

14. Moreau et al., *Introducing World Missions*, 16.
15. Hiebert, "Worldview Transformation," 28. Hiebert acknowledges there are certain problems with the use of the term "worldview," but supports its use because he feels

about contextualization, Gilliland points to the importance of worldview as a framework for communication,

> Contextualization means that the Word must dwell among all families of humankind today as truly as Jesus lived among his own kin. The gospel is Good News when it provides answers for a particular people living in a particular place at a particular time. This means the WORLDVIEW [caps in original] of that people provides a framework for communication, the questions and needs of that people are a guide to the emphasis of the message, and the cultural gifts of that people become the medium of expression.[16]

The above statement clarifies that the goal is that Jesus as the Word is as naturally present in the lives of humans now as when he physically lived on earth. The gospel message is helpful when it provides answers and meaning for people living in a particular situation. Because of that, it is important to understand the circumstances people are living in, including their culture and perspectives, and utilize that as a framework for the communication of the message. It will be seen that modifications were made in the language and delivery of the Christian message in Cambodia, based on the culture, language, and worldview of the recipients, and with the purpose that the message was clearly understood and seen to fit into their existing culture.

This does not mean, however, that the message was not intended to influence the culture as well. In his significant article, "The Gospel as Prisoner and Liberator of Culture," Andrew Walls describes two principles which the gospel brings. The "Indigenizing Principle" is summarized by the ability of the gospel to make itself at home in a given culture. In contrast, the "Pilgrim Principle" relates to the fact that the gospel also calls people to be different than what they were before and different than their culture.[17] Dean Flemming discusses a very similar phenomenon as he explains the concept of contextualization and its implications.

> I take contextualization, then, to refer to the dynamic and comprehensive process by which the gospel is incarnated within a concrete historical or cultural situation. This happens in such a way that the gospel both comes to authentic expression in the

---

it is the best term available. He defines worldview as the "fundamental cognitive, affective, and evaluative presuppositions a group of people make about the nature of things, and which they use to order their lives" (*Transforming Worldviews*, 15).

16. Gilliland, "Contextualization," 225.
17. Walls, "Gospel as Prisoner and Liberator," 7–9.

local context and at the same time prophetically transforms the context. Contextualization seeks to enable the people of God to live out the gospel in obedience to Christ within their own cultures and circumstances.[18]

Flemming and Walls emphasize that the gospel needs to be authentically displayed in individual contexts, yet also challenge and change those contexts. The purpose is that individuals and groups can legitimately live as followers of Christ in their local context. The way in which the Christian message is communicated impacts the way in which it is understood and to what degree it is viewed as personally relevant. It also has the potential to influence to what degree someone considering the gospel feels they can be a sincere follower of Christ and still remain involved in their home culture and customs.

What adjustments were made in order to contextualize the message in Cambodia? Decisions were made about what was communicated and which methods were used in communication, with the purpose that the message would be understood and meaningful to the one hearing it. The use of the Bible, for instance, corresponds to the Muslim belief that certain portions of the Bible have divine origins.[19] Communicating stories from these books, including stories about characters such as Adam and Abraham, both of whom are known by Muslims, fits with their understandings and values. In addition, the use of pictures, diagrams, and media can be viewed as a method that takes into consideration the hearer and seeks to communicate the message in a way that is easily understood and remembered. The research revealed that the gospel message was contextualized in three significant ways: the choice of language, the use of experience-near terms and concepts, and communication within the framework of understanding of the listener.

---

18. Flemming, *Contextualization in the New Testament*, 19.

19. The specific portions are the Pentateuch (*Tawrāt*), the Psalms of David (*Zabūr*), and the Gospels of Jesus (*Injīl*). It is understood many Muslims believe that the New Testament used by Christians is incorrect or corrupted. At the same time, the *Tawrāt* has not been ignored by Muslims (Glassé, *New Encyclopedia of Islam*, 100). For a scholarly response to the issue of "corruption," see Nickel, *Narratives of Tampering*. In Cambodia, I have observed a general respect for the *Tawrāt*, *Zabūr*, and *Injīl*.

COMMUNICATION AND CONTEXTUALIZATION OF THE CHRISTIAN MESSAGE

Contextualization Through Choice of Language

The Cham language is the mother tongue of most of the respondents. Because they live in Cambodia, interact with Khmer people, and are educated using the Khmer language, they are also usually fluent in Khmer. In some cases, however, especially in rural areas or locations where there is a concentration of Muslim communities (and thus not as much interaction with Khmer people), some individuals are not very fluent in the Khmer language. Interviewees reported hearing the message in different languages, and with different effects. Some individuals heard the message in the Khmer language and experienced no difficulties in understanding. Narin, who recently decided to follow Jesus, reported that he heard the message in both the Khmer and Cham languages. He heard in Cham from those in his community who were speaking with him. He also listened to the radio and received information in the Khmer language. For him, there was not a problem regarding language, and he was interested in the message regardless of what language was used. As he said, "I was interested [in both Khmer and Cham]. Even though they are speaking in Cham or Khmer, they are only talking about the one Jesus."

Other respondents, however, experienced difficulty when the message was communicated in Khmer. Tahira, previously introduced, is middle-aged and lives in a rural area near the banks of the Mekong River. She discussed a video CD that some neighbors had recently viewed. That particular CD was produced in the Cham language. She was then asked if it was clearer for her to hear the story of Jesus in the Cham language as compared to the Khmer language. Her quick and simple response was, "Yes, when they use the Khmer language with deep words, I cannot understand. I can understand when they use the Cham language."

Ibrahim, in his twenties, also reflected on viewing a video CD. His experience occurred in his remote home village when he was young. In his case, the CD was in the Khmer language, which was not his mother tongue. As he remembered the experience, with a laugh he said that he did not understand much at that time. When asked why, he responded that young children didn't yet understand much about the Khmer language. Because of that, he did not know about Jesus. He later added that he also was not interested in Jesus then. When he was older and more fluent in Khmer, he met with a cross-cultural worker, who spoke of Jesus. In addition, Ibrahim was treated for a long-term illness in a hospital where there were many Christians and materials about Jesus. He began to understand much more of the

Khmer language and also about Christ. He remarked that he began to be interested in Jesus during that time. The cross-cultural worker introduced him to a Cambodian believer who taught him more about Christ. After continual teaching, Ibrahim noted that he began to believe, and gained more and more clarity about Jesus. He added, however, that there was a difference between simply understanding and believing, "Understanding in one thing, believing is another thing." For Ibrahim, the Khmer language was an initial barrier to understanding the Christian message, but with increased abilities in Khmer, and more input about the gospel over time, this barrier was greatly reduced.

It was previously observed that as an adult Pes received a Bible in the Khmer language from a cross-cultural worker. The content of the Bible was not explained at that time but was later made clear by another person. Pes said that he did not understand the meaning of the Bible because it was in the Khmer language. Moreover, talking about people later explaining the message, he remarked, "They used the Khmer language. That's why I didn't understand the story." He adds that a later version of the Bible included some religious terms that were used by Cham speakers. One example is the term "Allah," which, although written in that Bible using the Khmer script, when spoken was pronounced as Muslims commonly do. He noted that using those terms made the message easy to understand. This use of familiar terms will be discussed in the upcoming section. The use of Khmer language is a hindrance to understanding for some. For others, the difficulty goes deeper than a mere misunderstanding; it actually affects one's attitude about the message itself.

Rony is aged in his twenties and has been following Jesus for approximately four years. He heard the message from cross-cultural workers, who spoke and taught in Cham. When discussing his hearing of the message, he commented, "I do not look down on the Khmer language, but if he [the cross-cultural worker] had taught using the Khmer language, it would have been difficult for me to accept it." When asked why this was the case, he replied, "In the Khmer language, the message is understood in a similar way. But when they speak, I understand that they are talking about a different God, not the one and only God. Because in my heart I think that I have God (Allah) already. When we know more about who that God is, then we easily understand." Although he noted that it was a similar message discussed, regardless of the language used, Rony pointed out that the use of the Khmer language led him to feel the person was talking about a *different* God than the one he knows of. How this occurs was revealed later in the conversation, and it revolved around the use of a certain Khmer term, *preah*. *Preah* is the Khmer term for "God," but Rony pointed out it can have many meanings. Because in his mind it did not refer to the one true God, it led him to assume the speaker was talking about something far different than God (Allah). The term *preah* is commonly used in Cambodia, primarily by Buddhists but also by non-Buddhists. Although Christians use the term to refer to the Christian God, its range of meaning for others also includes lesser deities and spirits. It is thus not surprising that Rony interpreted the use of this Khmer term as referring to spirits or powers which were not all-powerful, and that this was not appealing to him, as he holds to a strong belief in one true God. In his case, the language used affected his attitudes about and openness towards the message. In contrast, the cross-cultural workers who taught him spoke in the Cham language. The final portion of his quote above reveals that when he was taught more deeply about the God that he already knew some about, he was able to understand the gospel message more easily.

The contextualization of the gospel message was accomplished in part through the choice of language. For some, the message was communicated naturally to others in Cham, without a conscious decision to use that language. For native Cham speakers, this method is usually the easiest. This approach also applies to Cambodian Muslims fluent only in Khmer who naturally communicated the Christian message to others like them using Khmer. The Cham language is the mother tongue, however, for the majority of Cambodian Muslims. Some who were not native Cham speakers deliberately decided to communicate the language to Cham speakers in the Cham language. This procedure involved activities ranging from learning the language itself to having the message translated into Cham as it was being communicated. One example of the latter was given by Sagy, who described a Malay-speaking visitor whose words were translated into Cham as he taught. Much effort was involved in the above activities of either learning Cham or translating the message into Cham. For some who received the message, the choice of language simply increased understanding, which is significant in itself. For others, such as Rony, the choice of language also impacted their attitudes and interest regarding the message.

Contextualization Through Use of Experience-Near Terms and Concepts

The use of experience-near language was also an influential method of contextualization. The experience-near concept was described by anthropologist Clifford Geertz as one which people "naturally and effortlessly" use to define how they think or feel, and in which they easily understand when it is used by others. He contrasts this concept with that of "experience-distant," which is not familiar or naturally understood, but specific for the purposes of specialists such as ethnographers or priests who are often different than the general population.[20] Robert Priest draws on Geertz's writing and notes that experience-distant concepts are usually more abstract or theoretical than experience-near ones, which are often more concrete. His research among the Aguaruna-Jívaro ethnic group in Peru revealed that ordinary and commonly-used words from their own culture were used to describe deep personal realities such as a sense of sinfulness.[21] This terminology could be referred to as experience-near. The choice of language also affects the understanding of and potential interest in a given message. In the Aguarunan culture, when words which were not experience-near were used to describe morality and sin, and connections were not easily made between the message and the personal lives of the listener, then the message was not clearly understood and often was not compelling, but was rather "tasteless" (*sakam*).[22] The choice of terminology that is easily understandable and naturally connects with human experience assists in communicating the Christian message and in making it personally relevant.

Experience-Near Terms

Several terms were deliberately chosen in order to communicate the Christian message in a way that is understandable and meaningful. The most prominent term was that of *Nabi Isa*, which means the prophet Jesus. This term is a Cham one, with Arabic origins. The Khmer term for Jesus is *Preah Yesu*. Because the Christian Church among the Khmer is larger and more visible than the church of BMBs, Muslims often hear the term

---

20. Geertz, "'Native's Point of View,'" 223.
21. Priest, "Experience-Near Theologizing," 183; Priest, "I Discovered My Sin!," 96–97.
22. Priest, "Experience-Near Theologizing," 189.

Preah Yesu. Those seeking to communicate the gospel to Muslims, therefore, have a choice to make regarding the use of *Preah Yesu* or *Nabi Isa*. Approximately one-fourth of those interviewed discussed this choice of words. For some respondents, both terms are easily used. Sofia says that both terms are good, because the Khmer word *Preah Yesu* is used when speaking with Khmer people, and the Cham term *Nabi Isa* is used when speaking to Cham. Tewi introduced the concept of *bangii pang,* translated as "sweet to listen to." Certain terms and phrases are more appealing and less offensive. In short, they sit more easily with someone. The term *bangii pang* captures this concept. I thus often asked what terms were "sweet" to listen to. For Tewi, both terms were easy to use, although she did say that when she identifies her faith to others, she remarks that she believes in *Nabi Isa*. Nabeel, in his fifties, has followed Jesus for several years. For him, the Khmer term *Preah Yesu* is also "sweet to listen to," because it refers to Jesus, whom he follows. He is not discussing his communication with others, but his personal feelings about the term.

The majority of those interviewed identified a clear preference about which term to use when talking to others about the Christian message. That preference was *Nabi Isa*. Hassad had previously discussed contextualization with another BMB and used the English term "context" to refer to this topic. He identified three terms he felt were important to use when explaining the Christian message to others: *Isa* (Jesus), *Allah* (God), and *Roh Allah* (God's Spirit). In his opinion, using these words established a better connection to the listener than if other ones were spoken. He related a story about a BMB who deliberately avoided the use of *Isa*, and strongly used the Khmer term *Preah Yesu* with those in his community. In Hassad's opinion, this man did not use contextualization, and it contributed to some of the problems experienced by him and his group of Christ-followers in that community. He also later explained that only certain people such as older individuals of high socioeconomic status, and those educated and familiar with the stories of God's prophets, know that *Preah Yesu* is actually referring to the Jesus they have heard about in Islam. In his opinion, normal people without a high status or level of education do not understand terms such as these well.

Others also preferred the use of *Nabi Isa* for reasons of understandability. Chenda, responding to a question about the theoretical use of those terms in a book for Muslims, said, "If *Nabi Isa*, good. If *Preah Yesu* [was used], not so good." She clarified that because of her location in a Cham village, others could more easily understand if they used the Cham term. That is the term that is "sweet to listen to." If they used the Khmer term, older people might not understand as easily. Kosal, living in a Cham village in central Cambodia, expressed a similar mindset. He clearly understood that both terms referred to Jesus, but when speaking to others he noted, "I don't use the word *Preah Yesu*. I use the word *Nabi Isa*. People understand more when we talk about *Nabi Isa*."

For others interviewed, the choice of this term was connected to acceptability as well. Amir, in his thirties, lives in a village located near the Mekong River and stated that he has followed Jesus for over ten years. He noted that because God has told his followers that others would hate his name, actually both terms could be used, and both will be hated. However, since the term *Isa* (Jesus) is related to the Arabic language, "only a few people will hate the term '*Isa*'. When we use the term '*Preah Yesu*,' more people will hate it." Isak also explained that Cham people know the term *Isa*, and understand that he is in the line of the prophets they know of, from Moses to Abraham and onto Jesus. However, "if we talk and say *Preah Yesu, Preah Yesu* like that, they will not be interested even though they already know that *Preah Yesu* is *Isa* (Jesus). *Preah Yesu* is what the Khmer call him. If we use the Khmer word, people are not interested, not interested . . . ." For Isak, the choice of words is not simply a matter of understanding. It affects one's sense of interest in Jesus. Even if one does understand that the Khmer term is referring to the Jesus they know about, the use of the Khmer term is not sweet to the ears. This is an example of contextualizing the message by using a term which is experience-near because it is familiar and easily understandable. There are parallels with other religious terms used, where the Cham or Arabic-based terms for God (*Allah*), and the Holy Spirit (*Roh Allah*) are used instead of the Khmer terms, which have often been influenced by Buddhism. Other examples of familiar terms used are those for sin (*duhsa*), heaven (*sorga*), hell (*naraka*), Satan/spirit (*Iblih*), and sacrifice (*kurban*). These words, deeply ingrained in the thoughts and common vocabulary of Cambodian Muslims, are instantly recognized and meaningful.

In this study, contextualization was also accomplished through the use of simple and commonly-used language. Experience-near terms are ones which are readily understood, naturally used, and resonate with one's personal life. Respondents spoke of both hearing and communicating the message through the use of simple and easily understood language. Minat was previously introduced as one who was quite interested in listening to the MP3 recordings from the Bible. When asked about the words used in the recordings, she replied that they were just "usual" ones, essentially referring to basic terms that are normally used. She further clarified that this use of words did make it easier to understand the message. Kari, speaking about how she communicates the gospel message to others, noted that she explained the story clearly, little by little, and that she used only simple or colloquial words. If more difficult words were used, people did not understand. Another female, Chenda, also remarked about how she told the message simply, discussing such topics as Jesus, doing good deeds, and belief. From the above, it is seen that the message is contextualized both through the use of simple, familiar terms as well as a simple method of presentation. Both of these approaches fit the culture and assist in clear communication. They also dovetail with the findings of Adams, Allen, and Fish who reported on fruitful practices for those working in Muslim contexts. One survey statement they asked three hundred practitioners to respond to was, "When communicating the gospel, I intentionally use terms that local Muslims will understand from their own culture, language, or religious background." The results from their survey suggested that the use of understandable terms did have a positive impact on the number of fellowships started.[23]

Experience-Near Concepts

In any culture, there are topics and concepts that are close to the hearts and minds of many of that group. Those topics are often ones which people are familiar with and concerned about. In the present Cambodian study, the gospel message was seen to address several topics important to Muslims. Four of them will be briefly discussed: spirits, heaven, good deeds, and sin.

Approximately twenty-five percent of interviewees talked specifically about spiritual forces. Nida, a young adult, spoke for many when she said, "... most Cham people believe in *cay* [a type of spirit] or believe in those things which we cannot see: spirits, evil spirits . . ."[24] Nida was previously afraid of these beings, so she respected them. She and others used a variety

---

23. Adams et al., "Seven Themes," 79.
24. Trankell and Ovesen note that belief in the *cay* exists among the smaller *Jahed* subgroup of Cham, and explain that "The *cay* spirits are the royal spirits of their ancestors in Champa." Nida belongs to the *Jahed* group. The other types of spirits she identifies are also referred to by the other groups of Cham ("Muslim Minorities," 23).

of both Cham and Khmer terms to identify these beings. One way in which the Christian message was presented to Nida was through telling the Bible story of a person who was demon-possessed and who trembled with fear before Jesus. During her interview, Aisah described a history of belief in spirits and fortune-tellers, and of requesting assistance from them in times of sickness. The following quote reveals that information she came to believe about Jesus's victory over Satan influenced her decision to believe in him, "Satan cannot persecute us when we believe on Jesus. For example, when we do not feel well in our body, just pray to God, and then we will feel better. That's why I believe strongly in him." Aisah heard that the gospel message addressed the spirit world. This was personally helpful to her. Amir related how he was exposed, both through reading and through watching a film, to the story of Jesus in the Bible. Remembering the story and the teaching that Jesus can be called upon if there is any problem, Amir specifically requested help from Jesus during a time of spiritual attack. His incidents of calling out to Jesus will be examined further later in this paper. What is clear is that he felt teachings he received about Jesus related to the spirit world, of which he was already aware.

The concept of heaven is personally important to many Cambodian Muslims. Hamat described how the BMB who shared the gospel message with him spoke about two things: sin and heaven. He was told that believing in Jesus would save him from sin, which Jesus accomplished through being hung on the cross. In addition, this crucifixion and shedding of his blood was to "help us go to heaven." Hamat stated that Muslims who pray five times per day are not sure if they can go to heaven or not. They are not brave enough to say they will enter heaven, though this is their desire. This illustrates that the concept of heaven is familiar to Cambodian Muslims, and for some, heaven is longed for. Sofia heard the Christian message from many, including Khmer people in Phnom Penh. She noted that one detail communicated was that those who believe in Jesus go to stay with him in heaven after they die. Imran, who heard the message from cross-cultural worker Timothy, remembered him explaining about sin, Jesus, and the straight path to heaven. Messengers frequently included the topic of heaven in the conversation when communicating the Christian message.

Those explaining the gospel message also discussed the topic of sin. As noted above, part of the message communicated to the fisherman Imran was that of personal sin. Malik recalled that the discussion of sin was often tied to information about Jesus, who could remove sin from people because of his crucifixion on the cross. The general concept of sin is understood by many Cambodian Muslims. Sukry is in his thirties and lives in a remote community in western Cambodia. He described experiences in which he learned about some aspects of sin,

> Older people in this village always talked about the story of Eve and Adam. When I was a child, I always went to play around the older people's homes. Sometimes when I go . . . I went to listen to them talk about Eve and Adam. They talked about the story of Eve and Adam, but they just talked about sin. They do not talk about the topic of being freed from sin . . . They talked about Eve and Adam having sin when they committed wrong towards God, but they did not talk about the topic of being freed from sin.

Sukry has clear memories of hearing about sin, through the story of Adam and Eve's disobedience to God. Some individuals, like Hamat, reported a sense of personal sin before ever hearing the gospel message. Isak provides further clarification about sin. He noted that he previously used to define sin as wrong actions such as murdering someone or stealing the belongings of another. Isak then added, "Cham mostly think like that," to explain that this is their general understanding of sin as well. His stated that his personal understanding of sin has greatly widened to include many attitudes and activities not previously recognized, but he felt that most Cham hold to the same viewpoint he previously held. In contrast to Sukry, Isak did not feel that sin is discussed very much. Rather, another topic was more prominent. He revealed that in the Islamic teaching he knew of, most did not frequently discuss sin, but they did often talk about carrying out good deeds, including following the religious law. Regardless of how prominent the topic is in discussions, sin appears to be an experience-near concept in Cambodian Muslim culture. The topic of sin is central to the content of the Christian message, and, by recognizing the experience-near nature of this concept for Cambodians, gospel messengers were able to make the message more relevant and understandable.

The topic of being good and carrying out good deeds was also discussed by Christian messengers. As previously noted, the concept of doing good deeds is valued in Cambodia. The term "good" is often used in common speech. Respondents spoke of how those who communicated the gospel couched the message in these terms. Abdul reflected on what Steven and Isak told to members of their community, "Then Steven and Isak came and said that Jesus is good. To follow Jesus is good. Jesus remained on the wooden cross to help us." Malik remembered that cross-cultural worker Kevin said that Jesus did good deeds and that if we followed him and did good deeds, we would be good like him. He added that Kevin explained that Jesus was one who commanded his followers to do only good, and not bad. Narin, when describing his decision to follow Jesus, used the term "good" and its concept many times, "I think that [this teaching] is true because Jesus taught people to do good [deeds], not to walk in the wrong path, but to walk in the good path. The people who believe in Jesus are kind, do not do bad things, and also help other people. So I decided that I would walk this path, the true path, the good path." Although there are many reasons for his decision to believe in Jesus, the terminology he used revealed that the words and concepts of "good" and "doing good deeds" are experience-near for him. Those communicating the Christian message discussed a variety of topics, but they did utilize this terminology and concepts in some of their explanations. Some common themes were: Jesus is good, Jesus did good deeds, Jesus taught his followers to carry out good deeds, Jesus's followers are good and do good deeds, and it is good to follow Jesus. Communicating in this manner illustrates that Christianity values many of the things that Cambodians already consider important. Honoring and following Christ is therefore not as foreign as one may have expected.

The four topics of spirits, heaven, sin, and doing good deeds have been reviewed. These topics can be considered to be 'experience-near," as they are close to the hearts of many and quickly understood. I have argued that communicators of the Christian message contextualized it by using these experience-near concepts. For some BMBs, this contextualization may be naturally done and without thought. Regardless of whether or not deliberate thought was given, this method allowed quicker recognition and deeper understanding of the message.

Contextualization through Communication within the Framework of Understanding of the Listener

Paul Hiebert reminds us of the critical importance of communicating the gospel message according to the language, worldview, and culture of those listening in order to facilitate understanding.[25] Cambodian Muslims have complex pre-existing frameworks of understanding,[26] which includes cur-

25. Hiebert, "Worldview Transformation," 28.
26. It is understood there is not a simple, singular "framework" of understanding.

rent beliefs and values held. Those seeking to present the Christian message to Cambodian Muslims utilized and honored this pre-existing framework of understanding. This method enhanced communication and made the message more personally relevant and acceptable. The interviews revealed that communication within the framework of understanding occurred primarily through honoring the existing religious understandings and perspectives of those hearing the message.

Honoring Existing Religious Understandings

The Christian message was communicated to some in such a way that their current beliefs and perspectives were honored and acknowledged, instead of being quickly dismissed. This approach, while certainly not agreeing with all the person's beliefs, was meaningful to many and prompted increasing openness to the message. It allowed the gospel message to fit into their current understandings about the things of Allah, and add to them. The perspectives and beliefs of the hearers were therefore respectfully acknowledged. The Christian message was not presented as something totally foreign to one's current understanding, but instead it built upon beliefs they already had. In short, it was communicated as news that fit into their existing framework. This phenomenon is seen in three different examples.

The first example is most complete and is found in the life and words of Isak. Previously in this paper, there have been only brief introductions to interviewees. In order to provide a more full-orbed picture of the lives and experiences of interviewees, some of their stories will be told in depth. These more detailed biographies will be shared in conjunction with specific topics they illustrate. Isak's experiences illustrate communication within a pre-existing framework. Excerpts from his long interview are included below. His biography will be written in the first person. Much of the following material is a summary of his words. Exact quotes, however, will be noted with quotation marks. Isak began as follows:

> Initially, I did hear stories about Jesus. But Muslims say that Christians are wrong, as they declare that Jesus is actually Lord. So at that time, I also felt that Christians were wrong. Through a relationship with a Cambodian friend of the family, I was introduced

---

Many beliefs and factors are at play, which vary by individual or group. For the remainder of this paper, however, the less cumbersome term "framework" will be used, with the understanding that it describes dynamic and very complex beliefs and values.

to Steven. I knew that Steven was a follower of Jesus, but I did not speak with him about that. We did, however, work together on a development project in a rural area. One time we were driving together in a car and we spoke about Jesus. I had listened to a cassette player and heard the words, "the King Father and the King Son," [God the Father and God the Son]. "I was thinking at that time that if he immediately told me that Jesus [*Isa*] was God [Allah], then I would not believe him." I asked, "Who is the King Father?" Steven said, "The King Father is Allah [God]." I asked him if he believed that Allah or a Lord exists, and he said "yes." When I asked about the King Son, he began to talk about Jesus. So I was interested when he said that the King Father was Allah. These people who follow Jesus, they also believe and accept that there is Allah. Because of these things, I began to be interested in following Jesus, and I began to research this, but I did not yet believe in Jesus. "If he had told me immediately that the King Father was Jesus, I would not have believed him. But he told me that the King Father was Allah, and the King Son was Jesus." I asked him if he believed there was a Lord [Allah], and he said "There is. The Lord created the sky and the land." Because of this, I began to be interested in the story of Jesus. If we talk to Muslims and say that Jesus was the one who created the sky and the land, they would not believe us and will refuse us. Before, when I was in the car with Steven, I thought he was walking in the wrong way. But it was not like that. He believed that Allah exists. And when I asked him if he believed that God [Allah] created everything in the world, he said yes. I then became interested because of that topic.

I was wondering about our good deeds and our worship five times per day. I wondered if the Lord would accept these or not. This caused us to think again. We see that the Qur'an tells us what we should do, but it does not show us if the Lord accepts us or not. We do not know. At that time, we started to do research about Jesus. We saw that Jesus said that for people who have faith in him, God will release them from judgment. We thought about this as well. I read the Qur'an and saw that it talked about Jesus as well, and I began to become interested, continually interested. I saw that this Jesus was not from the outside, but he is in the Qur'an, which also talks about him. We cannot depend on our good deeds if we want to go to heaven. I also began to change my heart and believe in Jesus. I said that I now believe. At that time I had a feeling that I believed, and my heart began to be very happy because when I was following Islam, we worshipped but we did not know if we would enter heaven or not. But I heard that Jesus said, "Whoever believes, [they] will enter heaven." So I was interested. I acknowledged in my heart that I believed and had faith in Jesus. And I told Steven that I already had faith in Jesus.

I did not initially think much about personal sin, because I thought that sin was if we did actions like kill someone or steal their property. That is what we call sin. Most Cham think like that as well. I thought that since I did not murder and steal, I did not have sin, but after studying more about the story of Jesus, I know that there are many types of sin.

I want to depend on Jesus because I want to see the way to heaven. Because in the law of Islam, people say that there is nobody who can help us. In the future, Allah will judge us and there is no one we can depend on. What helps us is the good works which we have done and spiritual merit we have. We will receive according to the good deeds we have done. We cannot ask someone to help us. So if we think about the final judgment, it will be difficult for us. So I thought that only Jesus can help me because he said that whoever accepts me, I will be their substitute [and forgive]. So those two paths help people to understand and to be willing to follow Jesus.

When I did not yet have faith in him, I did not have problems. But when I started to believe, I had some problems, first with my coworkers. One person told me that I was walking in the wrong way, "You're Christian. You already knew about the good religion [Islam]. Why are you walking in this way?" The second problem I had was with my family. My wife did not yet believe in Jesus, and we had trouble in the family. We were against each other.

Also at that time the place where I worked closed. After they closed, I did not have work. So it was very difficult. I continued believing, and at times I wondered in my heart as well. Before I believed, I had a job, a family, and no problems. Just when I believed, I had problems. But when I studied in the Bible, there is a verse that said, "When we believe, God will test our faith." Whoever believes in Jesus, God will test their faith. So I began to read the Bible and ask for his help, and after that, I saw that God helped me. I didn't know where to go and was in a difficult situation, but God helped me. I had a friend who introduced me to a small business, and I found that I was able to make good money on my first day. I thought that perhaps God was solving this for me. The Lord, God, Isa truly helped me. I saw that I made money in a short amount of time, and I was happy and thankful.

Much is included in the above narrative from Isak. At the beginning of the discussion, he said he was prepared to reject Steven's message if Steven quickly pointed to Jesus being God. Isak was surprised that Steven acknowledged Allah and that the God he knew of was also the creator. His expectation was that Steven would only dismiss Isak's understanding of Allah. Steven's words to the contrary contributed to Isak's new interest in learning about Jesus. Steven's approach can be seen as presenting the Christian message within the framework of understanding of the listener. He acknowledged that Isak had beliefs in one almighty God he called Allah. Instead of rejecting that framework, Steven worked within it and added further information. He clarified about Jesus. Isak was encouraged and somewhat surprised to see that the Qur'an teaches about Jesus. This realization created interest, as Steven was working within his framework, teaching more about someone Isak was already familiar with, instead of presenting him as foreign and new. Later in the interview, commenting on how to communicate the gospel message, Isak noted that people already knew about Allah. He added that if someone used terminology which indicated there is another Allah, the listener would not be interested and would feel looked down upon. It would be as if the messenger were saying "This person does not know anything!" While discussing this topic during another conversation, Isak emphasized that those of his group "already know about Allah and are wanting to find him." He also explained the principle that if people have already heard of a particular subject, they are more interested in learning more about it. He gave two practical examples of this, referring to a popular movie, *Titanic*, and to a well-known Cambodian political party. His point was that because these are already known topics, people are more interested in them, in contrast to that which is unfamiliar. Isak's comments, while focusing on communication within a framework of what is already known, also touch on the importance of demonstrating respect for current beliefs.

Imran's experience also illustrates communicating the Christian message within the framework of the listener. As previously noted, he was exposed to the Christian message earlier in life, but was not interested at that time, partially because of the use of the Khmer language for religious terms, which made the message seem foreign. Recently, however, he expressed much interest, "[I am] very interested because this story is the story of Allah . . . we respect and believe in Allah. So we are much interested in him." Similarly, reflecting on when others talked about Jesus, he said,

"Jesus, I understand is within Allah also. Because of that, I take it to heart." Two other times during his interview, Imran mentioned that this story is the story of Allah. There are many fundamental differences between the Islamic teachings Imran was raised with and the gospel teachings he recently heard. He is aware, for instance, of the importance of Christ for forgiveness and eternal life in heaven. Nevertheless, Imran saw the gospel teachings, including information about Jesus and his work, as fitting in the framework of topics concerning Allah. Because of this, he was interested.

A final example of placing the Christian message within the framework of the listener is found in the natural comments of a BMB who addressed a group consisting of both BMBs and non-BMBs. I participated in this meeting, which was similar to others that occasionally took place at that home. People gathered one evening to study and discuss the Christian message. Many onlookers were present, the majority of which did not follow Jesus. On this occasion, Sukry, a member of that community, suggested a question-and-answer session of sorts, pointing out that the older people knew much about the culture and history of that people, and some of the younger ones knew about the teachings of Jesus. People could thus learn from each other. In this context, Sukry simply stated that the book they are studying is a book about Allah. He did not say that what they were studying was new and foreign, but rather that it gives further information about Allah, whom they knew. He utilized their existing framework of religious understanding.

Discussion

The above approaches of contextualizing the message and honoring existing frameworks intersect with the studies of other scholars. David Greenlee's "Theory of Congruence" emerges from his research of conversion to Christianity and church growth in Morocco. By "congruence," Greenlee is describing, "the overall fit and the ease of transition between the old and the new, between the former faith and set of values and Christianity." He also refers to this as "a low level of barriers to conversion and church growth."[27] Based on his research, Greenlee provides two principles regarding congruence for conversion and church growth. The first principle is more important to this study as it concerns initial conversion. It is stated as follows: "An individual tends to be drawn to Christianity by elements in the Christian

---

27. Greenlee, "Christian Conversion from Islam," 208.

faith and in the nature of the sources of witness that are congruent with that individual's personal values. These values may both stem from and conflict with the individual's culture."[28] This principle highlights the importance of similarities between teachings about Christianity or the sources of those teachings with the values that an individual holds. This Cambodian study differs from Greenlee's. For example, only conversion is examined, and not church growth as in the Moroccan study. However, the concept of congruence is significant in the Cambodian study and is revealed in several ways. In short, the present study demonstrates the importance of a congruency of values, of ideas, and of a framework of understanding. A congruency of values is seen in the examples of individuals commending good deeds and good character, and discovering that the Christian message also honors this. In addition, the ability to enter heaven is valued, and the gospel message attends to this topic. A congruency of ideas is seen where concepts such as sin and the spiritual world are both known to be important to individuals and also addressed in the Christian message. A congruency of framework of understanding is seen where interviewees see the gospel message as fitting into their broad pre-existing framework instead of lying outside of it. In all of the above, there is a sense that, at least to a degree, the gospel message resonates with the values or perspectives already held by an individual. These types of congruency, although broader in some ways than those described by Greenlee, also exhibit similarities to his findings.

Previous to Greenlee, Kraft and Rambo discussed the concept of congruence or cultural similarities as impacting conversion. Kraft's research was among the Higi ethnic group in Nigeria, where he discovered several cultural factors that led them to have a positive attitude towards conversion to Christianity. One of these was a general disinterest in Islam that was influenced by historical tensions with the Fulani, a nearby Muslim group. Another factor was titled "The Cultural Fit Between Higi and Christian Worldviews."[29] Although Kraft's study focused on conversion from traditional tribal religion, not from Islam, it does illustrate that congruence and cultural similarities between the old and new religions can have a positive impact on conversion. Rambo views congruence as fitting into the "context"

---

28. Greenlee, "Christian Conversion from Islam," 211. The second principle, regarding church growth, is "Churches tend to grow when there is congruence between the congregation and the surrounding community. Congruence may be perceived in mutually meaningful cultural symbols, but may also be practically displayed in the response of Christians to the needs of the community."

29. Kraft, "Cultural Concomitants of Higi Conversion," 431–32, 436.

stage of conversion, and he interprets Kraft's study as demonstrating that various aspects of the context contributed to an openness of conversion to Christianity.[30] The congruency concepts described in the Cambodian study above not only relate to background cultural factors, but also to the manner in which the message was communicated.

In a more recent publication, Warrick Farah identifies eight separate contemporary missiological themes impacting MBB conversion. One of these is, "The Congruence of Cultural Values." He writes of conversion and church growth being encouraged among those who share common experiences, values, and social connections. Farah refers to Greenlee's study above and notes that the congruence of cultural values is a key factor influencing conversion.[31] This Cambodian study demonstrates that a congruency of values, of ideas, and of a framework of understanding was used in the communication of the Christian message.

Daniel Hoskins identifies seven research findings from his study of BMBs living in post-Soviet Central Asia. Finding number two, significant for the Cambodian study, is stated as, "For many Central Asian Muslims, Jesus is inaccessible until he, as *Isa*, enters into their culturally-constructed metaphysical landscape. The primary example of this linguistic phenomenon is the change of the Russian religious figure *Yesus Christos* into *Isa Masih*."[32] Hoskins explains that the term *Jesus* was seen by Muslims to refer to the Russian god. As such, it is inconceivable one would believe in him, even if one were attracted to him. However, when the one presenting the Christian message used the Muslim-background term *Isa* instead of *Yesus Christos*, the reception was much different. Hoskins provides an excerpt from an interview to illustrate. An individual was asked about the terminology used to discuss Jesus. The "location" of Jesus was changed when the person speaking used Muslim-background terms such as Jesus being *Kurban* (sacrificial victim) instead of common Russian terms. The interviewee noted that this was the first time terms like that had been used by someone when speaking to him. When the interviewer asked "Did that make a big difference for you?" the individual answered, "Yes, of course! Of course because I thought he knows really. He became a little bit closer to me. He did not say Jesus, *Jesus* in Russian, but he said *Isa Masih*."[33]

30. Rambo, *Understanding Religious Conversion*, 37–38.
31. Farah, "Emerging Missiological Themes," 16.
32. Hoskins, "Conversion Narratives in Context," 194.
33. Hoskins, "Conversion Narratives in Context," 117–18.

Hoskins findings connect to both the previous discussions of experience-near terms and communicating within a framework of understanding. The Cambodian use of the Khmer term *Preah Yesu* has similarities with the *Yesus Kristos* phrase in the Central Asian study. Both terms refer to the "god" of the majority people and are in the language used by the majority people. Both terms communicate a sense of distance and foreignness and are not experience-near for the Muslims living in those locations. It is thus not surprising that these terms illicit little interest in the minds of Muslims and do not resonate in their hearts. However, the use of familiar Muslim-background terms such as *Isa* does foster a sense of closeness and openness to the message. Hoskins's statement that Jesus must enter the Muslim's "culturally-constructed metaphysical landscape" in order to be seen as accessible has connections to the principle of communicating within a framework of understanding. Hoskins describes Jesus entering into an existing framework, and as *Isa*, he is known and accepted. Similarly, communicating the Christian message within the existing framework of Cambodian Muslims allowed Jesus to be seriously considered. He was already known to them as *Isa*. Thus the message was not foreign. Although not fully understood, it was already within their metaphysical landscape. This Cambodian study, although unique, connects with research conducted by others.

Materials Demonstrating Contextualization

In the course of this study, four types of materials were discovered which demonstrate contextualization. It is appropriate to review these materials now, as they illustrate many of the contextualization approaches discussed above. While the development of some of the materials was spearheaded by non-Cambodian cross-cultural workers, local BMBs were commonly involved in the design, updating, and use of these materials. The four materials are: a contextualized Bible, a film about Jesus, a tract to communicate the Christian message, and a large cloth printed with illustrations of ten Bible stories.

Contextualized Bible

A contextualized Bible was produced for Muslims in Cambodia. This Bible was printed in the Khmer language and was based on the Khmer Standard

Version Bible (KSV).³⁴ Although the majority of the contextualized Bible is identical to the KSV Bible, changes were made to make the Bible more acceptable and understandable by the Cambodian Muslim community. Main changes included using different religious terms that are familiar to Muslims. For example, the term Allah was used instead of the original Khmer term, *preah*. Cambodia is predominately Buddhist, and the term *preah* has a range of meaning. It does not simply refer to the existence of one omnipotent God, but may also denote other lesser spirits. Cambodian Muslims, therefore, do not necessarily directly think of a single all-powerful God when they read that term. Thus the use of Allah was seen as more appropriate than *preah*. Of course, there are many different words in the Bible that refer to God. All of these were not simply replaced with the term Allah, but different combinations were used to most accurately refer to the original biblical meaning and also be understandable and recognizable to Muslims. Many other terms were changed as well. Buddhist-based Khmer terms for heaven, hell, sin, sacrifice, and Satan, for instance, were replaced with Muslim-background terms for these topics. These new terms were the ones regularly used by Cambodian Muslims and were usually Arabic-based. Other terms such as the names of Bible characters and Bible books were similarly changed in the contextualized Bible. One BMB involved in producing this Bible noted that whatever it is that people already know, those are the things that we put in front of them. When asked if people are interested when they read this Bible version, he exclaimed,

> Interested. Ninety-nine percent interested. Why? Because they have heard about this book, but they have never seen it . . . And in the Qur'an, there is information about the Pentateuch, the Psalms of David, and the Gospels of Jesus . . . and it talks about Jesus. So that means they have this already. They know already. So what do we do in order to match what they already know? . . . So, because of that, this translation is important to give to people.

For him, contextualizing the message, including using familiar terms and names, is important in both facilitating understanding and interest in the message.

---

34. *Khmer Standard Bible.* An initial version of the contextualized Bible consisting of the New Testament was published approximately 2007 (no date provided in the publication itself). The second version including both the New and Old Testaments was published in 2014.

Film about Jesus

In the mid-2000s a film about Jesus, based on the New Testament book of Luke, was contextualized for Cambodian Muslims. The original film was produced in English and has been translated into many other languages of the world.[35] A standard Khmer language version of the film was produced before the contextualized versions discussed here, which were specifically made for a Cambodian Muslim audience. Two contextualized versions of the film were made. The first was translated in much the same way as the contextualized Bible above. The existing Khmer translation was used as a basis, but certain words and names were modified. The second version, however, used the Cham language exclusively. Several Cham recorded their voices to represent the various characters in the film. The original film was then re-voiced with these recordings. An introduction to the film specifically created for Muslim audiences was used. Cross-cultural workers, as well as Cambodians, were involved in the translation and production of these films.

Tract to Communicate the Gospel Message

Two cross-cultural workers developed a foldable ten-panel tract for Cambodian Muslims who are not fluent in the Cham language. The tract was written in the Khmer language. The front panel of the tract is green in color and, in addition to the Khmer words, includes a stylized Arabic phrase in the center. I interviewed Alex, the cross-cultural worker most responsible for creating the tract. He noted that this tract was based on one previously done for the Khmer ethnic group, but there had been modifications in focus, language, and images. Whereas he used the theme of "authority" with the tract for the Buddhist-background Khmer, he chose the theme of "heaven" for the Muslim group. The reason for this is found in his words, "and so we felt like the desire to go to heaven is a very big focus. Religiously it is a very big focus." His interaction with Cambodian Muslims led him to this conclusion, and this influenced the design of the tract, which discussed man's sin, Jesus's death on the cross to remove it, and the ability to be forgiven and have the right to enter heaven. Regarding modifications of language, four key Khmer terms were replaced with those used by Muslims.[36]

---

35. Krish and Sykes, *Jesus*.

36. Regardless of whether or not the Muslims speak the Cham language, they are familiar with these terms, which are usually Arabic-based and often used for religious

COMMUNICATION AND CONTEXTUALIZATION OF THE CHRISTIAN MESSAGE

The Muslim-background terms used were *sorga* (heaven), *duhsa* (sin), *Allah* (God), and *Isa Al Masih* (Jesus the Messiah). In addition, the phrase, "straight path," was used in the tract. This phrase, while written in Khmer, often resonates with Muslims as it is used in the Qur'an.[37] The images used were also modified from the original tract intended for the Khmer. Three of the pictures used are the same (separate ones depicting the power of Jesus to heal, his death on the cross, and his tomb). Other pictures were not used, such as ones which depicted the face of Jesus (at times offensive to Muslims), or ones tied with the theme of authority. This flip tract was deliberately contextualized for Cambodian Muslims, and its author notes that in its limited use thus far, people have reacted well to it and were able to understand its meaning as it was explained.

Cloth Illustrated with Bible Stories

I attended a training session for approximately ten BMBs as a participant observer. The session was led by a BMB, and a prominent topic was the understanding and use of a tool for communicating the Gospel message. This tool was a white cloth illustrated with ten Bible stories. The cloth can be conveniently hung vertically and measures approximately five feet high by three feet wide. Five Bible stories are depicted on the left, descending from top to bottom. Stories numbered six to ten are found in the right column. Each illustration has a title, printed in three separate languages. The first is in the Cham language, written using an Arabic-based script.[38] The second is in the Khmer language, using the Khmer script. The third is in English. As the leader Tinak noted, the stories on the left concern biblical prophets and characters that Muslims are already aware of. The stories on the right provide new information and focus on the life of Jesus.[39] A photograph of

---

vocabulary.

37. An example of this is the very first surah (1:6), when the worshiper asks Allah to, "Show us the straight way." Ali, *Meaning of the Holy Qur'an*, 15.

38. Although most Cambodian Muslims are not able to easily read the Arabic-based script, they would tend to identify the content as religious and in a positive manner. Muslim religious materials books in Cambodia are often written using the Arabic-based script.

39. English titles of each story printed on the cloth are as follows: 1) God created Adam and Eve, 2) Adam and Eve sin by eating the forbidden fruit, 3) God destroyed all people with a Flood except for Noah and his family, 4) Abraham obeys God's command and takes his son Isaac up the mountain to sacrifice him, 5) Moses leads the Israelites out

the cloth is included in Appendix B. During the training session, the leader asked a specific participant to explain one of the stories. After that person spoke, Tinak provided comments or more detail, and then invited another participant to explain the next story. This method was used to review and gain skill in using this tool. Referring to the concept of preparing well, Tinak told those present, "If we want to cut [wood] in the forest, we need to sharpen our ax." He summarized the left column as teaching about the law, and the right column as telling the good news about Jesus, with the overall theme that it is God's plan to help all people in the world to be freed from sin. His main teachings about Jesus centered on Christ the Savior's birth, Jesus's death as a sacrifice, and his resurrection, which will also occur for those who follow him. Tinak's encouragement to those present was that they should be telling others this information.

In a separate interview, I asked Tinak about the value of the above tool in helping people understand clearly about Jesus. He responded that the cloth helps discuss two concepts, two parts to the story. The first is about the law and sin, found in the teachings on the left of the panel. People sin, and even if they seek to follow the law, they will not be saved from that sin. The second part, however, is the news that God promised Jesus and that he is the powerful person able to help all people. The stories on the right provide proof that God is able to help us. When asked if others were interested when the message was explained using this cloth, Tinak responded strongly, "very interested . . . sweet to listen to, interested. So this story we talk about, when someone talks about it, people are interested." This particular tool is one used by BMBs in Cambodia. Along with others, it illustrates the manner in which materials were contextualized in order to communicate clearly without bringing undue offense.

How do BMBs Communicate the Christian Message to Others?

Interviewees were asked about their experiences of hearing the Christian message. The reality is that for many respondents, the message was heard years ago. Not surprisingly, some indicated they did not remember the interactions clearly. However, it is easier for people to remember and

---

of Egypt, 6) Isa (Jesus) was born in a stable, 7) Isa raises a man (Lazarus) from the dead, 8) Isa dies on the cross to save people from their sins, 9) After 3 days, Isa rises from the dead and appears to his disciples, 10) Isa goes back up to heaven.

articulate what they are presently involved in. In order to understand more about how BMBs communicate the gospel, additional questions were asked. First, "Have you told others about this news of Jesus and your decision?" Second, "If so, what do you tell others in order for them to understand clearly?" This section of the book seeks to present the responses of BMBs to these questions. Much of what is discussed clearly connects to material presented above, and it provides a deeper understanding of the present-day communication of the gospel message in Cambodia. What and how the message is communicated is discussed first. Following that, comments from respondents about their motivation to tell others about Jesus and the motivation of others to listen are examined. Nine approaches and methods of communication used by BMBs will be reviewed.

Communicating in a Natural and Non-Threatening Manner

Hassad, who was baptized approximately a decade ago, stated that he works on building relationships with people before speaking to them about Jesus. After a relationship has been established, he tells them that he is someone who follows Jesus's religion. In a similar way, Ali, aged in his forties and living far from Hassad, noted that when he travels to other communities, he seeks to greet the people and talk about normal topics. He said he did not want to talk about Jesus immediately, as the people have strict beliefs. He related that it was difficult to explain the gospel initially, but now they understand and some currently experience beautiful lives since they have believed. Pes, an older gentleman, pointed to an informal approach to sharing, "When we have a meal, we tell them. Jesus is like this or that." Amir is concerned about health care and he desires to discuss health issues with individuals. He noted that after talking about those topics with them, he might have further conversations, and present them with a Bible or a book about health care. Nabeel described a slow and steady approach, saying that he sought to speak good things little by little each day, month to month. In his experience, over a long period of time, some people follow him and others in their beliefs about Jesus. Shaza lives in a rural community where there are other BMBs. When asked if she tells others information about Jesus, she replied, "[I] tell, tell, tell. I told people that stay near my house. Some people follow, and some do not." She understands that some are interested in the message and others are not. At the same time, she stated that she did seek to tell them and that they heard the message from someone they already knew. This method is more natural than hearing from a stranger. The above approaches, while varied, demonstrate familiar methods of communication in which the recipient is not threatened.

Using Experience-Near Language within the Existing Framework of Understanding

Respondents commonly and naturally used experience-near terms as they spoke not only about previously hearing the message but also about their current beliefs and how they tell the Christian message to others. Terms discussed above such as *Isa* (Jesus), *Allah* (God), *kurban* (sacrifice), and *duhsa* (sin) were used when they described how they explained the gospel message. The experience-near concept of doing good deeds was mentioned by Chenda. She noted that when she does talk with others, she mentions that Jesus asks us to do good, and not bad. She stated that this declaration was at times followed by telling the person the Bible story about the poor widow woman who donated all she had (Mark 12:41–44). This concept of the poor widow giving up all she had interested Chenda, and she communicated it to others. This story is also a natural example of someone doing good deeds and demonstrating a good heart.

Cambodian Muslims honor the Qur'an. Two respondents discussed referring to the Qur'an when they sought to talk about the Christian message. When Maria talked about meeting with other university students, she said she told them that the Bible was before the Qur'an and helped explain the Qur'an. Maria stated that when she read the creation story from the Bible, others often assumed it was from the Qur'an because of similarities. After she stated that is was from the Bible, others had an increased interest in reading it. She also told others about her practice of worshiping on Sunday, and that this worship is directed at Jehovah God as found in the Bible. She explained more and felt encouraged when others deduced that the Jehovah God she was talking about was Allah, which they already knew. Maria spoke more to them about other truths such as the importance of seeking after God, but her words and actions demonstrated the desire to initially help place the gospel message within an existing framework of understanding.

Inviting Others to Meetings

In certain locations, BMBs gather to study the Bible and for fellowship. As a way to promote hearing the gospel message, Fatimah walked through her community and directly invited others to come and hear the teacher talk about Jesus. She noted that some people were willing to come. She stressed that those that were not interested were not forced to come; it is their right to do what they desire. Those who did come, however, were able to directly hear people teach. Fatimah is an example of someone who invites others to meetings in order to give the opportunity to hear Christian teaching.

Inviting Others to Request Help from Jesus

Yasmin is a young woman who has recently begun following Jesus. In explaining how she and other older believers talked about the gospel message, she started by saying that we told them the (Bible) story from beginning to end. Her subsequent words revealed her heart and an additional approach, "I want them to pray. For example, if someone has a sickness, at that time we tell them about Jesus (*Nabi Isa*). People don't believe us, so I want them to pray to Jesus and ask Jesus for help. And if Jesus helps that person so they are healed of their sickness, I want others to believe. I want Jesus to stay in that person continually." As will be seen later, Yasmin suffered from a sickness and felt that Jesus helped her. Her desire is that others specifically ask for his assistance and experience his help in their lives. She feels these actions can contribute to sincere faith in Jesus, and she invites others to pray.

Teaching from the Bible

Kosal received Bible teaching from Isak and Steven. Regarding others who have not received much instruction, he said, "Whatever I know from the Bible, that is what I explain to them." His approach centers on using the Bible, even though his knowledge is limited. Sara, around fifty years old, said that when she talks to others she explains by means of the Bible. She added that most in her area do not think that the words in the Bible are true, for instance, the teachings that Jesus came and died and lived again. At the same time, she feels that her role is to share the gospel message, "When I tell other people, they can either believe or not. . . . I just proclaim the good information. If other people do not listen to me, I do not force them."

Sara, in talking about different events in the life of Jesus as portrayed in the Bible, introduces the concept of telling stories.

Telling Stories

Stories were commonly told as a way to communicate the Christian message. Two types of stories were prominent: Bible stories and personal stories.

Bible Stories

As BMBs talk about the gospel, they often focus on simply telling Bible stories, rather than explaining Bible doctrine. For individuals such as Hamat, one reason for this is because he is illiterate. As he said, if he was able to read, he might be able to remember and have many lessons to talk about. However, what he does remember he tells others, and these are stories from the Bible. Omar identified two main things he tries to communicate with others. Both concern events in the life of Jesus and both contain doctrinal truth and personal implications. First, he explains that people nailed Jesus to the cross. His blood flowed and it cleans and saves his followers from sin. Whoever follows him is saved from sin. Second, he tells the Bible story of Jesus's followers traveling on a boat with him and encountering a strong storm, which nearly caused the boat to capsize because of the large waves (Mark 4:35–41). His followers thought they would die, but after Jesus prayed and raised his hands, the storm calmed immediately and all were safe. Omar added that Jesus then invited people to follow him. These two events are ones that Omar seeks to explain to others. They are stories, and they have personal implications, including a challenge to believe in and follow Jesus. In responding to the question about how they communicate the message clearly, Amir explained that the first step is to tell stories from the Bible. His comments immediately following this statement reveal his rationale for the use of the Bible, as well as the challenges he faces in his particular location,

> If we tell personal stories, others will not believe. Even if someone dies and comes back to life, people in this area will not believe, because God has done this already. . . . People still do not believe, until their hands are pulled [they are led]. If others see two people [believe], they believe. If they see only one person [believe], they do not believe. It is difficult.

For Amir, telling stories from the Bible is much more effective than simply telling personal stories. I believe this is likely due to the principle that the Bible, as a book from Allah, is generally respected. Amir did not identify any particular story or stories as most helpful but talked about discussing all the stories. Amir has followed Jesus for over a decade and has lived in his community for years. He is clearly aware of disinterest in his area about the Christian message, and uses strong words to express this, even noting that a resurrection would not prompt a response! He does observe, however, that if people see more than just one person believe, they are more inclined to believe as well.[40] Although there are a few believers in his community, Amir's frustration with the apparent indifference to the gospel is evident. Communication with others is quite difficult, but telling Bible stories is a good initial step.

Personal Stories

Amir's de-emphasis on the use of personal stories contrasts with the perspective of Ibrahim. Ibrahim lives in a different location than Amir. His opinion is revealed in the following quote, "Mostly I tell my personal story to others. So maybe they will start to think, 'Oh, what should I start to do [in my life]?'" When asked if he has ever used Bible verses, he added that he usually does not, because the Cham do not often accept teaching from the Khmer Bible. He feels it is better to let others know bit-by-bit first, and then give them the Bible to look at. He says, "For people who have begun to understand, we use the Bible, and they are able to begin to understand more. But if they do not understand at all, if you use Bible verses to talk to them, they will not receive it." Ibrahim lives in an urban area and interacts with people in Khmer. The fact that some Muslims are not interested in the Khmer Bible partially explains his approach. The differing opinions of these two men demonstrate that there is no standard way BMBs are communicating the Christian message to others.

Two women talk about telling stories as well. Sofia refers to both stories about the Bible and also personal stories. When asked how she helps

---

40. While just an observation, this principle is likely valid across many areas and populations of Cambodia. It also intersects with the research of others about the influence social connections can have in conversion, e.g., Gray and Gray, "Paradigms and Praxis"; Lofland and Stark, "Becoming a World-Saver"; Snow and Phillips, "Lofland-Stark Conversion Model."

others understand the message clearly, she said that, in short, she talked about the beginning of the planet and how Jesus created all things. She goes on to discuss his death and resurrection after three days, followed by his going to be with God his Father. She also added that early on she also talks about her personal story and how she believed in Jesus. Sofia noted that some people "opened their hearts" to listen after she told stories about Jesus and also related her personal story to them. Yasmin experienced "sickness" in her life that she attributed to Satan entering her body. As will be seen in a later section, she felt that Jesus helped provide lasting healing. Her desire to communicate her experience is found in her words, "I want to tell about the history of when I was sick, when Satan entered, and how difficult it was. And then I want to tell about how Jesus helped me." Yasmin also expressed personal interest in the story of Jesus removing Satan from the demoniac (Mark 5:1–120) and the desire to communicate this story to others. Clearly, it is important for Yasmin to tell others about her personal experience of suffering and of later being healed by Jesus.

Cambodian BMBs have used both Bible stories and personal stories to communicate the Christian message. Colgate discusses the impact that Bible storying has had in telling the gospel message in Muslim contexts. In a separate article, he relates how he used Bible storying in his work in Southeast Asia and he introduces the concept of relational Bible storying, which includes the three aspects of "Telling my story," "Drawing out his/her story," and "Telling God's story/Bible stories." Colgate writes that Bible storying should include storying from our own lives and asking good questions of others in addition to telling God's story.[41] The BMBs referred to above were not deliberately trained in Bible storying. However, they did tell stories which they knew, and they also included their personal stories. For Colgate, Bible storying is best done relationally. The Cambodian BMBs commonly told their stories in the context of relationship and demonstrated sensitivity to those existing relationships.

Adams, Allen, and Fish reported on the results of surveys collected during a 2007 meeting in Southeast Asia of three hundred practitioners who serve among Muslims. The purpose of the meeting was to examine practices learned from observing God at work. More specifically, they desired to understand practices that have proven fruitful in the formation of communities following Jesus. Adams, et al. identified seven themes of

---

41. Colgate; "Bible Storying," Colgate, "Relational Bible Storying," 138–40, 135.

fruitfulness, one of which focused on storying.[42] The authors noted that because many Muslims in those areas live in societies that emphasize oral communication more than written communication, the use of oral stories helps communicate the Christian message more effectively. They also highlighted the use of the Bible (theme number five), stating that both cross-cultural workers and communities of faith use the Bible as the "primary means of sharing the gospel, training new believers and developing leaders."[43] There is some evidence that in Cambodia cross-cultural workers used storying to teach and explain the gospel message.[44] This may explain some of the reasons why certain BMBs told Bible stories. The manner in which they heard the message is the manner in which they told the message. At the same time, their communication through stories, both Bible and personal stories, appears to be natural. They may see the Bible itself as primarily being a narrative containing many stories. This perspective is not surprising, as a large portion of the Bible is written in story form. Cambodian BMBs often communicated the Christian message through Bible or personal stories.

Using Metaphors and Illustrations

Ott writes that metaphors can both communicate meaning and touch the emotions and affect. He lists four different metaphors that relate to the gospel message: law, relationship, cleansing, and deliverance. Although each metaphor communicates aspects of the gospel, different metaphors may be appropriate to different cultures.[45] Respondents in this study mentioned topics related to three of the metaphors listed above. The term "law" was used, often as they described requirements of Islamic law, and also the breaking of God's rules as sin. The theme of "deliverance" was used by some interviewees, primarily those who had experienced God's help in dealing with a perceived attack or possession by a spirit/s. Descriptions of

---

42. Adams et al., "Seven Themes." The seven themes were: (1) Sharing the Hope within: Fluency, (2) Engaging Hearts and Minds: Storying, (3) Exemplary Lifestyle: Reputation, (4) Redemptive Bonds of Trust: Social Networks, (5) Getting the Word Out: Scripture Use, (6) Faith, Community, Leadership: Intentional Reproduction, and (7) A Holy Sacrifice: Prayer.

43. Adams et al., "Seven Themes," 77, 79.

44. One worker, for instance, utilized a poster which highlighted Bible stories in chronological order.

45. Ott, "Power of Biblical Metaphors," 360–62, 370.

"cleansing," however, were much more commonly used. The term "clean" was used by seventeen of the forty respondents, hinting that this concept or metaphor was significant to them in some way. Sara, for instance, said she was touched that Jesus was willing to die for our sin, and she tells others that he lived again to clean people's sin. Sagy spoke about being clean by means of an illustration. As we sat in the shade of his home discussing his decision to be baptized and his belief in Jesus, he said, "I wanted to change my mind and have a good heart. A clean one. We can compare that to before when we behaved badly, our mind was black like this [points to audio recorder], so I want to change my mind to be white like paper." Sagy focused on the themes of change and cleansing and described them by means of a practical illustration.

In addition to some references to metaphors, BMBs used a variety of illustrations to help explain the Christian message. In his interview, Sukry revealed three illustrations he uses with others, two of which will be discussed here. The first is regarding the topic of personal sin. He explains to others that even though he never killed someone, he should not think he is without sin. Sin originally came from Adam and Eve, and he compares this to his mother and father. He is the son, and if his parents were infected with HIV, the HIV virus would be transmitted to him when he was born. So we have sin from our parents already. A second illustration Sukry often uses relates to seeking important information. After mentioning that humans cannot escape from sin through religious acts, he said, "I talk casually with others, and to compare, I say if I want to go to the United States, I need to contact the U.S. Embassy. If [I] want to go to heaven, [I] have to contact and ask people who know about that." To elaborate, Sukry sought to communicate that the U.S. Embassy is the place to gain information and permission that will help one go to the United States. In order to enter heaven, people need to be first released from sin, but this is not done by our own good actions. It requires the assistance of someone outside of us. Another person, Isak, used a similar illustration, saying that if one has a problem, they look for someone who can help fix that problem. For instance, if their car is broken, they seek out a mechanic who can repair it. Isak pointed to the need to seek after and receive the assistance of others. He explained that Muhammad instructed humans to do certain good deeds, but he said he was unable to personally help people. In contrast, Jesus is able to help. Thus it is reasonable to seek his help for an issue he can address. The examples above illustrate the use of illustrations and the prominent metaphor of cleansing referred to by BMBs when they seek to communicate the Christian message to others.

Giving and Using Contextualized Materials

Rahman, around thirty years old, remembers when Steven initially came to his rural area. At that time he did not believe and had never read the Bible. After following Jesus, in cooperation with Steven and another BMB, he distributed copies of the Bible widely to two different districts. He described a Bible or book that was printed in the Khmer language on one side and the Cham language on the other.[46] Although there were initial opposition and suspicion of teaching about Jesus, Rahman noted that after people received copies of the Bible and understood more, some of this opposition decreased. Rahman described how he used this book when meeting others. He would read one or two sentences, then explain the meaning, and continue in that manner. Other times he would allow them to read by themselves, and assist in explaining when needed. He noted that, whereas before many expressed the sentiment that followers of Jesus were very bad, after a period of time and greater understanding, some said that Jesus's followers helped others and did not discriminate. In his opinion, this led to others beginning to believe in Jesus in those areas. Suliman is aged in his fifties and has followed Jesus for approximately one decade. He also interacted with Steven, and, like Rahman, told of distributing Bibles to many areas. In his words, "I spread this good information about Jesus to all the villages." For some BMBs, giving the Bible or other materials was a key component of communicating the gospel message.

Contextualized materials were not only distributed but were used in teaching others. Suliman, mentioned above, talked about traveling to locations where believers live and teaching using the cloth with Bible story illustrations. He particularly makes reference to teaching the stories about Adam and Eve eating the forbidden fruit and also about Noah. Isak frequently uses the cloth as well, saying it assists him to explain the reality that humans do have sin, and that Jesus can help. In an earlier statement, Isak provided insight into what he discusses when trying to communicate the Christian message to others. In short, he said first they talk about sacrifice (*kurban*), using the example of Abraham. They identify a purpose of sacrifice as that of releasing one from sin, a concept that many Muslims

---

46. This may have been a book containing Bible portions or Bible stories.

are aware of. Isak and others continue by saying that God loves us and has provided Jesus to be a sacrifice for us. Isak shared that because this point related to the concept of sacrifice, it was interesting to others. To summarize his teachings, he said, "First, we talk so that people understand sin. Second, we talk about the topic of sacrifice." For Isak, these are foundational points addressed when seeking to communicate the message to Cambodians from a Muslim background. Isak's words provide a glimpse into how one individual seeks to make the Christian message understandable and relevant to others.

Kosal uses another contextualized tool, MP3 audio recordings of Bible stories. Personally, he enjoys listening to them. He also noted how he plays the recordings in his barbershop as he cuts hair. He remarked that others, as they listened, made statements like, "Oh, truly Jesus is really good." His natural use of a tool which he appreciates appears to communicate Christian truth is a manner which is inoffensive.

Demonstrating Love

As Razaa told his story of hearing about and eventually deciding to follow Jesus, a key early theme was love given to him by others, even when he behaved badly. He frankly said that early on, he was not interested in hearing others talk about sin and he did not agree with them. What was most interesting to him was the concept of love. This background informed his communication approach with others, an approach centered on love. When he described how he spoke, he said that other Christians commonly said things like, "God loves you," to a seller at a drink shop. In contrast, he did not speak, but rather cleaned up his mess, returned the cup properly, and said, "Thank you." He recognized that his approach is different. As he elaborated further, Razaa, speaking in English, said, "For me, I don't want to say, 'I am a Christian, please believe.' No. I think my way is different. For me, it is very hard to say that 'God loves you,' or say like, 'God serves you.' For me, different. I and my wife choose this way. . . . We don't have my love, but . . . love from Jesus. One day they can see. It's not about telling." The manner in which Razaa chooses to communicate the Christian message to others is likely connected to how he was initially attracted to Jesus himself. Razaa also talked of experiencing opposition in his home community because he followed Jesus. These events have also likely influenced his approach with others. However, it is clear that he emphasized the demonstration of love to others as a means of communicating the Christian message. Many BMBs talks about showing love. Razaa provides a poignant illustration of this principle.

Observations Regarding Motivation to Tell and Hear the Christian Message

Interviewees expressed opinions about their desire and willingness to tell others about the gospel message, as well as their observations about the interest others had in hearing it. This information provides deeper insight into the manner in which the gospel message is communicated. Some individuals are quite motivated to explain the message. Suliman is an example. When discussing how the message was good news to him personally, he stated,

> It is good for me directly, and, so that I can spread [the message] to others, it is good for them also. It is not just good for me. For me, things are good already. When I study, I know that myself, I am free from hell already. But what about my friends, my children, my grandchildren, and my group? I spread out this information in order to allow other people to be free from hell also.

Suliman's animated voice displays clear motivation to spread this message so that others may benefit as he has. Rahman's statement below reveals a motivation to communicate even in the midst of opposition. If others, in a mocking way, identified him as a follower of Jesus, he said, "I am not afraid to tell other people that I truly believe in Jesus." Aminah noted that all people need this good information, not just herself. She wanted to broadcast the message to others, as she wanted them to believe also. At the same time, she knew that some oppose their group, and she said she was not brave enough to talk to them. Aminah's experience included both a desire to and a fear of speaking to others about Jesus.

Other BMBs also exhibited some degree of reluctance to communicate the Christian message. Sok is married and lives in a Muslim village different from his home community. While some in his original community have chosen to follow Jesus, Sok feels he cannot tell others in his current village, which has somewhat different Islamic beliefs than his hometown. The reason is, "If they knew that we follow Jesus, they will cut us off." He explained that he would still be able to remain living in that community, but that he would be cut off from Islamic connections. For example, if he were to have a celebration at his home, others would not come and join. This is the reason for his silence in that community.

Some BMBs expressed a reluctance or fear of speaking to Muslims, but an openness to speak to the Khmer majority people, who have a Buddhist background. Srey Mum is an example. She stated that she is afraid if Muslims know she believes, and at other times realizes that she should not hide anything. Her struggle is not unique and is revealed in her words,

> When we spread the good news to others, we are glorifying God, and we know clearly who we are. But with Muslims, it is difficult and hard to face them, because I am from the Islamic group. If I was Khmer, I would not be afraid. . . . If I join with Khmer to share the gospel, I am not afraid, because they [the Khmer] do not ask us anything. They only ask us how to believe in Jesus. . . . but with Muslims, we have difficulties.

Srey Mum finds it hard to be open with those from her group about her faith, and at the same time, she feels conflicted about these feelings. She currently lives in a Khmer area. Her statement about the Khmer not asking questions relates to her experience that some Muslims deliberately ask who she is and where she is from, with the apparent intention of reporting her belief in Jesus to others. It is thus not surprising she states she experiences difficulties in communicating the message to Muslims.

Sara lives far from Srey Mum, in a Muslim community containing other BMBs. She has also experienced problems, in her case opposition from others that has impacted her desire and ability to talk about Jesus. She said, "[Some] other people do not believe us. They do not listen to us. They said that we can believe alone, but we are not to convince them to believe like we do. Since they said that, I'm afraid to do that again. I dare not talk about Jesus's story to [those] other people." Sara is understandably afraid to talk to those who oppose her. She did, however, discuss communicating the message to some individuals who are willing to listen. She tells Bible stories to others, even though she acknowledges that most in her area do not believe the stories about Jesus to be true. She added that "they can either believe or not . . . I just proclaim the good information to them. If other people do not listen to me, I do not force them." When she described her own conversion, Sara stated that no one forced her to follow Jesus. Rather, she made her own decision. In a similar way, she is sensitive to the decision process of others, knowing that she cannot force them to follow. Later in the interview, Sara insightfully noted that if people have *ea tai* (heart interest), you can talk to them. Otherwise, it is difficult.

Borey also discussed the importance of a sincere desire to listen. He stated that if people are not interested in listening, he does not talk to them. However, if they do genuinely want to talk, he will explain to them the gospel message. As he noted, "If someone listens to me, I will talk to them. . . . If they do not listen, what words do we have to tell them? If they do not listen, we do not have words to tell them, unless they agree to listen and to discuss. Then we have words to tell them." Borey is aware that many individuals are not interested in the Christian message, and thus words spoken to them have little impact. He does not personally know Sara, but his perspective echoes her comments about the importance of having a heart interest in the Christian message and the fact that many Cambodians they know do not appear to be interested. These realities affect the motivation and manner in which the message is told.

Conclusion

This chapter has examined the answers to the following questions: (1) Whom did the Cambodian BMBs hear the Christian message from? (2) What was communicated? (3) What methods were used in communication? (4) How was the Christian message contextualized? and (5) How do BMBs communicate the Christian message to others? In summary, the message was communicated primarily by Cambodian BMBs and cross-cultural workers from other countries, but also by Khmer Christians. Old Testament Bible stories and teachings about Jesus were often focused on, with the challenge to believe in and follow him. A variety of methods were used in the communication of the gospel, prominent among them being the use of the Bible, discussion in groups, and utilizing multimedia tools such as MP3 recordings and films. In many cases, the message was contextualized in order to make it more understandable and relevant. Various adjustments were made, such as choosing what language to communicate in and using experience-near terms and concepts. In addition, the message was commonly communicated within the framework of understanding of those hearing it. These contextualization practices intersect with the research of other scholars such as Greenlee and Hoskins.[47] Several types of materials were used which demonstrate the contextualization of the message, including a contextualized

---

47. Greenlee, "Christian Conversion from Islam"; Hoskins, "Conversion Narratives."

Bible, a film about Jesus, a tract about the Christian message, and a printed cloth containing illustrations of Bible stories.

Cambodian BMBs communicated the message to others in a multitude of ways, such as using terms and concepts which others naturally understand, being non-threatening, inviting others to meet and learn about the gospel, encouraging people to personally request assistance from Jesus, teaching from the Bible, telling stories, using illustrations, distributing contextualized materials, and simply demonstrating love. Many Cambodian BMBs demonstrated a clear desire to proclaim the Christian message, while others expressed reluctance to talk, at times fueled by personal feelings of inadequacy, a perception of disinterest or opposition of others, or fear.

The content of this chapter relates to the first research question: What role, if any, did the contextualization of the message play in clearly understanding it, and in the decision to follow Jesus? Few respondents explained the connection to contextualization as clearly as Isak, who stated that this interest was piqued when Steven acknowledged the existence of Allah and placed teachings about Jesus within his understanding of Allah's story. The evidence suggests that the contextualization of the message did contribute to three results: the message was better understood by the listener, it was seen as somewhat familiar, and it was viewed as personally relevant to their circumstances. Data about how the message was contextualized and how it was communicated by BMBs themselves demonstrates that contextualization was used, precisely because it was helpful. These conclusions are reinforced by findings discussed in subsequent chapters, which examines core themes important in the conversion of individuals and also how the message was personally meaningful to them.

5

Prominent Themes and Factors in the Conversion Process

AN ANALYSIS OF CONVERSION narratives is complex as individuals often speak about various aspects of the gospel together. The topic of sin, for instance, may be naturally tied to forgiveness, which may lead to a discussion about Christ and his work, and even heaven. It is difficult, therefore, to delineate clear categories and factors impacting conversion. Furthermore, there may be overlapping content between categories. Rather than confusion, this phenomenon can reveal a connectedness of various aspects of the gospel and cohesion of understanding for respondents. I will, however, seek to present the content of the interviews according to categories as much as possible, with the understanding that there is obvious overlap at times.

What did the respondents identify as important in their conversion process? Their narratives revealed several themes or factors. Respondents did not generally directly identify which themes or topics were most important during the process of conversion. However, as they told their stories and discussed their life of following Jesus, these themes emerged. Most respondents elaborated on more than one theme as they reflected on their path to conversion. The majority of these themes relate to the content of the message itself. Others relate to self-perceptions or desires, or the manner in which they heard the message or were influenced to embrace it. Four primary themes and four secondary themes emerge from the narratives and reflections of those interviewed. The primary themes are as follows: sin and cleansing, heaven and judgment, Jesus, and the Bible. Secondary themes include the witness of others, dreams, love, and the sense of God's leading. The use of the term "secondary" does not mean these factors were of less importance for each and every individual. For those who described them, they were often very important. Rather, "secondary" is used for those topics that were not referred to as often or by as many individuals as the primary ones. The delineation between a "primary" versus "secondary" theme is thus based on a combination of the number of respondents referring to it and to the intensity of their responses. Intensity refers to the degree of importance a respondent attributed to a particular factor/s. If a large portion of respondents referred to a particular factor, and many demonstrated intensity to their response, that factor was categorized as a primary one. Factors which were not as commonly referred to, or were not described by a large number of people as being quite significant in their conversion, were categorized as secondary ones.

Themes and factors were identified according to the reflections of respondents during their interview and their response to the initial open-ended question to share their story of learning about and coming to follow Jesus. Unsolicited themes and topics such as "heaven," "Bible," and "dreams" emerged during these discussions. Although questions were asked about specific topics such as "sin," themes such as "sin and judgment" were selected based not simply on how often the prompted topic was discussed, but rather on insights arising from the reflections and narratives of the respondents, including the intensity of their response. In addition, a summary question towards the end of the interview about why individuals chose to believe in Jesus served to reinforce or nuance previous comments. It is understood, however, that because several questions related to such topics as "sin," the "message," and "belief," respondents may have felt more freedom to discuss these at length. Questions such as these could potentially influence what topics were discussed and emphasized. A careful analysis of the data was thus required in order to accurately understand the perspectives and experiences of the respondents. Coding assisted in identifying themes and factors, and in revealing the number of respondents referring to a particular theme. The delineation between a "primary" versus "secondary" theme is ultimately subjective but is based on the above approach which focuses on the topics identified by respondents and the importance attributed to them by the respondents themselves.[1] In this chapter, I will initially

1. In his research on Palestinian Muslim conversions, Greenham identified "categories of greater prominence," and "categories of lesser prominence" as conversion factors. He refers to Monette, Sullivan, and DeJong's four categories for coding, (1) presence or absence of an element, (2) frequently of occurrence of an element, (3) amount of space devoted to an element, and (4) intensity of expression, and noted that for his research categories one and four were most instrumental in delineating between a category of greater or lesser prominence ("Study of Palestinian Muslim Conversions," 149; Monette et al., *Applied Social Research*, 175). While not specifically following Greenham's approach, my methodology contains parallels to his.

Primary Themes

Sin and Cleansing

Many interviewees spoke about personal sin and the fact that the gospel message addresses sin. Ibrahim is a single male in his mid-twenties who was baptized five years ago. When invited to tell his conversion narrative, his first words were, "I think that I have sin. So I have to believe [in] Jesus because Jesus helps to escape from sin." In a later statement, reflecting about his understanding of Islamic teaching and talking about his hope in Jesus, he said, "Yes, we have hope because . . . in Cham [religion] they don't tell us what to do to escape from sin. We don't know clearly; we just know that we have to go to the mosque every day to pray to Allah. But we are not sure that we can escape from sin or go to heaven." Other respondents also referred to their perspective that Islam does not clearly address this sense of sin. Ibrahim does wonder if he is somewhat unique, and his personal concern about sin is communicated in the following statement, "I do not understand . . . why some people don't care about the time when they die? They are concerned about this world, about having things in this world. But for me, I care about what happens after I die. I care so much about this."

Rony is also in his mid-twenties. When asked about his early impressions of the message about Jesus, he noted that initially he did not know anything at all, but when he heard the message, it was like "[I] was surprised [startled] and I also had a happy heart. Because I was a person that did bad things. Someone who would give me help to escape from sin without me having to do anything at all! Free!" Rony felt that he had done wrong things, and the ability to escape from this sin was good and surprising news, especially as it was freely given.

Early in her interview, Srey Mum spoke about times of reading the Bible to understand, and of coming to the conclusion, "If I believe in Jesus, then I will be saved and be released from sin. I am not able to depend on what I am able to do [by myself]." Again, the topic of personal sin and addressing it is important in the mind of many individuals as they consider the decision to follow Jesus.

The above discussion brings up the question: did people have a sense of personal sin before, after, or during the process of believing? One of the questions asked of interviewees was, "Did you have a sense that you had done wrong before you heard this message about Jesus?" Those interviewed provided a variety of answers. Some, like Borey, aged in his forties and living in central Cambodia, talked of a clear previous understanding of sin, "Before I walked with Jesus, I knew myself that I had sin. [I] knew I had sin, but did not know what to do to escape from that sin." When asked if their Islamic teachers talked about the concept of sin, some interviewees noted that this had been discussed and that this contributed to their initial awareness of personal wrongdoing.

Some interviewees, however, did not have a personal sense of sin before belief. Tahira is approximately forty years old and lives in a village near the Mekong River. Reflecting on her childhood, she said, "Before I know nothing [that I have sin or not]. When I was a child I never thought about that [sin]. I did not commit sin either. I always did good things from the previous time on." When asked about her thoughts as a young adult, her comment was similar, "I think that I did not commit wrong. I always did that which is good, because I knew clearly that when we do good, we also receive good, but if we think about doing wrong, that is sinful."

Still, others spoke of a sense of both being and not being aware of personal wrongdoing. Aminah, aged in her mid-forties, is a small business owner living in a rural community. In her spirited discussion, she said that before believing in Jesus, "we don't know when we do wrong." She clarified further, "We know that we are wrong, but we do not accept the mistake, and think that we are right." Soon after, she talked about what happened after belief in Jesus, "If we believe in Jesus, we do bad, just a little bit, we accept the mistake. We know that we have done wrong." Aminah added that this was her experience now, understanding that she did wrong even after committing a small offense. She said there is a difference between pre and post-belief in Jesus. This perception of not knowing clearly about personal sin—or not taking it seriously—before belief but of gaining greater awareness afterward was expressed by several respondents. Certain individuals had a clear sense of personal wrongdoing before they believed, and others did not. For some, the sense of sin came about during the time they heard the message or believed.

The concept of cleansing was also prominent and often tied to understandings about sin. This is illustrated in the words of individuals like

Kosal, who when talking about baptism, noted that he "wanted to clean or relieve my sin, to make myself clean". Rony, previously quoted as one who felt he had done bad things and was happy to hear that Jesus would freely help him escape from sin without specific actions on his part, noted that "Jesus the Messiah has washed us clean from sin." Sin and cleansing from sin are tied together, with Jesus as the actor who provides the cleansing. The metaphor of cleansing was discussed in the preceding chapter and was identified as meaningful for many, with approximately a third of all respondents using the word "clean." In most instances, this word is used in the context of being clean from sin or having a clean heart. Sagy spoke of desiring to be different, to change from behaving badly (represented by the color black) to having a clean heart and mind (represented by the white-colored paper). Respondents talked much about personal wrongdoing and sin, and they also frequently discussed cleansing from this sin. The words of Matt illustrate this and include the concept of forgiveness. When asked if anything struck him as odd or interesting when he heard the Christian message, he responded by saying that we are able to ask forgiveness, and when we do wrong, because of God we are made clean again. Things are all thrown away, and we are totally washed clean like before.

Heaven and Judgment

The concept that the gospel message includes an eternity in heaven was important for many individuals. Kosal, who is in his early thirties and has believed for ten years, reflected this perhaps most clearly when he stated,

> In the beginning, I did not believe. In my mind it's unsure. Where would I go? How can I go to heaven? I was not sure about that even though I practiced the religious precepts [prayed five times per day].... I was unsure that I could go to heaven or not. Nowadays, after believing, Jesus will bring me to God's heaven, and prepare [a place]. I know clearly. I also told my wife, and my wife also believes in Jesus. We are his believers. Allah [God] is God the father, Jesus is the Son, and we as his believers go together [to heaven]. God has prepared Jesus to bring us to God's heaven. We will be saved because we believed in Jesus.

Kosal communicated his uncertainty about going to heaven or not, even as he was fulfilling the activities prescribed by his religion. He also demonstrated an excitement about his present belief that he will indeed go to heaven, based on Jesus and his belief in him. Early in his interview, he stated, "No one can guarantee that they will go to heaven, even though they pray five times a day. But Jesus guarantees that his believers will go to heaven. He died on the wooden cross in order to bring his believers to God's heaven."[2] Kosal was passionate about the concept of heaven in his interview, evidenced by the fact that he used the word forty-five times. Kosal's experience with Jesus was not merely an intellectual one; it also affected his outlook and emotions, "Since I have believed in Jesus, I feel really happy. God makes me feel fresh in my body, makes me feel fresh because I can go to heaven when I believe in Jesus."

Others also spoke about heaven and final judgment. Isak, whose detailed story was introduced earlier, reflected on his decision to follow Christ and tell that to another person,

> I admitted the truth that I believed in Jesus. Why? Because I had been thinking about what are the differences between Islam and Jesus. Islam asks us to do this or that, but we don't know what we are to do in order to go to heaven. But for people who believe in Jesus, we know that we will go to heaven. So this is what caused us to change our mind quickly.

Later in the interview, Isak talked about the reality of heaven and hell. He emphasized that those who have faith in Christ will enter only one, which is heaven. He continued by explaining that those who believe will not be punished later by God (experience judgment), and he concluded by saying, "And this is the thing that really attracted me." Isak noted that, for him, the concept of knowing he could go to heaven was important in his decision. He emphasized that the concept of personal sin was not prominent in his mind, but the idea that Jesus could help him go to heaven was. Srey Mum also discussed heaven in context with a final judgment. She talked about the option for someone to depend on themselves but added that if they chose to believe in Jesus, they are released from sin and don't need to depend on themselves or do anything. Srey Mum said she recognizes that committing wrongdoing in this world may result in punishment from the state authorities, but not in eventual punishment from the Lord, as she has already been released from punishment. As she stated, "my soul won't go into the lake of fire. I have been saved by Jesus so I could go to heaven." The concept of heaven is tied to and contrasted with that of final judgment.

2. The term "guarantee" was used by many interviewees when talking about what Jesus does. This concept will be explored later.

Others also discussed heaven. Twenty-eight of the forty interviewees made a reference to "heaven." Although not all of them were directly claiming that the concept of heaven was instrumental in their conversion, this number does reveal that for many, heaven is a common topic associated with their life with Jesus and decision to follow him. This finding about heaven was corroborated with an additional interview I did with a cross-cultural worker, Alex. Previously introduced, Alex was not in the group of forty BMBs interviewed but was involved in drafting a tract to communicate the gospel message. His interview was done to gain additional information and triangulate data. He and a coworker sought to understand the values of Cambodian Muslims in their area and concluded, "We felt like the desire to go to heaven is a very big focus. Religiously it is a very big focus . . . But ultimately . . . what is the ultimate thing? . . . to be able to go to heaven." The concepts of heaven and judgment were significant for many respondents as they considered deciding to repent and follow Jesus.[3]

Jesus

A third prominent theme discussed by interviewees was the person of Jesus. This is not surprising, as Jesus is the author, means, and primary actor in Christian salvation. Gaudeul identified "Jesus is so attractive" as an important factor in the conversion of those from a Muslim background.[4] Similarly, Greenham listed "the person of Jesus" as one of the five categories which had greater prominence in the conversion of Palestinians he studied.[5] Those interviewed in this Cambodian study talked about various aspects of Jesus, which can be organized according to three categories: "Jesus is," "Jesus did," and "Jesus does." These three aspects provide a more nuanced description than the research noted above and more accurately represent the thoughts of those interviewed, who frequently referred to Jesus and his actions.

---

3. There are numerous references to heaven (also referred to as gardens of paradise), hell, and the final judgment in the Qur'an (examples from Surah 3 include 3:15; 3:133; 3:136; 3:12; 3:103; 3:9; 3:25). The details about these topics do not directly coincide with the information presented in the Bible, but the concept of a final judgment for acts done and an eternal location of either a place of reward or punishment is prominent in the Qur'an. It is thus not surprising that Cambodian Muslims are aware of and concerned about these topics.

4. Gaudeul, *Called from Islam to Christ*.

5. Greenham, "Study of Palestinian Muslim Conversions."

Jesus Is

When asked in conclusion what led him to believe in Jesus, Rony answered two things, "The first issue, the one which is the most important . . . that I know that Jesus is truly Allah [God] . . . I know that he is truly God because he died and lives again, according to the Bible that teaches this. This is the first issue. The second one is similar. He helps me to be separated [freed] from my sin." For Rony, the understanding that Jesus was the true God was critical to his decision to follow him. Previously he did not believe that Jesus was God but becoming convinced that was the case greatly impacted his decision. Amir, a father aged in his mid-thirties, explained various reasons for his interest in Jesus. He said, "And I love Jesus because he's not [just] a human being. He comes from God." He later clarified that he believes in Jesus because he is not like previous prophets, who come from humans. Jesus is different because he is located with God. In a similar manner, Nida talked about questioning who God was, and the answers she found influenced her actions. She said, "Who is Allah [God]? Now I know who God is. That God is Jesus the Messiah. So whom should I believe? I believe in Jesus who is Lord." Coming to believe that Jesus was truly her God and creator was personally meaningful and contributed to her decision to follow him.

Another individual focused on a different aspect about Christ. Borey emphasized that Jesus is alive. He noted that he actually asked Islamic religious teachers to confirm whether or not this was the case, and they did. The importance of this teaching for Borey is revealed in the fact that he referred to Jesus being alive nearly thirty times during his interview! For him, the fact that Jesus is living is tied to his ability to actually help him and to convey Borey's words to God. He described it this way, "Muhammad has died already. Who is there who can take our words to God? There is no one. . . . So I decided that I am going to follow Jesus. I pray to the Holy Spirit, and Jesus will send it to God immediately. . . . So I decided that, the living person . . . the person living is able to do things [for us]." Borey chose to believe in and follow Jesus, whom he came to understand is truly living.

Jesus Did

The second category about Jesus focuses on what he did while living on earth. Tewi is in her forties and lives near the Mekong River. Her emphasis is clear when she stated, "Jesus did much good. He did not know how to do evil to anyone. He did not know how to do evil." She noted that the fact that Jesus did good deeds was a key contributing factor to her believing in him. Tewi's sister Tahira, also interviewed, stated as well that she was interested in Jesus because he committed good deeds.

Several individuals mentioned they were impressed that Jesus did not discriminate against others while he lived on earth. Malik, in his mid-fifties and living in a rural village, highlighted this several times. He said, "Jesus did not discriminate based on social status to anyone. Whoever they were, Jesus accepted all of them. Jesus helped disabled and blind people. If we just pray to Jesus, he will help. Because Jesus does not make himself to be higher [than others]." Malik later said that some people claim that Jesus did wrong, but he responds by saying that Jesus never did anything wrong to others. In contrast, he asks us to love each other. These actions of Jesus impacted his decision to follow: "I accepted Jesus. He could truly save me and all people from sin because he never spoke evil words to anyone."

Sok, married and in his thirties, also discussed discrimination, relating a Bible story he was familiar with about a lady who was hated by everybody except Jesus. Sok remarked that Jesus even held the lady's hand, which caused others to question why he did that. Based on the story, Sok commented that Jesus did not discriminate against anyone and added, "This is one of the best points about him. So we can receive him [believe] with a happy heart." The perception that Jesus did not discriminate impacted Sok's decision to follow him.

Cambodian Muslims are a minority group in Buddhist majority Cambodia and comprise about three percent of the total population. They have experienced discrimination in various ways, including harsh treatment during the Communist rule of Pol Pot in the mid-late 1970s.[6] These experiences of discrimination may contribute to their quick recognition of Jesus's acts of non-discrimination and may increase their interest in him because he is seen as one who treats all people with honor.

A final activity Jesus did was suffering and dying on the cross. This act was admired by many respondents. Chenda is an example. When discussing what made her choose to follow Jesus, she first noted that Jesus asks us to do good deeds. She also mentioned answered prayer and followed with, "and the other amazing thing is that Jesus agreed to die on the wooden

---

6. Collins acknowledges the reality of "enormous, widespread suffering" experienced during the Pol Pot period by all Cambodians, and includes a discussion of various viewpoints about if and to what degree the Cham were singled out for persecution because of their religious beliefs ("Muslims of Cambodia," 53–57).

cross, to clean our sin." This statement reinforces an earlier remark by her expressing amazement that Jesus would dare to give up his life in order to cleanse people in the entire world from sin. Her words dovetail with those of many others, who express admiration of Jesus because of his suffering and sacrifice. For Chenda, this act contributed to her decision to believe in and follow him.

An appreciation of Christ's attitude during his suffering is found in the words of Ali. Aged in his mid-forties and living in a rural area of Western Cambodia, he stated, "Because he trusted God . . . he was not worried. . . . People crucified him. The reason he allowed his blood to flow was so he could save our people. He didn't worry about anything, even though people hung him on the wooden cross or did other things, because he loves everyone very much." In discussing the suffering and death of Jesus, Minat also added that Jesus was not angry with those who crucified him but rather forgave them. Respondents often tied Jesus's suffering to addressing the sin of humankind. Sofia simply explained, "Jesus died on the cross because we have a large amount of sin. Jesus died on the wooden cross in order to relieve our sin." The suffering and death of Jesus were discussed by many individuals. This previous act relates to what Jesus currently does.

Jesus Does

Several interviewees used the word "guarantee" (*tanaa*) when referring to Jesus and their belief in him. The sense that Jesus is able to guarantee something for his followers was seen as important. Omar, aged in his sixties, was interviewed in his home, located in a large Muslim village in central Cambodia. He related the story of Jesus being in a boat during a storm, with his companions being frightened. He noted that Jesus quieted the storm and forgave and saved those who came along with him in the boat. Then they arrived peacefully at their destination. Omar reflected and mentioned that the point in which he came to sincerely admire Jesus was when he heard this story. He recalled his thoughts at the time, "This Jesus truly saved us and can truly guarantee us. So it is good to follow him . . . we must follow Jesus."

Fatimah, approximately fifty years old and the wife of respondent Nabeel, also used the word "guarantee." When discussing what interested her about the religious message she heard, she reflected that following Christ is "easier" than following the local practices of Islam. She explained that according to local Islamic practices, one must perform the daily prayers.

It is unacceptable not to. However, followers of Jesus still receive benefits, (previously understood as resulting from performing prayers), even if they do not perform specific activities. Fatimah's following statement reveals her understanding of what Jesus does, "[Jesus] is willing, takes himself and guarantees! Guarantees, willing to do anything and willing to be a substitute for us." She later expands, explaining that others do not talk about guarantees. They simply note that those who do good will go to a good place, and those who act badly will go to a bad place. Fatimah quotes a Cambodian proverb, *"A person's head, that person's hair,"* which is interpreted to mean that one is responsible for solving their own problems. This proverb reflects what most Cambodians tell her, namely, "No one guarantees us." This principle contrasts with the message of Jesus and his work and interests her. He is one who does help others and provide guarantees.

The related topic of forgiveness was important to many respondents. As will be explored in more detail later, Chenda was struck by the idea that Jesus forgives, which she saw as illustrated in the Bible story of the prodigal son (Lk 15:11–32). Other interviewees commonly used phrases such as "ask Jesus to forgive us," "God will forgive me," or "I forgive others." It is evident that many respondents see forgiveness as a core theme of the Christian message, and an important action that Jesus does for humans.

The perception that Jesus currently answers prayer and provides help during times of need had much influence on some interviewees. Amir lives in Cambodia but has previously worked in both Thailand and Malaysia. Communicating his story about his path to belief, early in the interview he announced that he has called out to Jesus three times. These incidents, although lengthy, are included here because they provide insight into the thoughts and experiences of Cambodian BMBs. The first instance of Amir crying out to Jesus occurred while he was in Cambodia. He explained that at that time he had some exposure to Jesus, through the Bible and also through a movie about him. He next describes an encounter with evil forces and of Jesus's assistance. In his words,

> When a ghost or evil spirit came to bother me, I shouted and asked for help. But no one could hear me. I called to God and Mohammad, but they couldn't hear me. Then I remembered the story of Jesus in the Bible. When there is any problem, call his name. And I called on the name of Jesus. He said, "Do not be afraid." And I gave my soul to him. So Satan can do anything he wants [to me]. Go ahead and do it. Because I have already given my soul to Jesus.

Interestingly, Amir's encounter has striking similarities with someone located in an entirely different country. In reporting the experiences of forty-two female followers of Jesus living in the Middle East and France, Greenlee tells about Asma,

> Asma had a frightening experience which deeply affected her. She remembered that: 'My friend had just told me that there is power in the name of Jesus. I had a dream that a demon was attacking me. I cried out in the name of Allah and it retreated only to come straight back to attack me. Then I remembered what she had said and I cried out in the name of Jesus and the demon fled.'[7]

Asma's experience is included here because of its surprising parallels with Amir's. Although Amir did not specifically describe a dream, as Asma did, both incidents include experiences of attacks by an evil spirit, of calling out to Allah, of not experiencing resolution of the problem, of remembering information heard about Jesus, of then crying out for his help, and of receiving it. Amir's and Asma's experiences, while personal, are not entirely unique. Although living on separate continents, they both report seeing Jesus directly help them in dramatic and similar ways.

A second time in which Amir called out to Jesus occurred while he was on a fishing boat with sixteen people off the western coast of Thailand. He mentioned that other boats were present in the area, but then left quickly, and he was perplexed why they did so. Soon after, strong winds and rain arrived. The boat was tossed and was tilting at a steep angle. He said to himself that he was going to die. He describes what happens next,

> After that, all the people cried, and we didn't know whom we should call for help. Then I prayed to God. I screamed and called out to Allah and Mohamad to help me. I said that I would die here. But suddenly, I thought of Jesus. Then I talked to him, saying that I would give my soul to him. If Jesus is not dead, is God's Spirit, and is still alive, please come to help me right now, and I will follow you. And I called Jesus three times. Five minutes later, the storm disappeared. And the sun started shining again, quickly. I said he was amazing.

Amir immediately began telling the third and final story of him calling to Jesus for help when troubled by a spirit. This incident occurred while he was working in Malaysia. During that time he was regularly reading a small Bible that had been given to him. He noted that one evening he did

---

7. Greenlee, "Coming to Faith in Christ," 60.

PROMINENT THEMES AND FACTORS IN THE CONVERSION PROCESS

not read the Bible, as he was weary from working. He described an incident in which, while lying down, "Satan" came to him, slithering and sitting on him, with the appearance of having long hair and a face which resembled his uncle. However, he understood this was not his uncle. He continued,

> I was so nervous and my sweat came out like when you take a bath. I shouted and there was no one who could hear me. My friend stayed near me. I called him, but what could I do? My hand and legs were cool and could not move. . . . I was so scared. I thought, "What should I do?" I remembered the story of Jesus when he was on the boat. Waves came strongly. His friends shouted, "Jesus, help!" I thought about that story, and Jesus asked them, "Where is your faith?" Then I wondered about Jesus telling them not to be afraid. When there is any problem, don't be afraid. I stopped [being afraid], and I began to call on Jesus. I called on him in my heart. I called three times. This [spirit] went back very quickly, like lightning.

The above experiences are primary events referred to when Amir is describing his conversion and his life with Jesus. They included incidents of fear because of perceptions of being in physical or spiritual danger. They also involve clear calling out to Jesus for assistance, at times at the prompting of remembering a Bible story or something previously told to him. These events illustrate the importance of answered prayer in times of need.

Rady, aged in his seventies, was present at the interview of a female relative in a rural community. When I asked the original interviewee if she had any final comments or statements, I was surprised to hear this man state he had something he wanted to share. His experience, while unique, parallels some of those above, where help is requested in the context of a disturbing spiritual encounter. He said,

> When I was staying at that small mosque, one time I was praying alone, I heard a sound falling down from the sky. It was falling down very strong. This was not normal. I thought that this would destroy all parts of the mosque. I only just heard. I heard it falling from above. I felt myself shrinking back in fear, as I was praying alone. There was a teacher who said, "You should believe in Jesus. If you hear that sound again, you can pray to Jesus for help, and that sound will go away." So, I thought about that, about Jesus, and it was gone since that time. I have not seen it again. From that time it has not come again. It is silent nowadays.

It is unclear whether or not the teacher who gave Rady advice was present during the incident, or spoke to him at a later point. What is clear is that this man felt Jesus was able to help in his situation. He later pointed to the connection between this incident and his belief by saying, "An evil spirit frightened me. I prayed to Jesus, and it did not come back. It is very quiet until now. So that is why I believe."

Respondents referred to other activities of Jesus beside specifically answering prayer or assisting during a time of need. Some individuals were impacted by the various ways they received personal help as a result of following Jesus. Minat, for instance, talked about a time when she was deeply depressed after the death of her mother, losing even her desire to eat and bathe. Her siblings spoke with her and reminded her that she still had relatives to support her and that she was not alone. In her words, "after that I prayed to Jesus and Allah, to please give me hope and help me to win and struggle in this life." For her, hope in this life was needed and was an appreciated consequence of following Jesus.

Narin is a single man around thirty years old who was repeatedly invited to studies about Jesus in a nearby home. He attended some meetings and began following Jesus approximately one month before being interviewed. He spoke frankly about both a desire and an inability to act morally, "I want to do something good, but I still can't do it because of Satan." It is not surprising that the ability to act well was a motivating reason for him to follow Jesus. He explained, "I asked for all three of these things [forgiveness, to follow him, to enter into my heart]. . . . I asked Jesus to enter my heart and to not let me do wrong anymore, [but] lead me to do good. I asked for all of these things." Another respondent, Yusuf, while not tying his conversion to the ability to act morally, echoed the words of Narin about Jesus helping one to act well, "If we want to do good things, we have to follow Jesus. We are not able to do good just as people. We want to steal, we want to hurt others, and then believe that we have not sinned. But it is clear that is sinful. We should not do it."

Sofia spoke of a desire for a changed life. She acknowledged previous wrongdoing, some of which were related to "believing on Satan" and being involved with traditional practices related to him. Her desire for personal help in the form of a changed life was evident in her words, "There are many [reasons that I believe in Jesus]. In short, if we believe in Jesus, he changes our life a lot." This individual also spoke of another personal benefit she received, that of not being troubled any more by Satan as was formerly the case. She noted that previously she would need to give offerings to Satan in order to appease him, but after asking Jesus to prevent Satan from coming

PROMINENT THEMES AND FACTORS IN THE CONVERSION PROCESS

and troubling her, she is not bothered or scared anymore. For Sofia, following Jesus has brought relief from being troubled by evil spirits, who she formerly deliberately interacted with.

Yasmin also emphasized what Jesus has done in her life. She was introduced earlier, but more details on her narrative are provided here in order to paint a fuller picture of her experiences. As Yasmin related her story of salvation, one prominent component was that she previously was "sick," which she further elaborated as meaning Satan had entered her body.[8] She described this problem as occurring for some time, and as being known by others in her community. Yasmin noted that when the spirit would enter her, others were not able to control her, "Others were unable to catch me because I had much strength. At the time that the spirit entered, I had much strength, don't know where it came from. But I did not know, I did not know myself [not conscious of self]." She spent time studying in Malaysia, and a traditional healer there tried to cure her but was unable to do so. She returned to Cambodia, and a few months later became sick again. A traditional healer in Cambodia was also unsuccessful in treating her. Her grandmother sent her to a modern physician, and she was admitted to a hospital, but still, there was no improvement. Later she was taken to a Christian hospital, where one lady there shared information about Jesus with her. This lady prayed for Yasmin to get better, and also invited her to follow Jesus. Yasmin said she felt she could follow, though later she noted that at that time she was not really believing in Jesus.

The subsequent dialogue from Yasmin centers on her thoughts and experiences of having the spirit removed from her. A few nights after returning home from the hospital, she had a dream in which she described seeing "an old man wearing a white shirt. He came to remove Satan from my entire body. From that time until now I have not been sick anymore. I have not been sick." Several days later, she attended a church meeting in Phnom Penh. When all were invited to close their eyes and pray, Yasmin related that she was unable to do so, as Satan did not want her to pray, because he wanted to stay in her body. She continued,

> I tried to close my eyes, inside the [church] I cried. As I cried, an older person entered and asked me why was I crying, but I did not tell her. Soon after, Satan totally disappeared. After that, I prayed

---

8. There are several words in the Cham language which refer to spirits or evil spirits. One of them is "Satan" (*saiton*). When Yasmin says "Satan" specifically, I will use that term. For other original words, I will use the English translations of "spirit," or "evil spirit."

> to Jesus. I said that if Jesus truly loves all your children and grandchildren, I want to have Satan disappear from my body, all [spirits] that are in my body to totally disappear. So I cried. I started to cry. I cried because I was afraid, I was afraid that he would come close to me again. But from that day, nothing has come, nothing has come close again. It has been normal. There has been no sickness or anything since then.

During her interview, Yasmin repeatedly talked about Jesus helping her, about the spirits being gone since these incidents, and about her being happy and thankful because of it. She did not describe a one-time event where clear unbelief in Jesus was followed by belief. Rather there were times where she says she was following but was not truly believing, and times where she said she truly began to follow. Yasmin did, however, connect Jesus's actions in removing the evil spirit/s to her belief, as seen in her words, "The evil spirit left me, so then I believed in and followed Jesus. When the spirit was staying in my body, I asked Jesus to help. I did not yet totally believe. When I got better from being sick, I knew that, Oh, Jesus truly helped me." These incidents occurred approximately three months before Yasmin's interview with me.

Yasmin spoke about later attending a church meeting and hearing the story about Jesus removing the demons from an individual, allowing them to enter pigs, and restoring that person to normalcy (Mark 5:1–20). She stated that since the day of hearing that story, she truly and strongly believes. Yasmin sees a parallel between Jesus's actions in this Bible story and his personal help for her. This connection is powerful for her, evidenced by her comments that she desires to share this particular Bible story and her personal story of release from the spirits with others. Yasmin's experience and those of others above illustrate the importance of Jesus himself—who he is, what he did, and what he does—in the decision to believe in and follow him. They also reveal the sense that Jesus was personal and close. He was not merely a deity who is separate and uninterested about one's daily life, but one who is experienced as personal and concerned about individuals.

The Bible

As the original source of the gospel message and the medium by which many heard the message, the Bible was often referred to by interviewees.

Often Bible stories were discussed which were surprising or impactful (e.g., Jesus calming the waves, the story of the prodigal son). Besides simply being a vessel to communicate the message about Jesus, the Bible itself was also instrumental in leading to belief. Sara, a widow in her fifties who has followed Jesus for two years, talked about hearing the message over several years from a cross-cultural worker and reading the Scriptures. In her interview, she mentioned not being able to see Jesus directly with her eyes, but being able to see him through the Bible. When she talked about her belief, she simply stated, "This comes from me reading the Bible. I believe [because of] the Bible."

During the interview with Ibrahim, the fact that some people hear the Christian message and do not believe it is true was discussed. Ibrahim noted, however, that he personally felt this gospel information was true. When asked how he knew that, Ibrahim responded that he believed because the Bible says it originated from God. He elaborated that all the words in the Bible came from Jesus, who does not lie. The information in the Bible is true. For Ibrahim, feeling that the Bible is credible contributed towards believing its message about Jesus and salvation.

While communicating his story, Rahman stated that he believed it is only God who can guide the way and make someone believe in him. Explaining further about how God showed him the path, he said, "Show [the way] through the Bible. We know the story of Jesus by seeing it in the Bible. If we look, we know the story . . . God shows us through the Bible. So if we open [and read] it, we know." During his interview, Rahman referred to the Bible over thirty times, illustrating its importance to him. He resisted the concept that something besides God himself can lead him to follow him, and he explained that for him, God led him through the words of the Bible.

Others spoke of their interest in the Bible when learning about the gospel message. Suliman wanted to meet Steven. When talking about instruction he received from Islamic and other teachers, he said,

> "In the beginning, the books of the *Tawrāt* and *Injīl* [Bible] were all studied. But since then, people have not studied them. I have not studied them, so I don't know. They did not allow us to study. After that, we started to learn the Bible. After we began to return to it and learn again, we saw that this information [in the Bible] is all good. Why was it abandoned? I wondered about that. I researched that as well. I will not believe in Jesus [without researching]."

Suliman referred to the *Tawrāt* (Pentateuch) and *Injīl* (Gospels of Jesus), which are traditionally accepted by Muslims as originating from God. While investigating more about Jesus, he wondered why these books were not discussed by Islamic teachers. In his mind, the content of these "abandoned" books was important, and it spurred additional research about Jesus and his acts. Suliman eventually decided to believe in and follow Jesus. His concern about the de-emphasis of these books by Muslims exists to this day and is at times discussed when he shares the Christian message with others.

Ali was previously imprisoned in Cambodia with others. As he reflected on his experience, he referred to the prominent role of the Bible in learning about the Christian message. Ali said he told his fellow inmates that, although they were in jail, imprisonment was the path that God opened to allow them to learn about Jesus Christ, whom they had never heard of before. He said that while in prison, there was nothing to read except the Bible. As they read it over a long time, they came to see it as very good. Ali's interest in the Bible is revealed in the extreme measures taken to read it,

> They only gave us a short amount of time to read. People who came to share the news, when they left, they took the books back too. But I tore out some pages in that book to read. It was against the rule to sneak and tear out the pages ... After I tore the pages, I put them in my underwear. When I took a bath, I wasn't sure what to do, because before we enter, the guards would check everywhere on our body. So that's why I put it in my underwear.

Although there was a clear risk of getting caught, Ali wanted to read the Bible. He later noted that after reading the Bible regularly and carefully, page by page, he came to feel that it was greater than Islam's book. It is evident the Bible had a role in Ali's investigation of Christ and the decision to follow him. This experience was shared by other respondents as well. The topic of the Bible, along with the previous themes of sin and forgiveness, heaven and judgment, and Jesus, are four primary themes revealed in the conversion narratives of respondents. Four themes which were discussed with less frequency and/or intensity are addressed below.

Secondary Themes

The secondary themes include the witness of others, dreams, love, and the sense of God's leading. The themes are listed in no preferential order.

Witness of Others

Early in her interview, Srey Mum stated that she began to have faith in Christ because she heard the good news from her husband. She stated that initially she said she believed, in order to study about his religion. In the beginning, she just said she believed, but she did not yet understand. Later in the interview, Srey Mum revealed some of her thoughts at that time,

> I thought that if he loves me, perhaps he wants good for me. . . . If he hates me, he wants bad for me. So at that time, I loved him, and he loved me. I thought there has never been a husband who loved his wife and led her to walk in the wrong way. After that, I decided to believe and to study. I had another thought. He is my husband. If he leads me wrong, I am wrong, but if he leads me right, I am right. . . . I thought, he is my husband. He loves me. He leads me to walk on the right path. So I decided to follow him . . . [he] does right, I am right. That is how I think.

Srey Mum also said that after a period of time, she came to know more about the law, about punishment, and about the ability to enter heaven. As she read, she referred to Bible verses which touched her, such as God's promise that "I am the road." She noted that from her youth Islam taught her to worship diligently, and to work hard to follow God's commands. As an adult, she concluded that these things are not able to save her from sin. She was attracted to the concept of forgiveness and release from sin through belief in Jesus. The experience of Srey Mum reveals what could be considered a two-step process of conversion. In the first step, she was influenced by her husband, both through his direct words (believe in Jesus), and through her thoughts about the situation (e.g., he would not deliberately lead me on the wrong path). She refers to this as deliberately believing, though she also notes that she did not understand much at the time and that this "belief" included the decision to study and learn more. The second step of the conversion process occurred later, after reading and studying the Bible. She was motivated by a sense of personal sin, by the belief that her personal actions cannot release herself from sin, and by faith that trusting in Jesus would save her from sin.

In his research on the Urapmin ethnic group of Papua New Guinea, Joel Robbins describes a two-stage process of their conversion as a group. The first stage, identified as utilitarian, was in order to obtain potential benefits, including in their case regaining status in the context of humiliation. The second stage, intellectualist, occurred at a later point and took place when the religious message itself provided meaning about the people themselves and their changing context.[9] The example of Srey Mum above is of a single individual, a contrast to the Urapmin as a group. The stages experienced by Srey Mum exhibit both similarities and dissimilarities to those of the Urapmin. Similarities include the presence of two stages, and the observation that the second stage was tied to providing meaning. For Srey Mum, the second stage was precipitated by studying the teachings of Christianity more deeply, and concluding that this message provided a satisfying answer to being released and forgiven from sin. In stage one, Srey Mum was clearly influenced by her husband, and also by her belief that he was sincerely concerned for her well being. The first stage for the Urapmin was different, although others, including group leaders, did advocate for a conversion to Christianity. The examples of both Srey Mum and the Urapmin illustrate that conversion does not always occur at a single point in time, and that different motivations and influences are at times present.[10] However, for both the Urapmin and Srey Mum, the conversion to Jesus had a profound impact.

Shaza also referred to her husband when describing her own conversion narrative, noting that he believed before her, regularly attended meetings of BMBs in their community and that he told her the news about Jesus. She spoke with admiration as she explained that her husband followed all that he has learned, with the example that he did not blame or angrily criticize his children even when they did such things as crash the motorcycle or damage the cell phone. For her, these actions were evidence that he strongly believed in Jesus. Shaza noted that she now also believed, but in her opinion, her belief was not as strong as that of her husband. As she said, "I still strongly criticize my children. For my husband, he does not angrily criticize them at all." The words of her husband, and his actions as a good man had an influence on Shaza's conversion to Jesus.

Other respondents noted the impact of others. Narin said that his siblings and the owner of their house were the ones who told him about Jesus. His brother teaches about Jesus in meetings held in their community. It is not surprising to hear him report that his parents and relatives encouraged him to follow Jesus. His decision was not quickly done or dependent upon their opinion, however. Narin talked of desiring to live correctly and feeling that following Jesus would enable him to have victory over Satan. He also

---

9. Robbins, *Becoming Sinners*, 114–15.

10. Tippett, "Conversion as a Dynamic Process"; Hibbert, "Negotiating Identity."

pointed to another way in which others influenced his decision, revealed in his words, "Those who believe in Jesus are kind and good-hearted. They do not do evil. They help others. . . . At that time, I decided that I would walk in the true path, the good path." The actions of other followers of Jesus influenced Narin's decision to follow as well. In short, the words, encouragement, and positive behavior of others, coupled with his own evaluation of the Christian message (including Jesus's ability to provide victory over sinful behavior), led to his decision to believe in and follow Jesus.

Rahman also discussed the witness of others. When explaining his observations that Jesus did not discriminate against other social classes, he added, "Those who follow Jesus are good people. They do not tell lies. They speak truthfully. That is why I believed in Jesus." Rahman ties his decision to believe with the positive perceived actions of followers of Jesus. Although other factors such as the Bible and its teachings were significant for him, the activities and attitudes of BMBs were meaningful.

Several respondents indicated that others did have some influence in their decision to follow Jesus. This influence appears to be present, but not prominent. That is, while it occurred, and for some was an important factor, it was not the most prominent factor for the majority of respondents. For them, other factors were significant, often tied to the content of the Christian message.

Dreams

Dreams were reported by seven individuals. Four people described dreams they experienced before they decided to believe. These dreams were seen to have varying degrees of importance in leading them to a decision to follow Jesus. Minat experienced two dreams before and during her time of belief which were personally significant. In the first, someone was chasing after her with the intent to harm her. Then she saw an older man wearing a white shirt who called her and told her to come and stay in heaven so that no one could find her. She told her mother this dream, asking why she would have an odd dream like that. She mentioned to her mother that she has never seen Jesus before, but the man in the dream wore a white shirt like Jesus. Minat explained that she was initially afraid about this, but after cross-cultural workers came to explain about Jesus, she stopped being afraid. Later, during a time after she had heard the message but was unsure whether or not to believe in Jesus, she experienced another dream. In this one, an old man appeared, wearing white clothes like Jesus. He asked her to open her palm, placed sand in it, and then asked her to close her fist tightly with the advice: just as the sand did not drop out, your heart needed to be firm and calm. Upon awakening, Minat said she was convinced that Jesus had truly revealed the path to her. She interpreted these events as addressing her indecision about whether or not to believe in Jesus.

Razaa tells a humorous but impactful story about a dream which occurred previous to his decision to follow Jesus. In his words,

> But the last day I was going to finish grade twelve, I started to love Jesus because I had a dream one night. I was riding on a motorcycle with my friend, in the dream. It was very strange. My friend was not wearing a helmet while riding the motorcycle, and the police stopped us.[11] That dream was nine years ago, but I still remember it. In the dream, my friend was the driver and I was riding behind him. And the police asked us a question. He did not ask why we were not wearing helmets. He asked, "What religion do you believe in?" My friend, who was a Christian, said that he believed in Jesus. The police allowed him to go. I was so afraid. And I thought that "Oh my friend believes in Jesus, and they allowed him to go. I should also believe in Jesus." And I told the police that I also believed on Jesus, and police allowed me to go. When I woke up, I felt strange. It was as if it was not I who believed in Jesus, but Jesus who chose me.

The dream was clearly remembered by Razaa. While amusing, it contributed to his sober decision to follow Jesus. As he stated, this marked the beginning of his love for Jesus.

Dreams influencing conversion, such as those described above, were rare among those interviewed, but they were personally important to those who experienced them. More commonly, people related dreams they had which occurred *after* their belief in Christ, and which were an encouragement at the time. Early in her interview, Tewi, who suffers from health problems, told about a dream she had in which she was being treated in Vietnam, but Jesus appeared and said she was to return to Phnom Penh, as he was going to cure her there. Tewi was quite encouraged with these words, and related how, through the contact of a cross-cultural worker, she was later able to receive treatment in Cambodia, and that she is now feeling better. This

---

11. It is illegal to drive or ride on a motorcycle in Cambodia without wearing a helmet.

dream encouraged Tewi, who remarked that since then she has believed in Jesus, regardless of what difficulties she encountered.[12]

In her lengthy interview, Maria revealed three dreams she has experienced over time. Her story is complex, and yet it illustrates the varied experiences Cambodian BMBs have had. Because of its value in shedding light both on the varieties of dreams experienced and on the challenges one individual faced, Maria's story will be explored in some detail. The dreams will be presented chronologically as experienced. Here is her story: Maria was raised in a poor family, and a local Islamic charity provided for her education. This charity initially educated her in an Islamic school, but after experiencing financial constraints, was unable to continue directly caring for Maria and, unknown to her mother, placed her in a Christian school. Maria notes that she experienced a dream when she was six years old. She related the dream to her Christian teacher, who told her it meant God was perhaps preparing her to meet different people. He also said wait to see if in the future you will follow God. Maria remembered this dream but noted it was not significant at the time. Maria spent many years living and studying in a Christian school environment. As such, she was exposed to the gospel message. During much of that time, Maria continued to perform the Islamic prayers. She studied at that school until her graduation from high school. Maria described her heartache of not being quickly told when her father passed away, for fear it would upset her and affect her final exams. She was informed of his death weeks after it occurred. She also felt discouraged that because of her father's death and her mother's limited income, she would not be able to attend college.

Maria was able to attend college in a larger city, however, because she received a full scholarship and also because a relative in that town offered the opportunity to stay with them in exchange for her help in their home and in the family business. Maria did not describe a clear time or event in which she began her faith in Jesus, but she did remark that when she moved and began her college education, she was a follower of Christ and thus no longer performed the regular Islamic prayers. She related that her stay with her relatives was quite difficult at times because they criticized her belief in Jesus. After much of her Bible was deliberately set on fire by them, Maria was discouraged, "My feeling is like, I don't want to believe in God

---

12. In her interview, Tewi also clearly stated she began faith in Jesus upon viewing a film about him shown in her community approximately twenty-five years previously. I thus interpret this dream to be one which encouraged and strengthened her belief.

anymore. I feel so angry." She started visiting the mosque again and began a time of seriously considering returning to Islam. Soon after she began living in a separate location. She asked God to help find employment, and was surprised and encouraged when she was offered a good part-time teaching position. Maria's words describe an emotional and sometimes volatile walk with God. She exhibited periods of hope, pleasant surprise, disappointment, and anger. Maria returned to following Jesus.

In earlier years, her mother displayed anger towards her and her belief. At the same time, Maria described a desire that other relatives, including her grandmother, would hear about Jesus. The second dream spoken of by Maria occurred when she was staying with her grandmother, who was included in the dream as well. In the dream, Maria and her grandmother were going to purchase vegetables. One vendor was selling in a dark location and another in a light location. Maria went to the location which was bathed in light, but in order to go to that area, one had to scale a ladder. Her grandmother and many others were in the dark location. Maria invited her grandmother to come up and even attempted to assist her, but when she tried to pull her up, her grandmother fell down and was unable to climb. Eventually, her grandmother disappeared. At that point, Maria said she woke up. She told her grandmother she had a bad dream, and her grandmother directed her to share it. The grandmother was troubled by the dream, but also asked others about it and pondered it. For Maria, the dream was seen as God's provision of an opportunity to talk about him. As she said, "it's not yet too late because that dream . . . wants me to tell it to my grandmother. If she already passed away, and I had that dream, it is not an issue, but she is still living. That dream is serious to me, and this could mean that God is giving time for her to accept him." The perspective that a dream is intended for purposes of sharing the gospel message is rarely described in academic literature. However, both Maria and Yasmin as follows provide examples of this. Yasmin told of dreaming of someone wearing a white shirt who gave instructions which she interpreted as meaning to act good to others and to share news about Jesus to all people.

Maria told of other incidents in her life, including times of encouragement, discouragement, fear, and also interactions with others about the Christian message. She spoke of two other experiences where she was specifically encouraged through God's presence or a dream. In one of them, she dreamt of someone who encouraged her and didn't let her abandon the idea of believing in God. The importance of this is seen in her comments immediately afterward, "Because if there is no one to encourage me, to share the Word of God, to . . . allow me to know God stronger and stronger, perhaps I would have stopped believing." Encouragement is important for Maria and others as they face the sometimes-lonely path of following Jesus. While the majority of respondents have not reported dreams of any type, dreams have been significant for some.[13] In this study, these dreams have not only been related to leading one to repentance and the decision to follow Jesus, but have also provided encouragement after one has decided to follow Christ, and even assistance in communicating the message to others.

Love

The concept of love was instrumental for some in their decision to truly follow Jesus. Love from God was certainly important and generally falls under the category above—what Jesus does for humans. Love demonstrated by others was noted and appreciated by many. Razaa, approximately thirty years old, clearly exemplifies this perspective. In the previous section, his dream of riding a motorcycle with a friend was reviewed. That experience was personally significant, but Razaa also repeatedly circled back to the topic of love during his interview. He began his interview by stating that his reason to believe was not based on the issue of sin. Rather, it was love, including love and patience shown to him by Christians, even when he was often drinking alcohol and not behaving well. He related that while studying in grade eleven, his friends and their family welcomed him, treated him like family, and sincerely loved him. He then stated, "After that, I started to open my heart to learn more about, about God's Word here. After that, I say I believe." Razaa follows with a comment expressing uncertainty about the exact time he believed.[14] This was not uncommon among respondents. What is clear to him is that the theme of love was important to his decision.

---

13. As previously noted, the first question in the interview was an open-ended invitation for people to tell their story of conversion. In order to avoid prompting for an answer, I did not specifically ask early in an interview whether or not an individual had a dream or vision. If someone mentioned a dream in his or her narrative and discussions, I asked further questions about that. At the end of the interviews, I did ask several individuals who did not mention a dream during their interview whether or not they experienced a dream or God's supernatural actions. Two responded in the affirmative and provided details. The other interviewees replied that they had not experienced a dream.

14. Razaa's dream about a motorcycle occurred while he was in grade twelve, approximately one year after the experience noted above.

As he reflects later in the interview, he says, "For me, I have only two reasons that led me to decide to follow Jesus. There are two reasons. First, I see that Jesus loves me. 'One is about love. No love no peace. And second is about promise. Just two, these is enough for me. So God's love is so different, so wonderful. And he's always promise me.'"[15] Love is the resounding theme impacting Razaa's decision to follow Jesus.

Many other respondents expressed surprise or an appreciation of love shown to them by Christians. Examples include a Christian Korean lady providing long-term assistance while a respondent was hospitalized in that country, a group of BMBs donating funds to replace a stolen bicycle, and a cross-cultural worker providing connections in order for someone to be treated at a medical clinic. Although these actions were personally meaningful, respondents did not always describe if and to what extent these actions impacted their conversion. Razaa above is an exception to this.

Borey also describes a series of events in which assistance or acceptance by Christians influenced his interest in the Christian message and his desire to follow Jesus. Previously introduced as one who was deeply impressed with the concept that Jesus is alive, Borey has lived much of his life in poverty. He described a time earlier in his marriage when he and his wife were living in a small, leaky home and had little food. He knew Christians were providing donations of rice, and he was also suspicious, hearing others say that these people were attempting to "buy our hearts," meaning they were using their influence to promote Christianity. Borey stated, "For a long time, I thought that [they] are just buying our heart. But I had nothing to eat, so I got rice to eat." He followed by noting that after a long time (one year, three years, five years, ten years), he came to understand more, partially as a result of looking at the Bible. Borey is disabled and has received treatment at a variety of locations. Because of his sickness, he said he is a person that others often ignore. More than once in his interview, he remarked that followers of Jesus, often from the Khmer ethnic group, accepted and assisted him, whereas many Muslims did not. Describing the practices of Christians, he said, "Their advice is good. Why? . . . They do not discard the disabled person. They love us. They are friendly to us. They hug us. They shake our hand. They don't give up on us. They [say] we are needed . . ." Borey later highlighted contrasting experiences. He said,

15. The first portion of the quote was spoken in Khmer and translated into English. The second portion, in single quotation marks, is the interviewee's exact words, speaking in English. His reference to "promise" refers to a Bible passage which he feels God used to encourage him, "I'll never leave you or forsake you."

> The Islamic teacher, the leader of the mosque . . . they never came to talk to me about religious teachings. Not at all, because I have a sickness. They did not come near me. That is the first story. Now about the story of Jesus [Christians], they don't think about the issue of people's physical bodies. They want to come to discuss things with me and talk with me so that I understand clearly about Jesus. So, since I was born, God has separated me already, between Cham and Jesus. . . . Why? . . . Ismael [Muslims] do not need us. They look at our body which is not pretty, and they don't need us. They see that we are not pretty, and they do not know us. About Jesus [followers], regardless of if we are pretty, or not pretty, they receive us. They want to speak to us. . . . They discuss with us so that we know about Jesus's words.

Borey drew a clear contrast between his perceptions of the actions of Muslims versus Christians. His experience and conclusion were that, because of his sickness and disability, Muslim leaders and teachers have not approached him to deeply discuss religious issues. Christians have exhibited different behavior, including an acceptance of his physical body. Having lived with a disability for decades, Borey is naturally aware of the response of others to him. His experience is only that of one individual, and his perceptions are his alone, but his words reveal the impact these actions have had on his life. Part of the content of his quote connects to the final secondary theme.

A Sense of God's Leading

For many interviewees, the direct involvement or leading of God was critical to belief. Based on his life experience, Borey concluded that God had separated him from those of his Muslim background and placed him with Jesus. An earlier incident in his life was instrumental, when he returned to his home areas in order for him and his wife to participate in a traditional Cham wedding ceremony.[16] Because he and his wife were not well known in those areas, however, the religious officials did not allow the ceremony to be conducted. These incidents impacted Borey, who noted that this contributed to his decision to fully follow Jesus forever. As Borey reflected, he said that God had prepared him to walk with Jesus. Through circumstances such as being disabled and experiencing rejection, Borey felt that God led him to

16. Borey was officially married to his Khmer wife before this, but not according to Cham custom.

follow Jesus. Borey has certainly encountered many inconveniences in his life, but his words divulge a sense of resolution and of being led by God, "I want to walk with Jesus continually because I am unable to be back [with the former people].... I decided that I would walk with Jesus forever, because my life, my life in this world, God... prepared me to be with Jesus."

Omar also spoke of God's influence. When asked about his thoughts when considering following Jesus, Omar discussed the importance of an honest heart. He followed by saying that Jesus brightened his thoughts and understanding, and this led to him having faith in him. Discussing his faith, he explained, "It came from Jesus. It came from Jesus, who saves us from sin and lights up our heart to believe in him." Hamat, aged in his late twenties, spoke in a similar manner when asked about what caused him to believe, "Allah [God] clarified this inside my heart. He confirmed to me that I should follow Jesus." Sara used the word "illuminate" often. When describing her path which began with disinterest in and ignorance regarding Jesus to an eventual point of interest, understanding, and repentance, she spoke of God illuminating her heart, "He [Jesus] illuminates my heart. In the beginning, I knew nothing. I didn't know who Jesus was. Now, I know that Jesus is God." As a follower of Jesus now, she asks God to continue to illuminate her heart. Sara has a sense that God was at work in order for her to understand, and that he influenced her decision to repent and follow Jesus. In relating his story, Razaa used phrases like Jesus choosing him or calling him. During a time in which he tried to leave Jesus, he said that God attempted to pull him back. Although some of these incidents occurred after the initial decision to follow Jesus, they reveal a sense of God being active in Razaa's beliefs and decisions. Other respondents referred to phrases such as "God's plan" when they spoke of their path to belief. Other factors were obviously at play in the lives of these individuals. For some, however, the sense that God was involved, illuminating, or leading impacted their decision to follow him.

During their interviews, respondents identified several factors as important to their conversion process. These factors became evident as people told their story and reflected on their path towards and walk with Jesus. The four primary factors and four secondary factors which emerged are summarized in the table below.

Table 4. Primary and Secondary Factors in Conversion

Primary Factors	Secondary Factors
Sin and cleansing	Witness of others
Heaven and judgment	Dreams
Jesus • Jesus is • Jesus did • Jesus does	Love
Bible	A Sense of God's leading

These factors can also be represented in the following diagram.

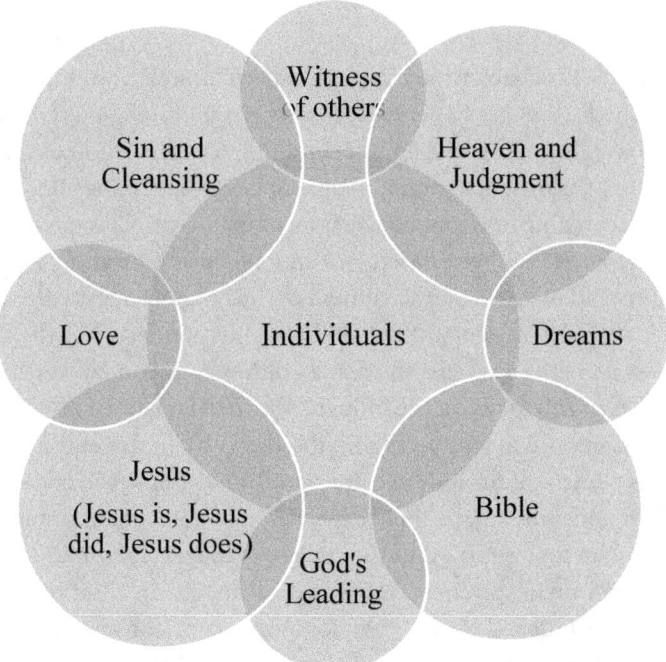

Figure 3. Primary and Secondary Factors Affecting Individuals in Conversion

The term "individuals" (plural) is placed in the center of the diagram, as it represents findings from all respondents, not just one. In Figure 3, factors affecting individuals in conversion are placed around the central circle, indicating that individuals interact with them. The primary factors are represented by larger circles and the secondary factors with smaller circles. Primary factors are those discussed by a larger number of respondents and interpreted to have more influence in the decision to follow Jesus. Secondary factors, while often critically important to those discussing them, were not as frequently spoken about by the group as a whole or with as much intensity. Figure 3 demonstrates the fact that many factors were identified as significant, that these factors commonly interact with each other, and that more than a single factor was usually identified as important to an individual. No respondent discussed all eight factors listed above. Figure 3 includes all of them, however, as it represents the total findings of the study group as a whole.

Discussion

The findings in this chapter interact with other research. Two topics will be discussed. The first relates to general reasons given for religious conversion. The second will be a comparison to the findings of others who examined the conversion of Muslim-background people to Christianity. Ines Jindra noted that when researching religious conversion, often the scholar's interpretation of the phenomenon has been based on factors such as education, a personal crisis, etc. instead of based on the content of the religious message itself. She argues that a theory of "religious beliefs," which is connected to the content of the message, better explains the results of her study on conversion than other theories which focus on the influence of social relationships. The findings of this Cambodian study support the thesis by Jindra and others that the religious content of the message does profoundly matter in conversion.[17] When asked generally about their experience of conversion, interviewees often brought up topics related to the *content of the religious message* [italics mine]: personal sin, forgiveness, sacrifice, heaven, etc. In addition, much of their discussion touched on the two components of conversion identified by Stott: repentance and belief.[18] The terms "*slih tai*," (literally translated as "changing heart,") or "*taobat*" (repent) were used by approximately one-third of the interviewees. Although there is evidence for other factors influencing conversion (e.g., the influence or changed lives of others, perceived benefits,

17. Jindra, "How Religious Content Matters," 275; Jindra, *New Model of Religious Conversion*, 21, 156.
18. Stott, *Christian Mission*.

etc.), the primary topic discussed by the interviewees themselves regarding their conversion was related to the content of the religious message, including the life and work of Jesus.

As previously reviewed in chapter 2, several researchers have identified various factors contributing to the decision to convert from Islam to Christianity. In the following section, the eight factors listed in this Cambodian study will be discussed in relation to the findings of these previous researchers.

The first primary factor identified in the Cambodian study is that of "sin and cleansing," and the second is "heaven and judgment." The content of both of these is related, as they concern topics such as sin, salvation, and forgiveness. These factors connect to other studies. Woodberry and Shubin directly discuss the topic of salvation. In their later article, Woodberry, Shubin, and Marks referred to the important concepts of salvation and forgiveness as part of the gospel message.[19] The content of the message was significant, especially as it related to salvation. Gaudeul also identified "the need for forgiveness" as one of the five motivations for conversion in his study.[20] In addition, Greenham reported "assurance of salvation" as one of the seven categories having lesser prominence among BMB conversion in Turkey.[21] Although having lesser prominence, it was seen as important for those studied. These concepts of salvation, forgiveness, and even assurance of salvation were commonly and prominently discussed among Cambodian respondents. The topics naturally found their way into conversations about sin, cleansing, forgiveness, judgment, and heaven. The belief that following Jesus led to one's sin being addressed, to cleansing and forgiveness, and eventual entry into heaven was important for many Cambodian BMBs. Other research reveals that these topics, although categorized in different ways, were also significant in other locations.

Related to the above factors is the subject of a personal sense of sin. In describing the Aguaruna-Jívaro culture in Peru, Robert Priest observes how some individuals came to the realization that they had personally committed wrongdoing. This realization contrasts with the previously commonly held perspective that sinful actions were primarily attributed

---

19. Woodberry and Shubin; "Muslims Tell"; Woodberry et al., "Why Muslims Follow Jesus."

20. Gaudeul, *Called from Islam to Christ*.

21. Greenham, "Study of Palestinian Muslim Conversions," 152–53.

to others. The hearing of words from God was instrumental in this process.[22] This Cambodian study demonstrates this phenomenon to be true for some individuals. Other respondents describe an earlier understanding of personal sin already present, with some noting that Islamic teachings influenced this perspective. For the majority of interviewees, exposure to the gospel message and/or their decision to follow Jesus brought a much deeper understanding of their personal sin, accompanied at times with a sincere thankfulness that this sin had been forgiven.

The topic of "Jesus" is listed as a primary factor in Cambodian BMB conversion. Woodberry and Shubin noted that the character of Jesus was attractive for those in their study, even mentioning the Qur'anic statement of Jesus being holy (Surah 19:19).[23] Gaudeul uses the phrase, "Jesus is so attractive" to describe a key motivation for conversion discovered in his study.[24] In addition, one of the five prominent categories for conversion identified by Greenham was "the person of Jesus." He stated that Jesus "played a key role in each conversion account," and described the person of Jesus as always central in the Palestinian conversion narratives.[25] Abraham Durán also discusses the appeal "the beauty of Jesus" has for some in conversion.[26] The theme of Jesus is prominent among Cambodian BMBs, and is nuanced by delineating three things about Jesus: "Jesus is," "Jesus did," and "Jesus does." "Jesus is" and "Jesus did" refer to aspects of his character and actions while present on earth. For Cambodians, the additional understandings that Jesus is truly God and is alive were significant. This was especially true as they compared him and his message with the Prophet of Islam and his message. Regarding Jesus's time on earth, Cambodian BMBs often discussed themes of Jesus being good and doing good deeds, including not discriminating against others. Previous studies did not specifically speak to these topics, although Daniel Hoskins's research did point to the impact context makes on religious conversion. The frequent responses by Cambodian BMBs regarding Jesus and his people not discriminating suggests that they were acutely aware of this aspect of

---

22. Priest, "I Discovered My Sin!"
23. Woodberry and Shubin, "Muslims Tell," 3.
24. Gaudeul, *Called from Islam to Christ*.
25. Greenham, "Study of Palestinian Muslim Conversions," 171, 169; Greenham, "Muslim Conversions to Christ," 227.
26. Durán, "Beauty of Jesus," 274.

their context, and their experiences of discrimination contributed toward their admiration of and interest in Jesus.

The aspect of "Jesus does" connects to and reinforces the findings of others. Woodberry, Shubin, and Marks identify the theme of a "lived faith," which includes the topic of God's power demonstrated through answered prayer.[27] Greenham discusses both "God's miraculous involvement" as a category of greater prominence and "personal crisis" as a category of lesser prominence.[28] In the Cambodian study, "Jesus does" took on many forms, including his provision of personal help during key times. This was often seen as an answer to prayer, at times during a personal crisis such as an attack from an evil spirit. Cambodian BMBs often spoke of prayers and answers to prayer. While most of the instances relate to their life as a follower of Jesus, some concern the time previous to their decision to believe. Several of the instances described in the category of "Jesus does" relate to a sense of God's miraculous intervention. The experiences of Amir and Yasmin, for example, illustrate this, where Amir relates Jesus's immediate assistance while in a dangerous situation on a boat, and also when oppressed by an evil spirit. Similarly, Yasmin describes Jesus's removal of an evil spirit/s which had long bothered her. Other researchers, as well as Cambodian BMBs, discuss the importance that Jesus's direct help had on their decision to trust in and follow him.

The topic of "Bible" is identified as the fourth primary factor impacting conversion in Cambodia. Greenham classifies reading the Bible in his category of "greater prominence,"[29] and Woodberry and Shubin use the heading, "A holy book: the power of the Bible" as one of the factors of conversion.[30] In his study of Muslims following Jesus in Turkey, one of Bultema's three main categories is that of "Word." A key conclusion he makes is, "the written Word of God surpasses other causes of conversion to Christ."[31] David Maranz, in his analysis of one hundred twenty written testimonies on the Internet of Muslims who have chosen to follow Jesus, concludes that in nearly all cases individuals spoke about the importance of the Scriptures in their conversion in some manner.[32]

---

27. Woodberry et al., "Why Muslims Follow Jesus," 82.
28. Greenham, "Study of Palestinian Muslim Conversions," 153–69, 171.
29. Greenham, "Study of Palestinian Muslim Conversions," 159.
30. Woodberry and Shubin, "Muslims Tell," 3.
31. Bultema, "Muslims Coming to Christ," 28.
32. Maranz, "Role of the Scriptures," 61.

Several Cambodian respondents pointed to the Bible as important in their personal conversion. For some, its content and stories were appealing. For others, the Bible was trusted and was seen as an instrument which revealed or confirmed the message. According to one female, Sara, it was a tool to reveal Jesus more, and it led to belief: "Even though I don't see Jesus directly, I can see him in the Bible which I read." Three-quarters of all respondents referred to the Bible. The focus of the interview was on experiences leading to faith in Christ, and many respondents discussed the Bible in that context, including its importance to them.[33] The topic of the Bible is thus identified as a primary factor in conversion for Cambodian BMBs as a whole. Several respondents also naturally spoke about the Bible regarding their daily life now, or in relation to how they shared the message with others. While most Cambodians can read the Bible, it is not yet fully translated into the language used by most Cambodian Muslims (Cham). Often individuals learned by studying the Bible in a group. Oral presentations, however, were common as well. These included passages, usually stories, of the Bible being told and explained. In addition, media such as MP3 recordings or even films or film clips, which were usually either directly from the Bible or based on Bible passages, were significant. These observations correlate with Miller's research about reasons for conversion.[34] More specifically, his second category of conversion factors, which are related to "missionary strategies and methods," includes topics such as oral Bible storying, Bible translation into the local language, and the use of media such as films about Jesus.

This study has identified four secondary factors influencing conversion. The first of these is the witness of others. Other researchers have pointed to the impact individual connections and social networks can have in religious conversion (e.g., Lofland and Stark regarding new religious movements, Snow and Phillips regarding conversion to Nirichan Buddhism, and Gray and Gray

---

33. Interviewees were not directly asked initially about the Bible. If the Bible was mentioned by them, follow-up questions were asked. I did, however, commonly ask about the message they received, including "How do you know that this message is true?" It is understood that questions such as these can offer an opportunity for respondents to more freely talk about the Bible, which may lead to an over-estimation of the actual importance of that or other topics. Care was given to select factors based not simply on the frequency they were referred to. Based on all the interview data, it is felt that the "Bible" is a legitimate primary factor.

34. Miller, "Living Among the Breakage," 101–6.

PROMINENT THEMES AND FACTORS IN THE CONVERSION PROCESS

regarding conversion of those from a Muslim background to Christianity).[35] Greenham identifies the "role of believers" as a category having greater prominence for conversion among those he studied.[36] Several Cambodian respondents spoke of the definite impact others had in hearing about and embracing the Christian message. They spoke more about the influence of an individual (such as a spouse) rather than an entire social network. This could be due to their experience that, while a wider network was involved, they were affected primarily by one or two other people. Those who pointed to the influence of an individual also spoke clearly about considering the message themselves. They often pointed to aspects of the Christian message itself as being prominent in their final decision, although they acknowledge that others introduced them to the message or encouraged them to receive it. Examples include Srey Mum, influenced by her husband, but later motivated by a sense of her personal sin and a belief that Jesus is the one who can release her from it, and also Narin, encouraged by family members to study the Bible and follow Jesus, who later noted that the ability to live a moral life as he desired was an important factor in his actual decision. Cambodian BMBs also pointed to the positive actions of others as influencing them. This phenomenon is also described in various ways by other researchers.

A second factor contributing to conversion is that of dreams. Miller identifies "transcendental factors," such as "prayer, God's timing, dreams, visions, and miracles" as influencing conversion in the Middle East.[37] Bultema points to the importance of God's "Word" in conversion and writes that he is referring to his word in all its forms, primarily that of the written word, but also through dreams and visions.[38] One article by Woodberry and Shubin and another by Woodberry, Shubin, and Marks both highlight the role dreams played among those studied.[39] They labeled one category as "I have had a dream," and they reported that one-fourth of those surveyed indicated that dreams did play a role of some type in drawing them to Jesus and in encouraging them to follow him.[40] Furthermore,

---

35. Lofland and Stark, "Becoming a World-Saver"; Snow and Phillips, "Lofland-Stark Conversion Model"; Gray and Gray, "Paradigms and Praxis."

36. Greenham, "Study of Palestinian Muslim Conversions," 161.

37. Miller, "Living Among the Breakage," 94.

38. Bultema, "Muslims Coming to Christ," 3.

39. Woodberry and Shubin, "Muslims Tell"; Woodberry et al., "Why Muslims Follow Jesus."

40. Woodberry and Shubin, "Muslims Tell," 4.

two types of dreams are described: "preparatory," which helps draw people to Jesus, and "empowering," which provides encouragement after beginning to follow Jesus. In analyzing data from all seven hundred fifty surveys, Woodberry, Shubin, and Marks wrote that twenty-seven percent indicated some type of vision or dream before deciding to follow Jesus, forty percent reported experiencing one at the time of their conversion/decision, and forty-five percent indicated a vision or dream occurring after they began believing.[41] In examining the conversion of urban youth in North Africa, David Greenlee observed that dreams were not a significant factor in the conversion process of those men. However, in gathering data on forty-two female converts in the Middle East and France, he reported that nineteen of them reported God speaking to them through a dream/s or audible voice.[42] The dream of one of Greenlee's respondents, Asma, was included above and was compared to the experience of a Cambodian, Amir.

Seven Cambodians (18 percent of all respondents) reported dreams of some type, either before or after conversion. Five of them were women, a significant percentage, especially as only forty percent of all respondents were female. While this finding parallels that of Greenlee's to some degree, clear conclusions cannot be formed at this time regarding reasons why Cambodian women reported higher incidents of dreams than men. While some Christians in the past have speculated about dreams, and viewed them as occurring at God's initiative,[43] the focus of this study is to understand the human decision about conversion. This decision does, however, include their experiences and perceptions about dreams.

For the individuals who experienced dreams prior to their decision to believe, the dreams were seen to have varying degrees of importance in their conversion. These dreams could be considered "preparatory," using Woodberry's term. Cambodians also spoke of dreams occurring after belief which were an encouragement to them, a category referred to by Woodberry and Shubin as "empowering." Another category of dreams which I

41. Woodberry et al., "Why Muslims Follow Jesus," 83.

42. Greenlee, "Coming to Faith in Christ," 53, 60.

43. For example, Greenlee agrees with a theory from Lilias Trotter, cited by C. E. Padwick, that God provides guidance through dreams primarily when other guidance is not available (Greenlee, "Coming to Faith in Christ," 61; Padwick, "Dream and Vision," 206). Woodberry and Shubin, make a similar statement, writing, "Dreams and vision may have been used by God in part because there is a dearth of flesh-and-blood witnesses for Christ willing to articulate and demonstrate the power of the Gospel in person" ("Muslims Tell," 8).

PROMINENT THEMES AND FACTORS IN THE CONVERSION PROCESS

title "evangelistic" were a reality for two individuals, who perceived them as either directly or indirectly leading to telling others about the gospel message. While significant for those who experienced them, dreams on a whole were not a major factor impacting conversion for Cambodians BMBs. In a follow-up discussion after all interviews were completed, one prominent BMB noted that he is not aware of many whose conversion has been significantly influenced by dreams. In his opinion, perhaps one out of one hundred people fit into that category. The actual responses from the interviews demonstrate a larger number than that. However, the factor can still be considered a secondary one when compared to other factors affecting the decision to repent and follow Jesus.

Love is identified as the third secondary factor impacting conversion. Woodberry and Shubin identify "love" as the most significant theme, noting that nearly half of those surveyed said God's love was important in their conversion.[44] This love was both demonstrated in the lives of others and also experienced directly from God. Other researchers, while not often precisely using the term love, do allude to the importance of people witnessing the lives of others, experiencing assistance from them, and also receiving love from God through actions such as answering prayer, providing forgiveness and assurance of salvation, and giving encouragement during a time of need. For example, Greenham identified the role of believers and the assurance of salvation as factors affecting conversion, and Bultema considered the experiences people have had in the local church, part of his category of "worship," as important in conversion.[45] Cambodian respondents spoke both of love received from others as well as love experienced directly from God. That which was received from others was often surprising, and long remembered. Razaa spoke clearly of love being a key factor in his conversion. In addition, Borey, contrasting the actions of many who avoided him because of his handicap with the actions of Christ-followers who spoke with and valued him, highlighted that love demonstrated to him personally was not only impactful but also an important part of his story. Cambodians did not directly speak of God's love as prominently as Woodberry and Shubin discovered in their study. They identified other aspects as important, such as the offer and assurance of salvation, and Jesus's direct actions toward them. These aspects are certainly tied to the concept of love. While not considered

---

44. Woodberry and Shubin, "Muslims Tell," 5–6.

45. Greenham, "Study of Palestinian Muslim Conversions," 153–61; Bultema, "Muslims Coming to Christ," 27.

a major factor influencing the decision to truly follow Jesus, love is certainly a minor factor among Cambodian BMBs.

The final of the secondary factors impacting conversion was the sense of God's leading. Other scholars do not specifically discuss this as a factor, but in the Cambodian study, several communicated that the sense of God preparing them, influencing, or confirming the message they heard was important during the time they were considering whether or not to follow Jesus. They relayed a sense that God was immanent, close, and active in their lives. Susan Harding, examining fundamentalist Christianity in the United States, observed the perception that many feel God's Holy Spirit is at work during the conversion process.[46] While the Cambodian respondents did not specifically use the term "Holy Spirit," they did talk as if it was God himself working. Miller's survey also revealed the category of "transcendental factors," which include the sense that God is working in his timing in the hearts of people, and the prayers of individuals influence this work. Besides identifying five themes regarding motivations for conversion, Gaudeul includes a chapter in his book titled "A Call from God?" suggesting that for some individuals, the sense of God leading or calling—whether through dreams, visions, or some other means—is significant in their conversion.[47] The perception by some Cambodians that God was illuminating or confirming the message, or leading them in some way, contributed to their later decision to follow him. Other researchers, while not using the above terminology, at times allude to the sense that God is working and influencing, at times through experiences such as dreams and visions.[48] Cambodian respondents often discussed God's leading in a manner which was much broader than just dreams and visions but included such aspects of God illuminating or confirming the Christian message.

Besides identifying significant factors in conversion, scholars have also commented on the relationship between the factors. Radford's research revealed that there were several factors, but one did not emerge as being key. Rather, "a combination [of factors] work together to impact

---

46. Harding, *Book of Jerry Falwell*, 36 ,60.

47. Gaudeul, *Called from Islam to Christ*.

48. Andreas Maurer, for example, identifies five conversion motives based on his research in South Africa of ten individuals who converted to Christianity and ten who converted to Islam. Labels he provides for the conversion motives are: religious, mystical, affectional, socio-political, and material. Dreams and visions experienced by individuals would fit into his "mystical" category ("In Search of a New Life," 293–99).

PROMINENT THEMES AND FACTORS IN THE CONVERSION PROCESS

the conversion process."[49] Woodberry and Shubin noted that "most of the prominent factors for conversion are interrelated."[50] Miller also discussed the phenomenon of the factors working together, and he added that this often had a synergistic effect, where the end result is more than simply the sum of the individual factors.[51] In his research, Maurer adds the observation that two to four individual motives were often at work and that the process may begin with certain motives, but other ones often take priority as time progresses. He notes this is especially true when the initial motive is for material gain, which is later eclipsed by other motives.[52]

Five observations will be made about the experiences of Cambodian BMBs in relation to the above research. First, there were many diverse factors which influenced conversion for Cambodians. Second, important factors were different for different individuals. Certain themes were highly significant for some interviewees, whereas other individuals identified different themes as personally meaningful. Third, respondents almost always did discuss more than one factor. That is, they were rarely influenced by just a single factor. Some, however, did appear to focus on one factor or relate that this single factor was critical to their decision to follow Jesus. Examples include Kosal and his singlehanded emphasis on "heaven," and Ibrahim's clear statement that he was concerned about personal sin and chose to follow Jesus because he was able to address this issue. The vast majority of respondents, however, naturally referred to more than one factor when discussing their process of conversion. Fourth, while they did not speak directly about the factors multiplying each other, there does appear at times to be a cumulative aspect to the interrelation of the factors during the process of conversion. One factor reinforces another. For instance, the concept of Jesus providing assurance of salvation may have been strengthened when individuals perceived he loved them and was helping them. Although not directly discussed by those interviewed, these observations can be made based on the words and stories of the respondents.

The concept of time is often related to this. That is, as time progressed, one's interest in the person of Jesus and in following him may have increased. Reasons may include increased or repeated exposure to the Christian message or to the activities of Christians. Respondents often used phrases such

49. Radford, *Religious Identity and Social Change*, 80–81.
50. Woodberry and Shubin, "Muslims Tell," 2.
51. Miller, "Living Among the Breakage," 115.
52. Maurer, "In Search of a New Life," 297.

as, "Before I did not know. But as I studied more and more, I came to understand." Time was a factor in the process of conversion, and perceptions and motives may change over time. One may only see Jesus as a good "prophet" initially, and later come to see him as one who is sent by God and can truly forgive. Fifth, for some, motives did change over time. One example is that of Srey Mum, who initially was influenced by her husband to consider conversion, but who later was impacted by other aspects of the message, such as Jesus's ability to truly forgive sin. While some shifting in the importance of factors likely occurred over time for a large portion of interviewees, the phenomenon is difficult to describe with clarity. Respondents at times spoke clearly about factors influencing their conversion, but they did not elaborate as often about if there was a change in the importance of factors as time progressed. Based on the narratives and reflections of Cambodian BMBs, several primary and secondary factors can be identified which contributed to their conversion. Individual respondents were influenced by more than one factor, and over time came to decide to follow Jesus. Finally, it is evident that the respondents often experienced God and the Christian message as personal and close. For example, Borey's comment that because Jesus is alive, he can specifically intercede for Borey, and Amir's reflections about Jesus's direct help point to a sense that Jesus is close and involved in their lives. Furthermore, Ibrahim's discussion that the gospel message addresses his personal concern about sin hints at a perspective that the message is not merely external and sterile, but rather personal and close. God and the gospel were experienced, not just intellectually evaluated.

Conclusion

This chapter has sought to answer the question, "What themes or factors do Cambodian BMBs identify as central to their decision to follow Jesus?" As a result of interviewing forty individuals, four primary and four secondary factors were identified. The primary factors refer to those which were more often discussed or which were seen as more influential overall. Secondary factors refer to those which, while sometimes critical to a few individuals, were not as often discussed or generally not communicated with as much intensity. The first primary factor is that of "sin and cleansing." The second factor is "heaven and judgment," and the third factor is that of "Jesus." Because he was so prominently discussed, this factor was examined in three parts, "Jesus is," referring to aspects about his identity, "Jesus did," referring to his actions while on earth, and "Jesus does," referring to his current activities in the lives of the respondents and others. The fourth primary factor was the "Bible." The first secondary factor identified was the "witness of others." The second was "dreams," and the third was "love," primarily demonstrated by others towards them but also demonstrated by God. The final secondary factor was "a sense of God's leading" as they considered following Jesus. For nearly all respondents, more than one factor was significant in their conversion process. These factors compare and contrast in many ways with conversion factors identified by different researchers in other locations. They also reveal that many respondents experienced the gospel message as personal and God as intimately involved in their lives. Identifying factors which influence conversion helps bring a fuller understanding of the process of hearing a message, considering it, and responding to it. Identifying factors, however, is not enough. A deeper discussion about the specific interaction one has with the gospel message is needed. How is it that the message is seen as personally relevant and compelling? The next chapter seeks to examine this topic further.

6

Personal Experience of the Christian Message

How did Cambodians experience the gospel message in personally meaningful ways? The focus of this chapter is narrower than that of previous chapters. In chapter 4, the way in which Cambodian individuals and groups received the message was examined. In chapter 5, prominent themes and factors influencing conversion were identified and discussed. Those factors are critical, and yet they are broad, often described as general categories. This chapter narrows the focus to examine the manner in which individuals interacted with the gospel message. Previous chapters have revealed some of this information already, and at times an overlap of material will be noticed. This is not surprising, as the previous topics certainly touch on the personal impact of the message. In addition, part of the answer to the question, "how was the message personally meaningful and compelling?" is found in an examination of how it was communicated to them and which factors they found personally important. This chapter thus will reinforce and interact with the previous chapters. It will provide a deeper understanding of the process Cambodian BMBs experienced as they interacted with the gospel message and came to see it as personally appealing and compelling.

This chapter is organized into three parts. First, the question of how the message was personally meaningful will be addressed, with five reasons given and discussed. Second, the ways in which respondents described their journeys to faith in Jesus will be examined. Third, the manner in which they describe their current beliefs and life with Jesus will be discussed. These final two topics provide a more comprehensive understanding of the process of conversion, including perceptions individuals have after they have begun following Jesus.

How was the Message Personally Meaningful?

The Christian message was personally meaningful and compelling in five ways. First, the message provided answers to life's questions and desires. Second, the message connected to someone in a personal way. Third, God's perceived actions were meaningful. Fourth, the method of communication was meaningful, and fifth, the messenger of communication was meaningful. The narratives and reflections of the respondents revealed that the above five factors, either by themselves or in combination, contributed to the gospel message being seen as personally relevant and appealing. These five reasons, although overlapping at times, will be discussed separately.

The Message Addressed Life's Questions and Desires

One of the ways that the message became meaningful was when it provided solutions to someone's concerns or questions. Early in his interview, Sukry spoke of his mother's involvement with the spirit world through traditional ceremonies. He noted that at one point she became quite ill. Some in the community declared her illness to be the result of a curse, with the solution being to hold a three-day ceremony where assistance was requested from the spirits. The ceremony was held, but his mother later died. Sukry did not think his mother's death was caused by spirits. He later spoke with a Christian about the illness, and Sukry himself was angry, feeling that the devil was not the cause of his mother's problems. He then stated, "Because of that, I had a feeling that I wanted to know what God is like and what evil spirits are like. I also began to ask him [the Christian] . . . began to ask him. He explained about God and evil spirits, and I believe." Sukry's sad experience about his mother produced questions about the nature of God and evil spirits. He asked these questions to a Christ-follower, received answers, and began to believe in God. The message he heard addressed real-life issues he was concerned about. Hearing an explanation about these issues was important and contributed to his believing in God.

Sofia, who acknowledged that she was often involved in the spirit world, experienced spirits bothering her. For her, this took the form of feeling physically sick, not of an actual spirit entering her. Sofia noted that Satan would cause some individuals to have stomach aches, indigestion, or cause them to laugh or cry. She remarked that she was often bothered, and would continue to be troubled unless she provided offerings of food (e.g., bananas) and lit incense sticks. One of the people who initially told her about the gospel message said, "Please believe in Jesus. Nothing can trouble us, and the devil cannot come near and trouble us as well." The person also added that following Jesus allows it to be easy for us after we die, and Jesus, not Muhammad, was the only one who could save us. Sofia later decided to follow Jesus, because of these and other reasons. During her interview, she spoke much about her experiences before and after following Jesus, "In the beginning, when I did not yet believe on Jesus, the devil always came to bother me like this and like that. This is true. But I believed in Jesus, I am not afraid of that anymore. I can go anywhere and the devil does not come near me." One of Sofia's concerns before hearing about Jesus was that of responding to spirits which were bothering her, causing sickness and fear. While news that Jesus could protect from evil spirits was not the entire Christian message told to Sofia, it is evident that this aspect of the message provided answers to some of her questions and desires.

It was noted that early in his interview, Ibrahim spoke about a sense of personal sin and of a desire to address it. He wondered out-loud why others were not concerned about what happens to them after death, because he was quite concerned. Ibrahim had these questions and desires prior to hearing the Christian message. Because the message directly answered some of these questions, it was meaningful and impactful. Narin also spoke of personal sin. He related a struggle with feeling that he was unable to act as he wanted, partially because of the influence of the devil. Finding out that following Jesus potentially provided strength to resist temptation was personally meaningful and relevant for him. He also noted that one of the reasons he decided to believe was because "I don't want to waste my time from day to day without any meaning." Although he did not elaborate on his comments, it is evident that he felt following Jesus would help provide meaning in his life, which was desired.

Isak spoke of a topic which he often pondered and yet did not have clarity on. This topic was important to him, but he did not see Islam as providing a satisfactory answer. The subject was that of the afterlife, more specifically heaven and whether or not there was an assurance of entering. Isak commented, "when I was following Islam, we worshipped but we did not know if we would enter heaven or not. But I heard that Jesus said, 'Whoever believes, [they] will enter heaven.' So I was interested." He also noted that after believing, he had much happiness because of these very concepts. Isak was concerned about the topic of heaven and salvation.

When he saw that the Christian message addressed these topics, it became personally meaningful and more compelling.

The Message Connected to Someone in a Personal Way

A second way that the message became meaningful was when it connected intimately to an individual. Many respondents discussed being moved in some way as they were exposed to teachings or stories about the Christian message. Sitting in front of her village home with her cow mooing loudly nearby, Chenda said she was impressed with certain Bible stories, one of them being that of the prodigal son (Lk 15:11–32). She was amazed that, "even the child wastes money and travels for himself, goes to different places and spends all the money, but he comes back and the father receives him well and forgives him." Consistent with the father's treatment of his son, she concluded, "even if we do wrong, Jesus always forgives us." This story personally touched her. Omar was impacted by another story, specifically the incident where Jesus and his companions were riding in a boat during a terrible storm (Mark 4:35–41). Omar noted that Jesus quieted the storm, saved all those in the boat, and even forgave them. In his interview, Omar said that hearing this story was the point when he came to truly admire Jesus. When he heard this story, he concluded that the Jesus in the story is one who does truly save and can guarantee us. Thus not only is it good to follow him, we must follow him. This story personally connected to Omar in a profound way.

Sara spoke of viewing a film about Jesus. At the time, she said she had not previously believed Jesus had died and been resurrected. Sara related her experience of watching the film,

> When I saw that movie, I started crying. I cried because I felt pity for Jesus. Older teachers told me, "You have a strong faith. That is why you are crying." I said, "Teacher, I do not yet have strong faith." My heart felt pity for the person whom they called Jesus. Then I thought, "Oh, that man is Jesus, is master, the one who died on the wooden cross, replacing our sin, as we as humans have sin."

Sara shed tears because she felt pity for Jesus, whom she came to realize was the one who was Master and who also died to address the sin of her and other humans. Others assumed she was already a strong believer, but she related that this was not the case. Viewing the film crystallized her understanding of Jesus.

Another female, Nida, also talks about weeping while viewing a film about Jesus. In her case, this did not occur before believing in Jesus but after. Her weeping was both because of regret for not understanding before, and also because of the reality of what Jesus suffered for humans. She noted that when watching the film before following Jesus, she did not believe what it said and simply watched it as one normally does. However, when watching it after following Jesus, she said she cried. In her words,

> When I had faith already and had seen evidence, I cried and felt regret. I was thankful because of how much he loved us. He was brave enough to die instead of us. And when he died, it was not a usual death. People hurt him, looked down on him, beat him, and spit on him. I did not want to watch it, because his death was instead of ours, because of the sin of humans, because of my sin. . . . At that time I felt like, Oh god, please forgive me. Let me repent.

For Nida, this experience was quite meaningful. It did not merely intellectually cement her understanding of what Jesus had done, but also emotionally connected her to him, including feelings of thankfulness and regret, and was even followed by her repentance and request for forgiveness. While Nida's experience was not one of leading her to initial belief in Jesus at that time, it does point to incidents where individuals were touched by the Christian message.

The above encounters provide illustrations of concepts Priest, Basso, and Stromberg refer to when someone interacts with a message about personal wrongdoing. Priest discusses two concepts regarding how someone receives a message about personal sin: communication of the message as a story, and seeing sinful actions displayed in someone else.[1] He illustrates these concepts with an example from the Old Testament. In 2 Sam 12:1–14, the prophet Nathan confronted King David about his adultery with Bathsheba by using a story in which someone else sinned by stealing a sheep. David emotionally entered this story, received its message about him, and repented of his own wrongdoing. Chenda above related how a different Bible story resonated with her, one of a wayward son. She applied the story about someone else who sinned to her own life, with the conclusion that just as the father in the story forgave his son, so God forgives her. Omar was also affected by a story, one about Jesus in a boat during a storm. This story was not directly about personal sin. However, Omar was able to connect the story to his own life, and it prompted him to feel he must follow Jesus.

---

1. Priest, "Tell Me," 5.

Sara was touched as she saw part of Jesus's story displayed on film. She connected his suffering with the sin of humankind and saw him in a new light. These examples connect to Priest's writings concerning interacting with messages about personal sin.

Priest also discusses the role one's personal conscience may play in interacting with the gospel message. He writes that the content of one's conscience is formed from "learned cultural meanings, norms, ideals, and values." Although one's internal conscience is tied to one's culture and socialization, it can also confirm an external message about oneself.[2]

Keith Basso's research on the Apache also makes connections to conscience, morality, and the impact of stories. His study highlighted the importance of geographical locations, stories associated with them, and how they were used to instruct about morality. His interview with one respondent revealed the sense of "stalking with stories," where an individual is told a story, and this story becomes like an arrow inside them, provoking them to consider their life and behavior, troubling them until they make decisions about their life.[3] Basso's description of this ongoing process of self-examination in light of a story about morality illustrates the role of one's conscience and the struggle with a message about oneself. Several Cambodian respondents discussed a personal sense of sin and the desire to address it. Some noted that their understanding of sin came from the religious teachings they had received as a child. Others described it occurring after they acted wrongly later in life, after being exposed to the Christian message, or as noted above, while reflecting on a particular story. While respondents usually did not directly talk about their internal conscience or the role of the Holy Spirit, they did reveal a process of pondering and evaluation, related to their self-evaluation and desires.

The above experiences of Chenda, Omar, and Sara also relate to Stromberg's discussion of "impression point," where, "A new understanding of self, a new understanding of a symbol system, and a feeling of commitment are all generated at once."[4] There is a crystallization of understanding, often paired with emotion and a personal commitment. Stromberg applies this concept to religious conversion. Many of the examples above demonstrate a sense of increased clarity and personal application, often accompanied by strong emotions. Both Chenda and Omar realized that the stories they

---

2. Priest, "Missionary Elenctics," 291–92, 294–95.
3. Basso, "'Stalking with Stories,'" 41–42.
4. Stromberg, "Impression Point," 61–62.

heard actually related to their own lives. In the case of Chenda, the concept was that of personal forgiveness. For Omar, it was the fact that Jesus could truly save and guarantee, even him. Their words reflect that these stories greatly affected them, which was unexpected at the time. Sara and Nida had emotional experiences while viewing films about Jesus. They also had a new understanding, coupled with a sense that Jesus's death was personally related to them. Sara's experience occurred before her decision to follow Jesus while Nida's occurred after. Both incidents, however, reveal powerful moments in their lives which are still remembered.

Emotions are often a window into what is personally meaningful. Some BMBs revealed experiences before deciding to follow Jesus which affected them. When speaking about her initial interest in the Christian message, Chenda said, "It was shining in my heart. I was interested because . . . Mary came and taught and explained. I felt strange, and was interested in reading the Bible on my own. . . . When I read the Bible, I feel brightness in my heart." Maria related emotions she had as she read the Bible as well, "When I read the Bible, it makes me feel very happy. I don't know why. I read Islam's book, and it makes my heart troubled. . . . My feeling is that I want to know the true God. What do I need to do so I can read the book and know what the content is like? [correct or not]." These ladies experienced strong emotions when learning about the gospel message, in these cases while reading the Bible. While they do not elaborate on the specifics, it appears these emotions influenced their attitudes about the message and willingness to continue to learn more.

The topics those interviewed expressed interest in as they heard the Christian message helps reveal what was personally meaningful to them. Imran, who said he had been following Jesus for four months, spoke of not being interested in the message about Jesus while younger, but of later having strong interest. When discussing how he knows the story of Jesus is true, he said that the fact he was interested in it was important. He said, "We are interested . . . deeply interested with Jesus like this, in our hearts, we [then] think that this is true already." The reason for his logic was that if the message was not true, he felt he would not have been interested in it. The genuine interest he felt helped confirm to him that the message was correct. Both the messenger of the gospel and the method of its presentation differed from when Imran was first exposed to it. When hearing the message recently, Imran expressed that he viewed it as part of the larger story of Allah. A fisherman, he was also was struck with two stories: Jesus helping provide an abundant catch of fish, and Jesus commanding the stormy waves to calm. After speaking about these two stories, Imran's immediate comment was that people should believe. Imran was intrigued with several aspects of the gospel message. For him, the fact that he felt sincere interest contributed to his viewing the message as being true. Although the process and logic of others may differ much from that of Imran, his perspective was personally meaningful and contributed to his decision to believe in and follow Jesus.

Other respondents expressed different types of interest. As a prisoner, Ali was intensely interested in reading the actual Bible, to the point he ripped pages out of the Bible and hid them in his undergarments in order to have access to them. He also related how he worked to compare the content of the Christian Bible with the Islamic Qur'an. At the beginning of his interview, Nabeel spoke about not having an initial interest in studying the Bible as he was busy seeking to provide for his family, who were lacking basic necessities. Later, however, when his financial situation was more secure, he became involved with a local body of believers. When asked about the length of time he thought about the gospel message before believing, he answered that for him it was brief, about two weeks, and was accompanied by an intense desire to know more. Describing that time, he said, "My heart was like it *wanted* [emphasis Nabeel's] to know about the reason, wanted to know at once. The Bible book, where did it come from? The book of Qur'an, where did it come from? I continued to read. Some things I understood, and some I didn't. Things that I didn't understand, I asked others. . . . Oh, I studied very hard then." After this period of study and questioning others, Nabeel committed to following Jesus. His keen interest to know more at that time indicates the potential importance the message had for him personally. This was not simply a message for others. The above discussion reveals how the content of the Christian message was meaningful to Cambodian BMBs. The interest expressed by individuals provides a window to understanding how the message was personally relevant. This message was not simply external information to be evaluated but was experienced in various ways, often with intimate connections to one's hopes, concerns, and emotions.

God's Perceived Actions Were Meaningful

Some respondents spoke of the sense God that was directly involved in their lives, influencing them in a powerful way. These perceived actions were often in the form of God's assistance or answers to prayer. Amir was previously identified as one who declared he had cried out to God three specific times. The first and third times were while being attacked and frightened by an evil spirit. The second occurred while Amir was on a fishing boat in the ocean, which was in danger of sinking. All of these incidents could be characterized as times of acute crisis. In each of these cases, Amir remembered a story about Jesus or thought of him, and specifically called out for his help. In each case, he was convinced that Jesus helped him. It appears that the first two incidents occurred before he began to follow Jesus and the third likely after. To Amir, the events were examples of Jesus's personal help in a time of need.

Rady also related an experience of Jesus's dramatic assistance. His experience of praying at a mosque, and then being frightened by an evil spirit, was previously discussed. At the time of the event, he remembered a teacher saying that he should believe in Jesus, and also that he should ask Jesus to help if he heard the sound again. Rady did deliberately pray to Jesus for help, and he noted that the sound went away. He remembers that story to this day, and it has strongly impacted his belief. As he said, "An evil spirit frightened me. I prayed to Jesus, and it did not come back. It is very quiet until now. So that is why I believe." Jesus's assistance that day and since has contributed to Rady's decision to personally follow him.

Other incidences of receiving help may not be quite as dramatic as the events reviewed above. However, they also assist in making Jesus and his message more tangible and appealing. Often this help was received in the form of answered prayer. Sok, speaking about why he looked to Jesus only for forgiveness and how he came to believe, elaborated about two factors. The first was answered prayer, and the second was documents which explain about the Christian message. He said he prayed to God specifically in the name of Jesus. Noting that his prayers were answered, he concluded that Jesus truly is a prophet. Sok explained that the vast majority of his prayers were answered, which he saw as very good. He continued by saying that God and his people have prepared the Bible and the Qur'an so humans can understand clearly. Moreover, one cannot expect to simply believe without evidence for belief. For Sok, the Qur'an even provides information as it speaks about the stories of the prophets across generations. He summarizes by saying, "It [information about Jesus] did not just pop up by itself. There are enough documents that lead us to believe, and we also have the good actions from God to lead us to believe as well." Sok talks of being led to firm belief because God both provides documents giving evidence about Jesus and also answers prayers in his name.

Maria speaks of the impact God's direct answer to prayer had on her belief. It was previously noted that Maria received a full scholarship to attend university in an urban area and initially stayed with relatives, who criticized her because of her beliefs in Jesus. At that time, she considered herself a follower of Jesus. Her story, however, included times of discouragement and withdraw from the Christian community. Her path was not simply linear, beginning with a belief which grew steadily stronger as time progresses. It was during one of those times of doubt that she was personally impacted by God's response to her prayer. Her perception of God's work and the significance it had in her life then is revealed in her words,

> So, when I was looking by myself [for work], [I] thought that there is a true God for me because when I prayed for a job, I received it immediately. I asked that I would be able to teach students. If I did not receive it, I would not believe . . . But, when morning came, I saw that the school principal called me, and asked me to teach at his school. So I thought that "Oh, God has prepared that for me." At that time, I thought that if I could not find a job, I would stop believing in God. I would do whatever I saw, according to what my heart wanted. If I had believed in Jesus, and also thrown away [belief in] the previous god I had followed for years, it was not possible to return and honor that god. So I thought that if Jesus did not help me, I would stop believing in all religions. I would only know and trust myself.

Maria appeared to be experiencing a crisis of belief. Although she had left Islam and embraced Jesus, she was considering leaving him and following only her individual beliefs and desires, not returning even to Islam. She was focusing on a specific prayer and determining her next steps of belief based on whether or not God responded to this prayer. Maria showed surprise that the prayer for a teaching position was answered, and even answered so quickly. The perception of God's direct involvement in her life spurred her back to believe again in Jesus. She concluded that "yes" there was a true God for her to follow. Although this incident did not lead to her initial decision to follow Jesus, it did impact her subsequent decisions to follow. Living in an urban area as a student, Maria had little contact with other Cambodian believers and almost none with Cambodian BMBs. Her up-and-down experience of following Jesus as a BMB was not uncommon among respondents. Borey, for example, expressed interest at one point to return to Islam. Part of the reason he did not return was due to his perception that Muslims were rejecting him by not allowing he and his wife to be married in a traditional Cham manner.

The above experiences illustrate how God's actions were seen as personally meaningful. Respondents described other actions of God which were not directly related to providing help or answering prayer. These actions created a sense that God was involved in their lives, and have been previously introduced. The first is that of dreams. Although respondents do not always attribute a dream to originating directly from God, they often communicated a sense that dreams had a spiritual component, meaning God was involved in some way. As was seen earlier, some dreams contributed to creating openness to the person of Jesus, to seriously considering the gospel message, or to deciding to ultimately believe in and follow Jesus. Dreams are obviously a deeply personal experience. Although they were but one facet in the lives of Cambodian BMBs, dreams helped some individuals view the gospel message as more intimate and compelling.

Another way in which God was seen to act in the lives of individuals was through his leading. In the previous chapter, a "sense of God's leading" was identified as a secondary factor influencing conversion. Examples of this phenomenon included Sara's use of the word "illuminate" to describe what God did. He illuminated her heart so that she would understand about Jesus. Hamat, talking about his path to belief, stated, "God clarified this inside my heart. He confirmed to me that I should follow Jesus." Omar talked of Jesus as one who "lights up our hearts to believe in him." It is evident that these experiences were deeply personal for those who describe them, that they were meaningful in part because of the perception that God was directly involved, and that they influenced the decision to believe in Jesus.

Charles Kraft defines religious conversion as a "lifelong process, consisting of continuous divine-human interaction and continuing series of human decisions."[5] This definition highlights three things. First, conversion is a process taking place over time. Second, "divine-human interaction" is involved. Third, human decisions are an important component. Cambodian BMBs do often describe a process of conversion, usually culminating in their changing their heart and deciding to follow Jesus. They discuss life afterward

---

5. Kraft, *Christianity in Culture*, 403.

as well. For some, such as Maria, this may include a wavering of belief or a period of unbelief. For most, however, different terminology is used to describe their life after their initial decision to follow Jesus. Though they describe a lifelong process of change, they do not describe it as a lifelong process of conversion, as Kraft writes. However, the sense of "divine-human interaction" dovetails with the narratives of some respondents, who do discuss God's involvement in their process of conversion. Moreover, there is also an acknowledgment of their "human decisions." They both speak about how God was involved and also how they decided to believe or follow. Their words provide an illustration of "divine-human interaction."

Gordon Smith defines Christian conversion in the following manner: "I am defining *conversion* [italics in original] as an encounter with Christ that leads to a new orientation that is Christ-centered."[6] He clarifies, as does Stott, that conversion is a human decision, a response to God's offer of salvation. Salvation, in contrast, is God's activity, wholly accomplished by him.[7] Smith describes conversion as a decision by humans, but one which is done in the context of God's actions toward them and offer of salvation.[8] Some Cambodian BMBs detailed their perceptions regarding God's activities towards them and the influence this had on their conversion.

The Method of Communication was Meaningful

The topic of communication was discussed previously in chapter 4. This section connects with earlier material and will focus on how the communication of the message led to it being seen as personally meaningful and compelling to those receiving it. How was the message communicated? One aspect of communication was the choice of language used. While most Cambodian Muslims speak the Cham language at home, they are also fluent in the national Khmer language. For those who speak Cham, some reported that hearing the message in their language assisted not only in clearer understanding but also in sensing that the message related to

6. Smith, *Beginning Well*, 128.

7. Smith, *Beginning Well*, 16; Stott, *Christian Mission*, 168–69. Stott uses somewhat different terms but communicates a similar idea: conversion is an act of man, whereas regeneration is one of God.

8. Further describing conversion, Smith writes, "Conversion is the act of believing in Jesus, choosing to follow Jesus and being united with Jesus as Lord and Savior," *Christian Mission*, 16. The phrases "believing in Jesus," and "choosing to follow Jesus" parallel those often used by Cambodian BMBs as they spoke about their conversions.

their personal lives. Rony is an example. He noted that if the cross-cultural worker taught the message "using the Khmer language, it would have been difficult for me to accept it." The reason is that he would have naturally assumed the person was referring to a different god than the one he is aware of. Thus the message would not be seen as personally applying to him, as he felt he already had a god (Allah) who he followed. Rony is referring to a cross-cultural worker, who expended the effort to learn both the Khmer and Cham languages. For Rony, this effort was not wasted, as it helped him view the message as more personally relevant. For those Cambodian Muslims who were fluent in the Khmer language but not in Cham, they naturally heard and understood the message as communicated in the Khmer language. However, the use of some non-Khmer religious terms which they were familiar with did assist in their understanding.

The use of experience-near terms helped lead to the message being viewed as personally relevant and appealing. The most common term referred to by respondents on this topic was the Cham word for Jesus, *Nabi Isa*, in contrast to the Khmer term with the same meaning, *Preah Yesu*. *Nabi Isa* is based on and essentially the same as the Arabic word for Jesus. Cambodian Muslims who do not speak Cham do understand this and other religious terms, as they are Arabic-based and commonly used in the mosque. Other examples of familiar terms understood by virtually all Cambodian Muslims are *duhsa* (sin), *sorga* (heaven), *naraka* (hell), and *Iblih* (Satan, devil, evil spirit). Isak noted that the use of these terms was not merely beneficial because of understanding. They also shaped one's potential interest in the message itself. As a BMB, Isak strongly advocates using the familiar Arabic-based terms for the person of Jesus and other key religious concepts. The use of familiar terms affects people's attitude towards the content of the message and by extension their sense that the message potentially has personal value.

The use of experience-near concepts also contributed to the perspective that the message was relevant, in part because the concepts were ones people were concerned about. Aisah, for instance, described a history of belief in and involvement with spirits and fortune-tellers. Coming to understand that belief in Jesus provided a measure of protection against Satan impacted her. She saw that this message she heard was one which affected her personal life and provided help. The concept of the spirit world, well known by many Cambodians, was discussed with the presentation of the gospel message. Furthermore, explanations were given about how belief in

Jesus affects one's interactions with the spirit world, including providing protection from evil spirits. Deliberate discussion of this experience-near topic helped Cambodian Muslims see that the Christian message was relevant and personally meaningful. Other experience-near topics were addressed, including the subjects of heaven, sin, and doing good deeds. These topics were close to the hearts and minds of many respondents. Similar to Aisah's experience above, hearing that the Christian message spoke to these subjects helped make the message seem more alive.

Other significant methods of communication were (1) communicating in a manner which respected the listener's previous understanding and (2) explaining the message in a way that fits within the listener's existing framework. As these two methods are related, they will be discussed together. Isak's experience illustrates both of these methods. As reviewed in chapter 2, he tells of his interaction with Steven, a cross-cultural worker he had been introduced to. Isak related a conversation he had with Steven, in which he asked Steven about the meaning of "the King Father and King Son." Isak was surprised by Steven's response that the King Father was Allah, whom Isak was familiar with. Contrary to Isak's expectations, Steven did not simply reject his belief in Allah and speak only about Jesus. Isak did not know Steven's exact beliefs about the God of the Bible as compared to Allah, but he interpreted Steven's words as acknowledging Allah and respecting his personal beliefs. Isak also clearly stated his response to this interaction: "Because of this, I began to be interested in the story of Jesus." Steven may have had various reasons for saying what he did, but his response to Isak's question demonstrated he was not simply trying to dismiss beliefs which Isak had come to embrace over his lifetime. In the Cambodian context, where Buddhism is followed in some manner by most citizens, Isak and other Muslims likely experienced some criticism of their culture and of their belief in one true creator God. In Isak's eyes, Steven did not deliberately try to devalue his beliefs.

As Isak investigated more, he came to realize this message about Jesus was not as foreign as originally thought. He said,

> The Qur'an says that we should do [good deeds], but it does not show us if the Lord accepts us or not. We do not know. So we started to do research about that and research about Jesus. We saw that Jesus said whoever has faith in him, God will release them from judgment. So we thought about this as well. I read the Qur'an and saw that it talked about Jesus as well, and I began to become

interested, continually interested. This Jesus is not from the outside, but he is in the Qur'an, which also talks about him.

Reading the Qur'an, Isak discovered more about Jesus, whom he saw was not outside Islamic teachings but rather is included in the Qur'an. The message about Jesus he was hearing—while different in many ways from what he was taught as a Muslim—was within his framework of understanding. It, therefore, made Jesus and the message about him more accessible. The experience of Imran the fisherman also reflects this concept. Communicating the message within Imran's framework of understanding helped him view it as part of a story he was already somewhat familiar with, instead of being totally foreign. It contributed to the message being perceived as more personal and accessible.

Another method of communication which contributed to the message being seen as more relevant and meaningful was the use of media. The film, *Jesus*, or video clips about Bible stories had a particular impact on some respondents. Tewi noted that she began believing in Jesus as a direct result of watching a film about him approximately twenty-five years ago. The film was shown in her small community by cross-cultural workers, and she traces her faith journey to that event. Sara was also stirred as she viewed a movie about Jesus, commenting that she began crying as she watched the movie. She felt pity for Jesus in his suffering, and through the film understood more clearly that he is the one who died for the sin of humans. Nida also speaks of a deeply personal experience of watching a film about Jesus, in which she wept and realized afresh that his death was because of the sin of humans, but even more specifically because of *her* [italics mine] sin. Through the medium of film, the life and death of Jesus became much more personal, understandable, and meaningful for Nida and Sara. Films did not always elicit these responses, however. Sara, who spoke about weeping as she watched a film, also noted that others expressed suspicion about the movie when she was younger, with older people saying that the movie was made to make the people believe (in Jesus). Although Sara also had some initial suspicion when watching the movie the first time, later in life the film had a significant impact on her life.

Audio recordings were important to some individuals. Minat, for instance, was quite happy to have MP3 recordings on her phone, which she often listened to. Isak listened to a cassette, which discussed the existence of the King Father and King Son. His interest was piqued, and he later specifically asked Stephen about these topics, which led to the deeper discussion reviewed above. Although not always clearly elaborated on by the respondents themselves, audio recordings of the Bible or Christian teaching appeared to be quite meaningful to several individuals. Some respondents reported recordings as significant before they came to believe in Jesus. Others, such as Najee, spoke of their value after they had already begun following Jesus. She listened at times late into the evening, and the recordings helped to both reinforce the message already followed and to prepare to explain it to others.

Other methods of communication, such as the use of the contextualized Bible and other materials, helped to make the message more personally relevant. The common reasons for this are described above in the discussion about the choice of language and the use of experience-near terms and concepts as methods of communicating the message.

The Messenger of Communication Was Meaningful

The fact that certain individuals or groups communicated the message contributed to it not only being taken seriously but also being seen as personally meaningful and compelling. Respondents spoke of hearing the message from many people, including cross-cultural workers. It appears that many were influenced when they heard the message from relatives or friends. The message was personal because they had close connections with these individuals, which was often accompanied with a sense that these people genuinely cared for them. Srey Mum is an example. As previously discussed, she heard the gospel message from her husband. The perception that her husband truly loved her and desired what was best for her was initially quite significant for Srey Mum. The message was personally compelling in part because she heard it from someone she deeply cared for and who sincerely loved her. It was also compelling later in her conversion journey because it addressed the topics of forgiveness and release from sin. Narin spoke of the fact that his relatives encouraged him to study and to follow Jesus. During his interview, Hamat identified another man (not related to him) as the one who had told him the message. Hamat expressed obvious respect for this person as he spoke about him.

Shaza is a mother who noted that her husband followed Jesus and was involved in local meetings where the Bible was studied. He told her the message. She also commented that she admired his life as a believer. In contrast to her actions, he would not angrily criticize the children, even when they did wrong. The message became personal to her because she saw its effects displayed in her household, even to the point of recognizing the contrasting actions between her husband and herself. Shaza's experience illustrates that communication is not limited to merely telling and explaining a message, but is also accomplished by living out and displaying it. This "displaying" of the gospel message may or may not be done consciously and deliberately, but it is often noticed. It was previously noted that Narin was encouraged by those near him to believe. In addition, his observations that followers of Jesus acted in kind and helpful ways influenced his decision to believe in Jesus. Their kind and good-hearted actions contributed to his decision to "walk the true path, the good path." This "good path" was more understandable, accessible, and relevant because it was lived out in front of him.

The cross-cultural worker Steven was previously introduced. Steven often facilitated mobile medical clinics in rural Muslim communities, often with the assistance of Isak. Medical personnel would spend one to three days in a community and treat community members or provide referrals as needed to larger clinics. Although respondents did not specifically discuss if or to what degree Steven's actions were tied to their decision to follow Jesus, many of them did informally comment that Steven assisted with these clinics and that they were much appreciated. People knew Steven was a follower of Jesus, and they noted that he carried out these good deeds as a Christ-follower.

The Christian message is not received by humans in a sterile fashion. It comes through the words of humans, often demonstrated by their hands and actions. In examining the narratives and reflections of Cambodian BMBs, it is seen that this Christian message became personal to many of them because it was communicated to them by those they knew intimately and respected, and because it was lived out in front of them.

Discussion

Cambodians in this study described the Christian message as personal, relevant, and valuable. At times this was due to the content of the message itself being seen as personally meaningful, either in addressing felt concerns or in touching someone in a personal way. In other instances, the method used in communication or the messengers themselves contributed to the Christian message being seen as personally meaningful. One underlying theory about how humans personally experience the message can be proposed as follows: *When the content of the message corresponds to or addresses topics which are important to the one hearing it, the message is more likely to be perceived as personally meaningful and compelling.* The content of the Christian message is broad, including topics such as creation, personal sin, shame, redemption, forgiveness, new life, restored relationships, etc. Not all of these topics will resonate with individuals in a given cultural context. Some may be seen as critically important; others may simply not be understood or be perceived as meaningless. However, when people discover that the Christian message includes topics which are personally important to them, they view it as more relevant to their lives. Furthermore, if the message actually provides answers or solutions to questions on these topics, it may be seen as more helpful or compelling. Topics of personal importance may have arisen because of previous socialization or religious teachings, current experiences, common cultural values, or individual longings. Examples of these from Cambodian respondents include topics such as sin, heaven, protection from evil spirits, hope, forgiveness, God's Word, God's prophets, and good deeds.

Craig Ott describes four New Testament metaphors regarding salvation. Citing Richard Mouw, he notes that one does not have to feel the need to communicate the comprehensive theological picture to unbelievers at one time. Rather, one can begin with the theological concept or metaphor which most relates to their understanding and lived experience. It is understood that eventually more teaching will be given, but one initially begins with the topics which are most understandable and meaningful for those hearing the message.[9] Dye and Priest, writing about communicating the gospel message to others, advocate understanding the conscience of those hearing the message and discussing topics to which their consciences are actually sensitive. In short, they suggest addressing issues which concern and/or trouble the heart of the listener, instead of the communicator.[10] In a separate article, Priest also discusses the importance of using "experience-near" terms, which are immediately recognizable and naturally used.[11] All of the above writings complement each other and reinforce three concepts related to the underlying theory stated above. First, the Christian message

---

9. Ott, "Power of Biblical Metaphors," 359, 362; Mouw, "Christus Victor Is Not Enough," 30.

10. Dye, "Toward a Cross-cultural Definition of Sin," 38–40; Priest, "Missionary Elenctics," 308–9.

11. Priest, "'Experience-Near Theologizing,'" 189.

includes not one but many important topics and truths. Second, each individual has certain topics, values, and longings which he or she is most concerned about. Third, when the content of the gospel message corresponds to topics which are important to an individual, the message is seen to be more relevant, personally meaningful, and compelling. This theory is illustrated in the experiences and narratives of Cambodian BMBs.

In addition to the content of the message being important, God's perceived actions also led to the message being seen as personally significant. Many individuals related a sense that God was involved in some way. For some, it was the sense that God was "illuminating" the message so they could understand and believe. Others speak of God's involvement through answered prayer or provision of assistance in a time of need. Yet others refer to the influence of dreams.

The manner in which the message was communicated had a profound impact for some. Often this was through the choice of language, use of experience-near terms or concepts, and communication within the framework of understanding. Some individuals reported being emotionally touched as they viewed a film or listened to an audio recording. For others, the message became personal and relevant partially because of the influence of people from whom they heard it. Both spoken words and actions were powerful. Lofland and Stark write about the potential influence social relationships have on religious conversion.[12] Lofland and Skonovd identify six conversion motifs.[13] One of them, affectional, relates to the current discussion. Many Cambodian respondents noted hearing the Christian message from friends or family members. More than one expressed admiration for the person who told them the message. The influence other individuals had on conversion is real. However, nearly all of those who spoke of being impacted by another person also provided *additional reasons* for their conversion, usually personal in nature (such as Narin's desire to have victory over sinful behavior). In the case of Cambodian BMBs, other individuals

---

12. Lofland and Stark, "Becoming a World-Saver."

13. Lofland and Skonovd, "Conversion Motifs," 376–82. The motifs and a summaries of them are: (1) intellectual, related to private research or thought about joining a different religion, often absent of outside contacts, (2) mystical, characterized by an emotional or powerful experience which cannot be explained logically, (3) experimental, described as trying out a new religious identity or belief, and discovering whether or not it seems to fit, (4) affectional, being influenced by others whom they are connected with or whom they admire, (5) revivalist, characterized by powerful experiences occurring in the presence of a group which is emotionally charged, and (6) coercive, described as forcing or "brainwashing" others.

PERSONAL EXPERIENCE OF THE CHRISTIAN MESSAGE

and groups, while influencing conversion, did not appear to be the primary or final reasons for conversion.

The phrase "experience-near" has been used to describe both terms and concepts related to gospel communication. This term also is appropriate to describe many of the respondent's interactions with God. The narratives and reflections of interviewees point to a sense that God is intimate. He is both concerned with and involved in the lives of humans. For example, Yasmin's description of being released from being troubled by an evil spirit points to her perception that God personally helped her. In addition, Amir's narrative about calling out to God three times and being answered each time depicts a sense that God is both aware of one's circumstances, is listening, and is willing to assist. Razaa expressed being encouraged by a verse which came to him one day during a season of discouragement. As he noted, "It's like a sound that God talks to me . . . like this verse is from Hebrews, 'I'll never leave you or forsake you.'" This became a meaningful verse to Razaa. For him, God was close and nearby. Some respondents expressed a sense of experiencing God as near and personal. Experience-near thus relates both to an individual's perceptions about God and also the manner in which God's message is communicated.

The factors contributing to the message being seen as personal and compelling are represented in the following diagram:

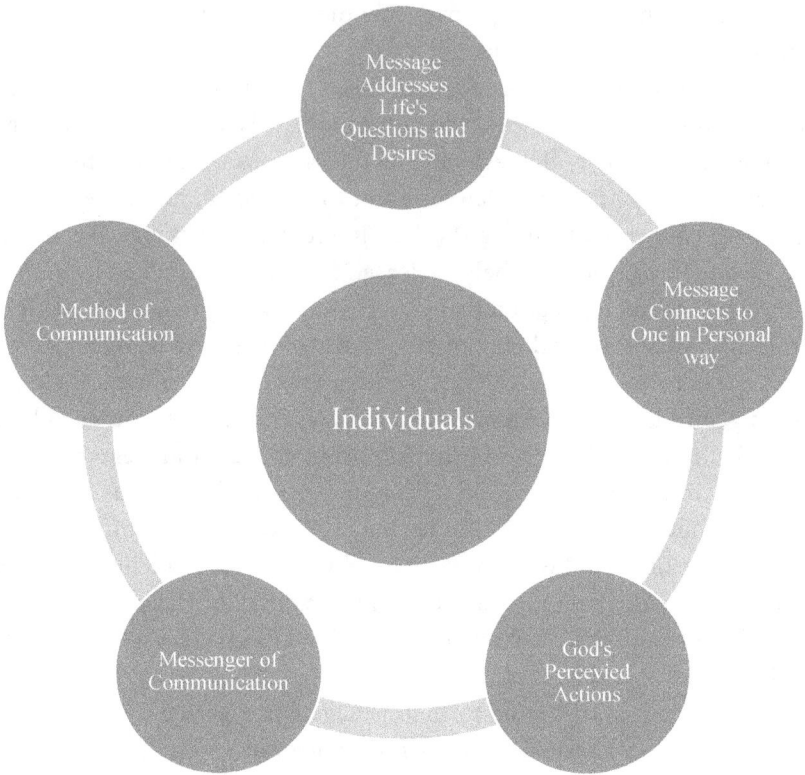

Figure 4. Factors Contributing to the Message Being Viewed as Personally Meaningful

The term "individuals" is placed in the center of the diagram, as it represents findings from all respondents, not just one. Individuals were commonly affected by more than one factor. For instance, from their narrative, it may be apparent that a respondent was influenced by all five of the factors. Certain factors were more important for some individuals than others. Additionally, it is noted that each of the factors is connected to others by means of a ring. This indicates that the factors may interact with or reinforce each other. For instance, the two aspects of communication, both the method and the messenger, can naturally interact and contribute to the message being viewed as personal and relevant. The factors which seemed to be most prominent for the largest number of individuals were those relating to the content of the message. In the diagram above, the two circles beginning with the word "message" in their title refer to the content of the message. The message itself addressed personal concerns or connected to individuals in a meaningful way. The figure above differs from Figure 3 of the previous chapter in that it is not identifying general categories influencing conversion, but specifically the manner in which individuals felt that the gospel message was for them, about them, and thus personally meaningful. The following sections complement the above information and provide more details about the journeys to faith and current perspectives of Cambodian BMBs in this study.

How do Cambodian BMBs Describe their Journeys to Belief in Jesus?

When Cambodian respondents told their stories and reflected on their conversion, they discussed many topics, often in a jumbled manner, as is often common during interviews. However, their words provide a deeper understanding of their journeys to faith. Ten observations will be made regarding the descriptions BMBs gave regarding their conversion. These observations paint a more comprehensive picture of the lives, thoughts, and experiences of Cambodian BMBs. Some of the observations have been previously referred to; others have not.

First, respondents frequently began their story by identifying the person or persons whom they heard the gospel message from. This was natural and at times done in an excited manner. People often appeared eager to tell about who communicated the message to them, or whom they studied with.

Second, individuals usually described a *process* of conversion. With the exception of Tewi, who said she believed years ago as a young mother when viewing a film about Jesus shown in her community, respondents spoke of a process before deciding to believe in and follow Jesus. Many used language of previously not knowing or understanding, to later coming to know, and eventually to believe. Suliman, talking about when he was younger, said, "I didn't know anything. Nobody at all let me know. My mother and my father did not teach me about that. I did not know [this] good news. When I met Steven in the mosque, I asked him. I asked him and he replied. When he spoke, I could hear and understand, understand, understand. Why? Because of [my] clear faith." Suliman and others spoke of not knowing or understanding which later developed into knowing, understanding, and belief. At times, words such as "study" are used, which point to a sense that for many, they categorize the process of believing in educational terms, such as not knowing, followed by study and greater understanding, and then a decision or series of decisions to follow Jesus. This is not surprising, for two reasons. First, the experience of many in learning about the Christian message was that of meeting in a small group for "study," where the Bible was taught and discussed. Second, these phrases fit into the larger Cambodian framework, where education is often discussed and is spoken of in terms of a process moving from "not knowing" to knowing, understanding, and/or being skilled at doing. This observation ties the experiences of many Cambodian BMBs with the common cultural perspective regarding education and growth.

The timeframe taken for respondents to hear, learn, consider, and embrace the Christian message varied. Although not all were asked how long this process took for them personally, many mentioned a period of time of approximately one month. Imran, for instance, who decided to follow Jesus about four months before being interviewed, told about a series of three discussions he had with a cross-cultural worker over several weeks, the third of which culminated in a personal decision to request forgiveness from Jesus. Isak spoke of a process of four to five months from his initial conversation with Steven to the point he truly believed. Others reported a much longer period of time, or that they could not remember how long their process of conversion took. For Ali, the timeframe was approximately one year. He reflected about that time and his reading of Bible pages, which occurred while he was in prison, "I considered and thought about the prophet [Jesus] who opened the path for me for about one year. For a year or a year and a half, I didn't go anywhere. I read it again and again. Only when it was time to eat did I get up. After I woke up, I read the papers [Bible pages] that I had stolen from them." Although Ali was likely involved in other activities besides reading, his words reflect an intensity to study and to know. One component of the process he used is identified in the next observation.

Third, respondents described comparing the path of following Jesus with their background religious practices and beliefs. This included considering the potential benefits of embracing and following Jesus. These acts of comparing were important for many in their decision to believe in and follow Jesus. Respondents most commonly spoke about differences they discovered, but at times they pointed to similarities as well. As previously noted, Isak discussed the concept of assurance, saying that the Qur'an instructed humans what they were to do, but did not tell them if they were ultimately accepted or not by God. He later heard about Jesus, and it was explained that believing in him allowed one to go to heaven. Isak said this created interest in Jesus. Kosal also discussed the assurance of going to heaven, stating, "They [other religions] cannot assure us that we can go to heaven . . . But when we believe in Jesus, it's not unsure like other religions. Jesus said that he will bring someone who believes in him to heaven." Later in his interview, reflecting on what led him to believe, Kosal says that before he simply carried out the religious practices as dictated in the rules, but "These days, I feel happy. Following Jesus is easy. Jesus also saves us and brings us to heaven. It is easy to go to heaven. It seems like a road with no bridge for someone who doesn't believe in Jesus. The person will fall down if they continue to walk. . . . For those who believe in Jesus, it seems like there are two roads linked together. God brings us to heaven . . . easy." Kosal's words highlight his personal focus on heaven, as previously discussed. They also reveal a sense that following Jesus is "easier" than their former path. The word "easy" is used by Kosal, and by other respondents as well.

Matt explained that the practice of praying five times per day was difficult, but the path of following Jesus is easy to follow. He emphasized that he made his own decision to believe and that the concept of being washed (from sin) and made clean again was critical. His decision was not simply based on what is easier, but he did observe differences between the religious rites of Islam and Christianity. When asked if there were aspects of the Christian message which initially interested her, Fatimah commented that following Jesus is easier than the practices of those who pray five times per day. She later noted that even if one [a Christ-follower] does not do anything (such as complete the prayers), they can still receive a benefit from God. Later in the interview, Fatimah spoke of tangible difficulties in following Jesus, including criticism by others and a lack of community support. She is aware of the hard road she has experienced as a result of her decision to follow Jesus. At the same time, her words reflect the fact that initially she, like others, compared the path of Jesus with its results to the path of her former belief system. Other interviewees conveyed their perception that Islamic doctrine did not address personal sin and forgiveness in a satisfactory way, including guaranteeing salvation. As previously noted, one respondent, Borey, focused on Jesus being alive, and therefore able to practically help humans. Other respondents utilized terms such as "easier," or "better," meaning following the path of Jesus was easier or better than continuing their previous path.

Scholars discuss various views regarding one's background belief system. Greenham lists the "rejection of Islam" as a category of lesser prominence for conversion.[14] This category implies that individuals evaluate belief systems. Woodberry, Shubin, and Marks include "dissatisfaction with the type of Islam they had experienced" as one of the components of the category titled, "seeing a lived faith," which was seen as the most important category influencing conversion among the seven hundred fifty surveys taken. Examples of dissatisfaction reported included such topics as unhappiness with the Qur'an, which was seen to focus on God's judgment, frustration with the need to conduct prayers in the Arabic language, instead of one's mother tongue, and disappointment that those involved in folk Islam commonly use amulets.[15] While the specific category of "comparison," did not emerge in other research about Christian conversion of Muslims, some of the themes which did emerge, such as a dissatisfaction with Islam, parallel the experiences of some Cambodian BMBs.

At times, however, the comparison of belief systems revealed similarities, which for some had positive connotations. Ali, who hid pages of the Bible in his underwear while imprisoned, talked about comparing the Bible and the Qur'an. One of his conclusions was that they were not that different from each other, although Islam's rules are stricter than those of Christianity. Ali noted that he came to believe in Jesus after comparing because following Jesus could help his entire life and decrease problems.

In contrast to expecting radical differences between Islam and Christianity, the perception by some that there are many similarities leads them to be less suspicious of Christianity. This observation connects to the previous discussion regarding contextualization, where the presentation of Christian teachings in such a way that they seem familiar to one's current understanding contributes to them being viewed as more accessible and personally relevant. Other respondents explained that, when sharing the message with others, one of the points made was that this Christian message is not that different from Islam. Tahira says, "I tell people that the books and rules are similar to what we have. I tell other people that following Jesus is similar to our religion."

---

14. Greenham, "Study of Palestinian Muslim Conversions," 154.
15. Woodberry et al., "Why Muslims Follow Jesus," 82–83.

PERSONAL EXPERIENCE OF THE CHRISTIAN MESSAGE

Although there are fundamental differences between Islam and Christianity, the presentation of similarities (at least initially) appears to help decrease suspicion to teachings about Jesus. The above discussion indicates that, for some respondents, considering the benefits of following Jesus, including comparing the practice and teachings of Christianity with their former belief system, was important in the process of choosing to follow Jesus. Because Muslims comprise only approximately three percent of the entire Cambodian population, they are commonly exposed to other religions, most significantly Buddhism, which the majority of Cambodians follow in some manner. Muslims in many other countries, especially ones which have a high percentage of citizens following Islam, have little contact with non-Muslims. In Cambodia, however, Muslims have much exposure to other belief systems. It is thus not surprising that many evaluate the teachings of their religion with that of others, and that individuals consider the perceived benefits of following Jesus.

A fourth observation is that many Cambodian BMBs emphasized they were not forced to believe but rather decided on their own. Remembering watching a film about Jesus shown by cross-cultural workers in her village years ago, Tewi said, "They only came to show the movie to us. They did not force us to believe. That depends on our own mind. If our hearts want to believe, then we believe. . . . This believing depends on whether or not we are happy to do it. It's about our own willingness." Tewi discussed not only the lack of pressure exerted from outsiders to believe but also the presence of personal agency in choosing to believe. This sense of personal freedom was perhaps expressed best by Matt. He used a vivid illustration of selecting clothing to wear when drawing a parallel between the freedom to choose to follow Jesus and other freedoms. Matt exclaimed that someone has the right to wear a white shirt, a black shirt, or even a shirt that is ripped. It is up to them. He argued that just as one has a right to choose which clothes they desire, they also have a right to choose which prophet or religious system they desire to follow. Several respondents expressed that they did not feel coerced by others to follow Jesus. Many spoke of an individual decision, with varying degrees of communicating the decision to others. Abdul talked about an initial personal decision. He knew he believed, and told his wife, but he did not know her thoughts and waited rather than aggressively sharing the gospel message. Aminah spoke about a decision to believe which occurred with other relatives. She, her uncle, and her nephew studied with a teacher and all three decided to believe together. While most respondents spoke about their personal journeys towards following Jesus, some of them noted others who also believed, whether at the same or at different times.

Based on his research in Melanesia, Alan Tippett describes group conversion, in which decisions are made through multi-individual social interaction.[16] Charles Kraft also discusses group conversion, noting that those who are involved in individualistic societies tend to convert in an individualistic way, whereas those coming from group-oriented societies will more likely convert in groups, after a process of group discussion.[17] Cambodian respondents did not speak often about significant group interaction before making decisions to follow Jesus. However, decisions were commonly made in the context of others. At times, groups of people met to study the Bible, and individuals were naturally aware when others were truly deciding to follow Jesus. While Cambodians were certainly aware of and influenced to some degree by others, the information provided by the respondents indicates that the conversions were likely not group ones, which are usually characterized by much group interaction beforehand.

Robert Montgomery introduces the aspect of volition in religious conversion. He defines "high volition" as occurring when an individual deliberately chooses to follow another religion, with "low volition" described as accepting a religious identity "more or less as a matter of course."[18] Lorne Dawson and James Richardson argue that conversion should be seen as a more active process than earlier thought. Dawson writes, "People are not so much converted to new religions as they convert themselves."[19] These authors discuss active vs. passive agency in religious conversion. Cambodian respondents, while influenced to some degree by others, demonstrated active agency in their decisions to follow Jesus. In the context of Islam, individual courage is at times needed if one desires to follow a different path, as most of one's companions will likely encourage them to stay within the fold of Islam. Several respondents spoke of some type of personal benefit they expected to receive after following Jesus, whether that be the entrance into heaven, strength to live right, or an easier path to God's blessing. Comments such as these indicate a sense of personal agency in their decisions, instead of simply agreeing to the suggestions of others.

16. Tippett, "Conversion as a Dynamic Process," 217.
17. Kraft, "Conversion in Group Settings," 262, 273.
18. Montgomery, "Conversion," 165.
19. Richardson, "Active vs. Passive Convert," 163; Dawson, "Cult Conversions," 309.

A fifth observation is that some BMBs spoke of times of turning away from Jesus or regression. Maria's previous comments illustrate this. She arrived at a point in her walk with Jesus that if her prayers for a job were not answered, she felt she would stop believing in Jesus. Although he did not clearly elaborate why, Borey frankly noted that at one point he was going to return to Islam. Researchers have discussed the reality that religious conversion is not always characterized by a linear progression, where one makes a single decision to convert and then continues to consistently follow that chosen path. Researching conversion into the Jesus movement, Richardson and Stewart use the term "conversion careers" to describe a process whereby people make a series of decisions as they try different religious options available to them.[20] Henri Gooren develops a model of conversion which incorporates potential phases of pre-affiliation, affiliation, conversion, confession, and disaffiliation.[21] Heinz Streib discusses six types of deconversion trajectories.[22] The narratives of Cambodian BMBs do demonstrate a series of decisions at times, and even doubts about continuing to follow Jesus, with three individuals seriously considering stopping their allegiance to Jesus. On the whole, however, respondents indicated their satisfaction with following Jesus and desire to continue to do so.[23] When Sofia was asked, for instance, about if she has had feelings about wanting to go back to her former religion, she stated, "I do not have any regret. Because nowadays I pray to Jesus to allow my parents and relatives to believe in him. Sometimes, my parents blame me [for belief in Jesus]. I don't concern myself with those words, because I ask Jesus to lead them to change their thoughts." While it is often assumed that converts out of Islam will be tempted to return to it because of criticism or persecution, Sofia stated that she did not regret her decision and is hopeful that family members who criticize her will also follow Jesus. Sofia's words do not discount the reality of criticism towards followers of Jesus, and of the emotional anguish that such criticism may bring. She, however, communicated a satisfaction with following Jesus. Others, such as Ali, spoke in a similar way, "Nowadays, I never think or dream about going back to Islam." Rather, he tries

20. Richardson and Stewart, "Conversion Process Models," 24–25, 32.
21. Gooren, "Towards a New Model," 154.
22. Streib, "Deconversion."
23. It is understood that because of reactivity by respondents and the fact that the interview itself focuses on the decision to follow Jesus, many individuals may want to communicate a satisfaction with Jesus and a desire to continue to follow him. I acknowledge these factors and have taken them into consideration in my analysis and conclusions.

to spread the gospel information he has to others. Few respondents spoke of deliberately leaving Jesus, though many did talk about difficulties they experienced after following Jesus, often related to criticism received from others. These criticisms did not appear to commonly precipitate crises of belief or strong desires to stop following Jesus, however.

A sixth observation is that when speaking of their conversion, participants did not necessarily give a sequential timeline, but spoke about different events or thoughts, at times jumping forward or backward in time. They understood that questions were focused on their thoughts and experiences of coming to understand the Christian message and choosing to follow Jesus, but their responses at times included perspectives and comments about events both prior to and following their conversion. Although clear conclusions cannot be drawn, some tentative remarks can be made. First, respondents did not view their conversion necessarily as a point-in-time event, but rather as a drawn-out process including many significant experiences. Second, Cambodians may not necessarily think sequentially about life and history, but rather in another manner such as cyclical. If that is the case, speaking about different events at different times would be more natural than simply giving a sequential timeline. Third, respondents have a clear sense that their conversion affects other aspects of their life, including the present. This comprehensive and interconnected view of conversion may lead to one easily discuss one thought or event and then jump to another occurring at a different time. What may appear scrambled to an outsider may be evidence of an integrated understanding of conversion to an insider.

The seventh observation is that some respondents frequently spoke of God illuminating or leading them to follow him. Pes spoke of God's leading, saying, "I know that my master pointed me to follow Jesus." He mentioned realizing this after he was actually baptized, which is a contrast to those who spoke of feeling that God was leading them before and during their decision to believe. This study has focused more on people's experiences leading to a commitment to follow Jesus. Pes's realizations complement these other experiences and illustrate the perception by many that God was at work in some way in their conversions, whether or not it was realized before or after their decision to follow Jesus.

Eighth, Cambodian BMBs spoke of incidents which were tied to their belief or the strengthening of their belief. These events were personally significant and were told during the interviews. Some were related primarily to initial belief in Jesus, such as Amir's description of him crying out three times to Jesus. Others were connected to encouragement after belief, such as the experience Isak had after he lost his job and was experiencing problems because of his belief in Jesus. He was struck with a verse about God testing our faith. When a friend introduced him to a small business, and Isak made money the first day, he felt God was helping him. This incident greatly encouraged Isak and prompted thankfulness to God. Regardless of whether or not they occurred before or after initial belief, these experiences were meaningful to Cambodian BMBs and were often told with excitement.

A ninth observation is that respondents often naturally used illustrations to describe their own journey. Kosal's emotions were evident as he said,

> Nowadays, I feel fresh when I believe in Isa. Before I knew nothing. It can be compared to walking along a thorny path and being pierced with thorns or walking along a path in darkness. Also, it is like walking along a road which has a bridge, but it is out, so you cannot cross but fall down. Nowadays, after I have believed, it seems like there is a new road which has just been built.

Kosal illustrates the contrast between his former and current perspectives. Whereas before the path ahead was fraught with obstacles, after believing in Jesus, the path has been smoothed and made new. Kosal spoke much about the path to heaven, and his comments above are related to that topic and his feelings that his sin has been taken away and that he is clean. Other respondents spoke about their belief in Jesus and present life through illustrations, such as Sagy's comments about desiring to become white like a piece of paper.

A tenth observation is that many individuals used the phrase "change heart" (*slih tai*) to help describe their conversion experience. The terms "change heart" (*slih tai*) or "repent" (*taobat*) were used by approximately one-third of those interviewed. The term "change heart" was used more frequently, in part perhaps due to the fact that many respondents did not easily recognize the specific Cham term I used for "repent" (*taobat*). However, the manner and frequency in which "change heart" was used demonstrated an understanding that is quite similar to that of the biblical meaning of "repent." Many authors highlight the aspect of "turning" or "change" as essential to the definition of conversion.[24] Danker et al. define the New Testament Greek

---

24. Walls, "Converts or Proselytes?," 2, 6; Peace, "Conflicting Understandings of Christian Conversion," 8.

term *epistrepho* as "turn around, go back," and *metanoia* as meaning "repentance, turning about, conversion."[25] David Kling identifies these terms as central to the Christian understanding of conversion.[26] The term used by respondents literally means "change heart" and is used primarily to discuss their belief in Jesus and the decision to follow him. Isak, describing what is meant by changing one's heart from Islam to Jesus, said, "It means we cannot depend on the rules [of Islam], but we depend on Jesus instead." Sara used both terms in her comments, "[I] repented, repented and changed my heart because I believed in Jesus. I believe Jesus, he died and was raised again. We have sin. We repent to Jesus, and he makes us clean." Sara's words illustrate the understanding of many regarding what it means to believe and follow Jesus. Isak adds the component of trusting Jesus, instead of putting trust in receiving benefit from following the laws of Islam.

Respondents used the term "change heart" not only to describe their conversion experience, but also to point to how their life was different after believing, usually in terms of conducting themselves differently than before. What is clear is that the concept of change is central to many BMBs when they reflect on their conversion. Scholars have discussed continuity and discontinuity in relation to religious conversion. In their research, Robbins and VanKlinken have each emphasized rupture as part of the experience of conversion to Christ, where significant changes occur in the lives of the converts.[27] Others have drawn attention to conversion as a process, which occurs over time and may involve a series of decisions, usually gradual and even spanning a lifetime.[28] A discontinuity may still be evident, but it may occur over time, punctuated by key experiences. The narratives and reflections of Cambodian respondents indicate that for many conversion was a process. It took place over a period of time, short or long, involved learning about a new message, evaluating it, seeing it lived in the lives of others, considering its impact in their life, and deciding—either at one time or through a series of decisions—to truly believe in and follow Jesus. It was not merely an intellectual consideration of an alternative belief system, but rather often included an evaluation of self and a focus on the person of Jesus. For most,

---

25. Danker et al., *Greek-English Lexicon*, 382, 640–41.

26. Kling, "Conversion to Christianity," 598.

27. Robbins, *Becoming Sinners*; Robbins, "Globalization of Pentecostal Christianity"; Van Klinken, "Men in the Remaking."

28. Rambo, "Psychology of Conversion," 165; Smith, *Beginning Well*, 31; Hibbert, "Negotiating Identity," 62; Richardson and Stewart, "Conversion Process Models," 24–25.

conversion was a process, although a variety of paths were taken. It was, however, a process which included change, often radical change. Although there was continuity in many ways in the daily lives of Cambodian BMBs after conversion, discontinuity was also apparent and was often spoken of, evidenced by the common use of words such as *slih tai*.

How Do Cambodian BMBs Describe Their Current Beliefs and Lives with Jesus?

While the previous section examined the reflections and experiences of respondents primarily up to and during the time they chose to follow Jesus, this section reviews their perspectives and experiences after that decision. Five observations will be made about how BMBs describe their current lives as followers of Jesus. First, respondents spoke of a definite belief in Jesus. Approximately one-fourth of those interviewed specifically remarked that they truly believe, or have a strong belief. While part of their motivation may have been due to the fact I was interviewing them about their beliefs,[29] several individuals often spoke about their genuine belief in a natural and casual manner. Although some appeared to deliberately desire to communicate they strongly believed in Jesus, others conveyed a strong belief without an apparent intention to do so.

A second observation is that respondents spoke of trusting not in themselves but rather in another. This was a fundamental understanding of many about the nature of conversion, and also a motivation for conversion. As previously noted, Isak said that he did not depend on the rules of Islam, but rather on Jesus. He, as well as many others, had a conscious sense that they were no longer depending on their observance of Islamic law as the avenue to gain spiritual merit, be cleansed from sin, or eventually enter heaven. Instead, they were deliberately depending on the person of Jesus.

---

29. It is understood interviewees and individuals, in general, may desire to project a certain image to others depending on the context (see also Erving Goffman's "front stage" and "backstage" behavior in Goffman, *Presentation of Self*). After completing all the interviews, I met with a prominent Cambodian BMB to discuss my research findings. I mentioned my observation that many spoke of the strength of their belief. He responded that this was not surprising, as those interviewed likely expected I wanted to know if they were truly following Jesus. I am aware of this potential desire for some respondents to over-emphasize their belief and have taken it into consideration as I have analyzed data and drawn conclusions.

Jesus's suffering and death on the cross were commonly referred to when discussing the above topics.

The concept of trusting in or believing in Jesus only was referred to by several respondents. Srey Mum said, "I want to believe in Jesus because I know clearly that it is only through belief in him that I can be released from my sinful actions and I can have a new life with him." Kari, talking about how she responds to others if they ask why she follows Jesus only, spoke bluntly,

> I answer that we love only him. We follow only him. We don't follow others. Yes, I love him like that. . . . We cannot love all, so we will love only one, we cannot love two. It is like when a husband and wife are married. We cannot love two. We can choose only one. If two, there will be problems, of jealousy! . . . If we have two or three [husbands/wives], we cannot say that we are honest. If we are double-minded, we will have arguments forever.

Kari's powerful words describe a sense of loving only Jesus and choosing only him. She illustrates her thoughts with the concept of marriage, of a spouse choosing only one other. When more than one other spouse is chosen, there is dishonesty, jealousy, and difficulty. Kari is clear regarding the person she has chosen. Early in her interview, Kari simply said she loved Jesus and was fulfilled in him. These words reveal both her motivation for initially following Jesus and her present-day lived experience with him. Kari's illustration of the relationship between husband and wife points to the perspective that God is near. In contrast to one who is removed and disinterested, God is close and concerned. She uses experience-near terminology to discuss her relationship with God, as God himself is near and personal to her.

A third observation is that people spoke of changes in their lives occurring as a result of following Jesus. Sukry, for instance, spoke of two changes, one directly leading to the other. First, he used to go to KTV (karaoke television) establishments to drink and then lie to his wife about it. At that time, he considered himself a Christian, but more recently he came to a renewed commitment, what he saw as true belief and trust in Jesus. Since this renewed commitment, he no longer visits KTV locations. This change in lifestyle has led to another change: his wife now trusts him. Sukry noted that even after his change, others were suspicious if he went out carrying a lot of money. They asked his wife why she allowed him to go out with such a large amount of money, as they felt he would spend it for KTV entertainment and drinking. Sukry, however, remarked that things have changed. Speaking about his wife's trust in him, he said, "Before sometimes she did not trust me. But now she truly trusts me, like the Khmer say, one hundred percent."

Others speak of different types of changes. Aminah remarked that before believing in Jesus, she would not accept mistakes or wrongdoing which she did, but rather would think she was right. After believing in Jesus, her perspective about personal wrongdoing has changed, "If we believe in Jesus, we do bad, just a little bit, we accept the mistake. We know that we have done wrong." Sofia frankly states that believing in Jesus changes our lives a lot. That was one of her motivations to believe in him. One specific change she identifies is that she is no longer troubled by or afraid of evil spirits. Formerly, she was involved with spirits, including appeasing them at times when they troubled her. Sofia now says that, after asking Jesus's help, much has changed. Sofia's experience relates to the next observation about the current lives of BMBs.

Fourth, respondents spoke much about prayer as a part of their lives. Although respondents were not specifically asked about prayer, approximately half of those interviewed spoke about praying to God and/or Jesus. The topic of prayer to God and Jesus was discussed more commonly in the context of their lives after following Jesus than their lives before following him.[30] The theme of simply asking for help in times of need was familiar. Minat, for example, spoke about previously feeling that demons would coax her to be angry with others. Now there does not seem to be a problem, and she prays when angry, "If I was angry with someone, I prayed and said please cool down my heart, and please let my mind calm down, and allow me to forgive those I am angry with. After a little while, I started to feel better." Minat said that she feels prayer has practically affected her life.

Shaza tells of an incident in her life involving prayer which, while frightening, had a profound impact. While visiting a medical clinic far from home, she entered a bathroom and got stuck in it when the door did not open. She began to panic and felt that she was going to die, as she had high blood pressure. Her description of what happened inside the small restroom, while lengthy, is included below, as it provides insight into her perceptions and conclusions.

---

30. Cambodian Muslims are familiar with Islamic prayer rites. Besides noting that they previously prayed according to the Islamic pattern, respondents did not commonly describe their former prayers. They did, however, discuss their prayers to God after deciding to follow Jesus.

> I said, "God, Jesus ... please help me now. I am going to die now. My arm and legs are getting colder." I was stuck in that place. Nobody saw me. I pounded on the door and called, "Doctor! Doctor! I am stuck in the bathroom." The doctor was inside [the other building] and did not hear me.... Someone came and said, "Aunt, are you stuck in the bathroom?" ... It seemed like Jesus and God helped me. I just turned the door a little bit. Finally, it opened. It was like I was able to live again. I believed. I truly believed. At that time, I thought I was going to die, but I started to think about God.... I prayed to God and asked him to please let other people see me.... Then I was helped by other people. It was because God helped me. If nobody helped me, I would have died in five more minutes.

Minat was not merely describing an answer to prayer, but an experience which greatly increased her trust in God, at a time in which she was already following Jesus. She perceived that God was directly involved in helping her escape from the bathroom, and she said her belief in him was strengthened as a result. God was close, listening, and active in her life during a time of need. Minat's experience provides an example of answered prayer in the lives of Cambodian BMBs.

Although, generally speaking, respondents pointed to God answering prayer, they did not assume he always answered, or did so quickly. Sofia spoke about formerly needing to offer food to evil spirits when they bothered her, but not needing to do that after believing in Jesus. She then said, "When there is a problem, just pray to Jesus, then he will reply. Sometimes, Jesus replies quickly.... Sometimes, he does not reply quickly." Sofia recognized that God does not always respond quickly to prayers. She, like many other BMBs, does speak of prayer when she reflects on her current life with Jesus.

A fifth and final observation is that many respondents displayed persistent belief in Jesus, even in the midst of criticism or persecution. One of the interview questions asked was, "Since you have decided to follow Jesus, have you experienced any difficulties or obstacles?" This question elicited many responses. Surprisingly, approximately a third of respondents noted that they had experienced no significant problems such as criticism or persecution. Those who replied in this way often lived in a context where other family members or relatives were also believers in Jesus. While more difficulties may have been experienced than actually reported, the information received from these respondents is important. This is particularly true when many people perceive that there is intense persecution of BMBs worldwide. Although a significant percentage of Cambodians reported no serious persecution, approximately two-thirds of those interviewed referred to difficulties encountered of some type, most commonly in the form of criticism. Some BMBs experienced this criticism directly through words of anger. Others spoke of more subtle criticism, where individuals in the community disliked them but did not communicate this face-to-face. One respondent expressed concern that her parents could potentially suffer if her belief in Jesus was uncovered. Her parents, who are Muslims, would likely be shamed by others in the community if it became known that their daughter followed Jesus. Another individual noted that he has not told others in his community that he believes in Jesus, for fear of being expelled. None of the Cambodian BMBs reported experiencing physical violence or the threat of violence as a result of following Jesus. This lack of physical persecution may be due in part to the Cambodian context. Although Muslims in Cambodia generally hold quite firmly to their faith, there does not appear to be a history of physically harming those who leave the fold of Islam.

In spite of criticism, many Cambodian respondents revealed a desire and intention to continue to follow Jesus. Sara said, "Even though my neighbors talk and discriminate against me, I have already entered Jesus![31] They can say what they want, I still depend on Jesus. . . . Even though I may be able to support or not support my family . . . I am willing to give my body to Jesus. If Jesus dies, I also die." Sara is aware of clear opposition, but she also demonstrates a resolve to continue to follow Jesus. Aminah also acknowledged the reality that some strongly criticized her, accusing her of following a religion from another country. However, she also stated that she was not to be angry with those who scolded her. The bold words of Shaza illustrate resolve in the context of criticism. Although she was told by others that if she followed Jesus, people in their community would not bury her after she passed away, she bluntly stated in the interview, "When I die, God will prepare something for me . . . You can bury me or not. It's up to you. . . . I don't care because I will be gone. The people in this village can organize my corpse as they want. I'm not angry." In a context where normally individuals are quite concerned about being properly buried, Shaza communicated a lack of worry—and a lack of anger towards others—because of her different perspective on the afterlife. She believes that after death her soul

---

31. The term "enter" is used by some Cambodians to refer to joining or entering a different religion.

will leave her body, and she is therefore not deeply concerned about the specifics of her burial. As previously noted, many Cambodian BMBs spoke about the Islamic perspective that entrance into heaven is not guaranteed and that one, therefore, does not know whether or not one will enter heaven. Cambodian Muslims are aware of and seek to follow specific Islamic burial practices for those who have died. In light of these practices, Shaza's words are powerful, precisely because she is discussing the topic of not being honored and cared for by others in her community after her death. Pointed opposition regarding her burial did not influence Shaza to stop following Jesus. Although some Cambodian BMBs experienced criticism and persecution for choosing to follow Jesus, many spoke of their desire to continue to believe in him, at times highlighting the personal freedom one has to choose their own path.

Conclusion

This chapter has sought to answer the question, "How did Cambodians experience the gospel in personally meaningful ways?" The message was meaningful and compelling in five ways. First, the content of the message answered life's questions and desires. Second, the message connected to someone in an intimate way. At times this was indicated by an emotional response or a sense of clarity and commitment. These first two factors relate to the content of the message itself, indicating its relative importance to Cambodian BMBs. Third, God's perceived actions were meaningful. Several respondents spoke of a sense that God was involved in their lives and in their process of conversion, often through him personally assisting them, answering their prayers, or leading them to believe in and follow Jesus. Fourth, the method of communication was meaningful. In addition to communicating the message within the framework of understanding of those listening, the use of mother tongue language, experience-near terms and concepts, and media were significant in making the message not only understandable but also personal. Fifth, the messengers of communication were meaningful. The identity and actions of those communicating the message contributed to it being seen as personally relevant and accessible. The respondents not only expressed the idea that the Christian message was accessible, but also that God himself was nearby and personally concerned about them. The above observations interact with and complement the research of others regarding the human hearing of, interaction with, and response to a religious message.

In order to provide a fuller picture of the experiences of Cambodian BMBs, this chapter also investigated the ways in which respondents described their journeys toward believing in Jesus. Ten observations were made, including the fact that many respondents described a process of conversion which included a sense of freedom and personal agency. Times of doubt did occur for some individuals, and many also spoke about events which encouraged them in their belief in Jesus. Finally, many respondents used the concept of "changing their hearts" to describe what occurred to them as they came to believe in and trust Jesus.

Cambodian BMBs also described their current beliefs and lives with Jesus. Many included a sense of depending on Jesus alone to address their sin and cleanse them. In addition, changes in their lives after following Jesus were often discussed. These were usually positive but at times included the fact they experienced criticism from others precisely because of their belief in Jesus. In spite of this, many respondents revealed a desire and intention to continue to follow Jesus. In summary, this chapter demonstrated how Cambodians came to see the message as personally relevant and compelling, and it described how they characterize both their path towards following Jesus and their current walk with him.

7

Summary, Missiological Implications and Recommendations

Summary

THIS PAPER HAS INVESTIGATED the conversion of forty Cambodian BMBs and has been organized according to the following topics: (1) examining the role of contextual adjustments made to make the Christian message more understandable and compelling, (2) identifying core themes or factors that converts report as central in their own conversions, and (3) exploring and analyzing the ways in which the message itself was experienced as personally meaningful and appealing. Chapter 4 centered on the first topic, the communication and contextualization of the Christian message. Interviews with respondents revealed that they heard the message from both Cambodian BMBs, Cambodian Christians who were not from a Muslim background, and also cross-cultural workers who are not originally from Cambodia. Individuals reported various methods used to communicate the message to them, including the use of media and audio recordings, distribution of Bibles, and studying Christian teachings in groups. The message was contextualized in a variety of ways. The most prominent methods were: choosing to communicate in the mother tongue language of the recipients, use of experience-near terms and concepts, and communication within the framework of understanding of the listener. Contextualized materials used to communicate the gospel message were reviewed. The above methods were significant in not only allowing Cambodians to understand the Christian message and its implications but also in contributing to it being viewed as personally relevant and appealing. Cambodian BMBs communicate this message to others, using a range of methods such as communicating in a non-threatening manner, inviting others to meetings, telling Bible and

SUMMARY, MISSIOLOGICAL IMPLICATIONS AND RECOMMENDATIONS

personal stories, using illustrations, giving and using contextualized materials, and demonstrating love.

Chapter 5 identified themes and factors instrumental in the conversion process as revealed in the narratives of Cambodian BMBs. Four primary and four secondary themes emerged. The difference between "primary" and "secondary" was due primarily to the number of respondents referring to that theme and also to the intensity of their responses. This includes how important the factor was, in relation to other factors, in their decision to follow Jesus. Two primary themes were the paired concepts of "sin and cleansing," and "heaven and judgment." Another theme was that of "Jesus" himself, which was further described through the subcategories of "Jesus is," referring to aspects about his identity, "Jesus did," referring to his actions while on earth, and "Jesus does," referring to his current activities in the lives of the respondents. A fourth primary factor was the "Bible," as it played a prominent role in the conversion of many. The four secondary factors identified were the "witness of others," "dreams," "love," and "the sense of God's leading." These factors, while not discussed by as many BMBs, often played a vital role among those who did speak of them. As the respondents discussed the above factors, they often revealed a sense that they experienced God as personally concerned about their lives and willing to help.

The focus of chapter 6 was exploring how the gospel message affected the respondents in a way which was personally meaningful and compelling. The message was experienced as personally meaningful in five ways, the initial two which relate to the content of the message itself. First, the message addressed life questions, felt needs, or topics important to the individual. Second, the message connected to individuals in a personal or emotional way. Third, God's perceived actions were meaningful. For some, the sense that God was working in some way, through personal assistance, answered prayer, or illuminating the message, for instance, helped contribute to the message being seen as directed towards them. Fourth, the method by which the message was communicated was meaningful, including the choice of language, individual words, and medium of communication. Fifth, the messengers of communication were important. Their words, actions, and living example of the gospel message made it personal and concrete to others. Respondents often experienced God and the Christian message as close and personal. Although God was viewed as holy and powerful, he was also seen as being concerned about the daily lives of individuals. In order to provide a fuller picture of the experiences of Cambodian BMBs, ten observations were made about how respondents described their paths to deciding to follow Jesus. In addition, key reflections about their current beliefs and lives with Jesus were introduced and discussed.

Missiological Implications

Several important missiological implications arise from this research. Most of them are directly connected to recommendations, which will be addressed in the next section. The first implication is that the Christian message itself profoundly matters in conversion. Other authors have pointed to the importance of the religious message and doctrine itself in conversion.[1] This study reinforces those conclusions. What the message says about oneself, about humanity, and about the results and implications of following it greatly influences an individual or group's decision whether or not to believe it or to investigate it further. As respondents told their individual stories of conversion and reflected on their decision to believe in and follow Jesus, they frequently focused on topics which related to the Christian message itself. Aspects of the message such as the concepts of sin and cleansing and the person and work of Jesus were highlighted without outside prompting. Research on conversion often focuses on other factors influencing conversion, such as sociological phenomenon or psychological factors. While factors such as these do play a role in conversion to Jesus, this study has demonstrated the important role the Christian message itself plays in conversion. The content of the message is often critically important and needs to be explored in conversion studies. While extremely significant, however, the message itself is not the only factor in conversion to Christianity.

The second missiological implication is that the decision to believe in and follow Jesus is influenced by a multitude of factors. Some factors are important for certain individuals but seemingly irrelevant for others. Individuals may be influenced by one, a few, or many factors at the same time. Furthermore, the separate influences or topics may work together, reinforcing and building on each other, resulting in more clarity and an increased desire to truly believe and commit to Jesus. The context of an individual or group, combined with their personal understandings, questions, and desires,

---

1. Jindra, "How Religious Content Matters"; Jindra, *New Model of Conversion*, 17, 21; Hefner, "World Building," 12; Robbins, *Becoming Sinners*, 101.

SUMMARY, MISSIOLOGICAL IMPLICATIONS AND RECOMMENDATIONS

affects the manner in which they consider the Christian message. Srdjian Sremac writes, "Almost no other religious phenomenon is as complex as conversion."[2] This discussion about the various themes individuals report as important to their conversions is an illustration of the complexity Sremac refers to. This Cambodian study challenges both practitioners and researchers to consider a variety of factors as influencing conversion. Furthermore, it invites investigation into the manner in which humans interact with and experience the gospel message, as this interaction is often not simply that of being influenced by certain factors. Rather, it is an encounter with a message which speaks about the world, humanity, and themselves as individuals. This encounter is often more intimate than businesslike, personal than impersonal, and emotional rather than merely intellectual.

The results of this Cambodian study connect to the research of others, both studies about conversion in general and also specific studies about the conversion of individuals from a Muslim background to Christianity. This study occurred in a specific context and among a specific group of people. It is not surprising that it confirms some research of others (such as Jindra's theory of the importance of the religious message in conversion), challenges the findings of others (such as Lofland and Stark's discussion about the critical importance of social networks in conversion), and complements the results of others (such as significant factors identified by Muslims in their conversion by Woodberry, Shubin, and Marks; Gaudeul; and Greenham).[3] This Cambodian study adds to the body of knowledge about the life experiences of those from a Muslim background who have decided to follow Jesus.

The third missiological implication is that the contextualization of the message matters. This study demonstrated that the method used to communicate the gospel message, including the way in which it was contextualized, contributed to the message being not only more clearly understood but also being viewed as personally relevant to the lives of those who heard it. The method in which a message is communicated can profoundly affect the manner in which it is perceived, including if and to what degree it is viewed as authentic and personally applicable. The principle of communicating the Christian message within the framework of understanding of the listener

2. Sremac, "New Model of Religious Conversion," 265.
3. Jindra, "How Religious Content Matters"; Jindra, *New Model of Conversion*; Lofland and Stark, "Becoming a World-Saver"; Woodberry et al., "Why Muslims Follow Jesus"; Gaudeul, *Calling from Islam to Christ*; Greenham, "Study of Palestinian Muslim Conversions."

allows for quicker recognition of the message and also can potentially decrease suspicion. Other methods are significant as well, such as the use of illustrations, stories, media, and experience-near terms and concepts. While the importance of contextualization is broadly understood, this study provided more insight about the contextualization of the gospel message among a Muslim-background population in a specific context.

This research interacted with Greenlee's theory of congruence and demonstrated the importance of a congruence of values, ideas, and framework of understanding. One underlying theory about how humans personally experience the Christian message was posited as a result of this study: *When the content of the message corresponds to or addresses topics which are important to the one hearing it, the message is more likely to be perceived as personally meaningful and compelling.* This theory and the additional empirical findings of this study undergird the missiological importance of contextualizing the Christian message.

A fourth missiological implication is that context matters in the encounter individuals have with the gospel message. The respondents in this study live within a specific context. Most of them identify with the minority Cham ethnic group in Cambodia. As such their population is dwarfed by the majority Khmer ethnic group. Moreover, Muslims are a religious minority in Cambodia, compromising only approximately three percent of the total population. Because they are surrounded by many who follow Buddhism or other religions such as Christianity, they are exposed to other religious messages besides Islam. As minorities, many respondents remarked that Jesus acted in certain ways towards others, and they admired him for these actions. The specific comment that "Jesus did not discriminate" was spoken by several respondents, who appeared to draw parallels between Jesus's actions toward others with their experiences as minorities. The cultural context of the respondents appeared to make them more attentive and appreciative of certain aspects of the gospel message, including the actions of Jesus. This study thus invites others to consider how the context of specific populations may influence their understanding of the Christian message, including which aspects of the message resonate with their lived experiences. Some minority groups may experience the gospel message in ways which are different than non-minority groups. The findings of this study are potentially applicable to other minority populations in the world, including diaspora populations or refugees living outside of their home locations.

A final missiological implication relates to the way in which conversion is viewed. The experience-near concept is helpful in understanding and studying conversion. Scholars often look at factors or variables influencing conversion. This approach yields beneficial information, but the process of conversion itself is often one of interaction with a message which contains information about both humanity and the hearer, and which invites a response. In conversion, individuals are often not as much impacted by external factors as much as they interact with and experience the message, often in personally meaningful ways. Furthermore, they commonly exhibit personal agency in making decisions about whether or not to embrace a new religious system. These commitments often arise from their experiencing the message and God as being near and personal. For many in this study, the Christian message connected with their lived experiences and concerns. Because of his personal actions towards them, God was viewed as close and concerned, not as distant and disinterested in their lives. The process of conversion involved not simply an intellectual examination of doctrine or teaching, but included an individual's affect, will, and emotions as they experienced God and the message. This study demonstrates the value of examining the manner in which individuals experience the Christian message, including investigating how its content and God himself is viewed as near and personal. Further studies can utilize this approach to understanding conversion.

Recommendations

Two types of recommendations arise from this study. The first is recommendations for communicating the Christian message to others. The second is recommendations for further research.

Recommendations for Communicating the Christian Message

The first recommendation is foundational, as most of the other recommendations are based on this one. It is to deliberately and deeply seek to understand those to whom one wants to communicate the gospel message. In instances where one is communicating the message to someone of their own background or from their own group, much is already tacitly understood. However, humans are individuals, and each individual has their own thoughts, hopes, beliefs, experiences, and perspectives. Communicators of the Christian message should seek to understand these nuanced feeling and perspectives of others, as even those living in similar circumstances and locations may demonstrate widely varied mindsets and beliefs. For the person seeking to communicate the message cross-culturally, it is even more important to learn about the "other," as a lack of understanding of them can hinder the communication of the message to them. Topics for possible study include the history, geography, means of livelihood, and religious beliefs about a group in general, as well as the hopes, experiences, disappointments, and daily lives of specific individuals. Another application for cross-cultural workers is to study the mother tongue language in the location where one works. This type of language study, while extremely time consuming, promotes both better communication and a deeper understanding of the culture and thoughts of humans living there.

A second recommendation is to communicate using familiar terms, ideas, and language. The use of experience-near terms and concepts assists in creating connections and a quicker recognition of what is being communicated. Many Cambodian respondents reported that the use of mother tongue language contributed toward the message being better understood and also viewed as personally relevant. Related to the above is the use of illustrations, metaphors, stories, and proverbs which are readily understood and which resonate with one's lived experience.

Third, communicators should seek to convey the message within the existing framework of understanding of the listener. When people view a particular message as being part of or contributing to their previous understanding, they are less likely to immediately label it as foreign or personally irrelevant. Of course, this recommendation pre-supposes that the one communicating the message is knowledgeable about the recipient's existing framework of understanding. This framework is not limited to the formal religious teachings followed by many in a particular area. Other religious practices or beliefs not formally associated with that religion might be a foundational part of the mindset and activities of individuals there.

A fourth recommendation is to develop and use contextualized materials in order to communicate the Christian message in a particular location or among a group of people. Cambodian respondents noted that various contextualized materials were utilized and that they contributed to the message being understood and seen as personally meaningful. Materials such as films, audio recordings, and pictures can be used.

The above recommendations relate primarily to the contextualization of the message. The following recommendations address the perspectives and attitudes of the communicator. Number five is to realize that those who are hearing the message are undergoing a process of hearing, understanding, and considering this message. This process can be quite rapid or even immediate, but more commonly it takes a long period of time. Richard Peace has written, "I have come to believe that *how we conceive of conversion determines how we do evangelism* [italics in original]."[4] He argues that those who view conversion primarily as a point-in-time dramatic event, like the experience of Paul the Apostle, will communicate the gospel message and encourage quick conversions like Paul. However, those who view conversion as a process taking place over time will follow a different path, one of seeking to identify where another person is at on their spiritual pilgrimage and assist them at that point. Other authors have highlighted the process aspect of conversion. Most Cambodian respondents took a significant amount of time before they understood and believed the Christian message, and decided to follow Jesus. Communicating the gospel with a "process" perspective can contribute to a longer-term and gentler approach to serving others. In addition, it can potentially increase one's desire to understand where another person is at in their spiritual journey, and an eagerness to address them at that point. It is noted that this process of conversion does not simply end when one believes in and deliberately decides to follow Jesus. Researchers have identified other events and stages which are significant in the life of the one who has come to believe. Realizing that those hearing the message are and will be undergoing a process helps the communicator embrace a long-term approach, which includes assisting people at various stages of their individual journeys.

A sixth recommendation is to realize that the lives and thoughts of individuals are extremely complex and that the Christian message may become important and meaningful to an individual through a variety of means. This study illustrates that there frequently were various factors at play in the life of a respondent. Although often the message itself had a significant role in contributing to a person's desire to believe in and follow Jesus, other themes such as the words and actions of others, dreams, and a sense of God's leading were powerful. Holding the perspective that varied factors may be involved in the process of conversion allows the communicator of the message to embrace a broader approach, with more openness

---

4. Peace, *Conversion in the New Testament*, 286.

to different factors and a curiosity about how people are interacting with the message. Plainly stated, individuals are *individuals*. They are unique, and they are complex. Communicators of the Christian message at times fail to realize or acknowledge this complexity, and rather resort to an understanding that an individual or particular group will be affected by certain themes and not others. The identification of these themes is often based on the personal experience or background of the one telling the gospel message. While this can be a starting point, it is important for communicators of the Christian message to deliberately adopt a broad approach where they recognize and appreciate that an individual may experience the Christian message as personally meaningful and compelling because of a variety of factors or teachings.

The above recommendations also can be applied to the instruction and training of individuals after they have decided to follow Jesus. It is helpful for one seeking to assist or train a follower of Christ to understand that an individual's walk with Jesus is complex and may include twists and turns. Those who have decided to follow Jesus can be encouraged to reflect on and understand their personal story, and also to tell that story to others. These processes, while not only providing information to others, are often encouraging to the individuals and can help them gain a greater understanding of their personal experiences. Furthermore, workers and leaders can encourage believers to broaden their understanding of salvation beyond just their personal experience. New perspectives are often gained as people meet and interact with other Christ-followers and hear their unique stories.

Recommendations for Further Research

Three recommendations for additional research are suggested. First, studies similar to this could be carried out in different locations and among different populations. This study has focused on one specific Muslim group in Cambodia. While other significant studies about Muslim conversion have occurred in different areas and countries, many groups in various locations have yet to be studied. Research could be done in areas where Muslims are a majority (e.g., in the Middle East, North Africa, and Indonesia), and also in areas in which Muslims are a minority (e.g., in Thailand, and parts of India and China). The approach used in this Cambodian study could, with some modification, also be implemented in the study of religious conversion for

SUMMARY, MISSIOLOGICAL IMPLICATIONS AND RECOMMENDATIONS

those of different backgrounds as well, such as individuals or groups with Hindu, Buddhist, traditional religion, or secular backgrounds.

Second, more specific studies on the contextualization of the Christian message are needed. This research could focus on specific ways in which the message has been contextualized, and to what degree those methods have contributed to the message being not only understood but also viewed as personally relevant and meaningful. Many methods of contextualization have been reviewed in this study, ranging from specific approaches such as using familiar words and illustrations to more nebulous approaches such as seeking to communicate within the framework of understanding of the listener. These methods were specifically identified in Cambodia and may or may not be widely used in other areas. However, research in other locations will certainly unearth contextualized approaches which are being implemented. Specific studies on the contextualization of the Christian message are valuable.

Third, additional research on the interaction individuals and groups have with the gospel message is needed. How can we better understand how humans come to see the message as being personally significant and compelling, and not just viewed as a message only for others? This research has attempted to answer that question, but more studies are needed in various areas, with perhaps a more specific methodology that will enable a deeper understanding of the lived realities of those choosing to follow Jesus and of the ways in which they have experienced the message. The content of the religious message is critical for many as they consider their decision to believe in and trust Jesus. It is thus important to conduct more research in order to better understand people's thoughts, fears, and emotions as they evaluate a message and determine if it speaks to them and demands a response.

Conclusion

T. M. Luhrmann researched the relationships American evangelical participants in the Vineyard Christian Fellowship have with God.[5] She begins her book by asking several fundamental questions, the first of which is "How does God become real to people?" She desired to understand the dynamics by which humans experienced God in real and meaningful ways. Luhrmann's study concentrated on the practice of prayer for those

5. Luhrmann, *When God Talks Back*, xi.

who already profess belief in Jesus. This Cambodian study has examined conversion itself, and yet there are parallels to Luhrmann's research. This study has essentially asked the question, "How does the Christian message become real and personal to Cambodians from a Muslim background?" Both Luhrmann and I have sought to examine the lived experiences of followers of Jesus in order to discover information relating to our questions. While the research focus differed, the desire to understand how people experienced God and his message was similar.

Around the world, many individuals and groups from a Muslim background are deciding to believe in and follow Jesus. Some of these people live within the borders of Cambodia. This research has revealed that Cambodian BMBs have not simply heard, reviewed and pondered the gospel message, but they have *experienced* it, often as a message which speaks to them and addresses their personal concerns. Their process of conversion has also often included experiencing God as near and personally involved in their lives. This demonstrates the need to seriously consider the role of the religious message in conversion. A large portion of Cambodian BMBs reported that the gospel message itself, including information about the life and work of Jesus, was of fundamental importance in their conversion. This study has further revealed the complexities of conversion, and it urges both the scholar and practitioner to recognize all the facets and factors surrounding it. At the same time, it points to a nuanced understanding of conversion, including the emphasis and study of how the gospel is experienced as personally meaningful. This Cambodian example has reinforced the value of contextualizing the Christian message and of communicating it in a way which is as clearly understood and personally relevant as possible. The manner in which the message was communicated was demonstrated to affect its understandability and desirability. This highlights the importance that local contexts have in influencing which aspects of the gospel message may be most appreciated. Cambodian BMBs live in unique circumstances, but their experiences reveal insights which may apply to other Muslim-background populations, including those living as minorities in various locations.

This study has communicated the stories, impressions, and joys and sorrows of Cambodian BMBs for the purpose of providing greater clarity about conversion to Christianity of those from Muslim backgrounds. Cambodian BMBs have experienced the gospel in some ways unique to them, and in other ways similar to others in various locations. Their

SUMMARY, MISSIOLOGICAL IMPLICATIONS AND RECOMMENDATIONS

stories help us understand the lived realities of humans around the globe who have chosen to embrace Jesus.

Appendix A
Interview Questions

FORMAL INTERVIEWS WERE CONDUCTED after first verifying that the individual met the selection criteria, obtaining consent from them, and gathering basic demographic data. Primary interview questions are listed below. Where applicable, the research question (RQ) associated with an interview question is provided.

Introductory Question

1. Please tell me the story of how you came to know about Jesus (*Isa*) and how you came to decide to follow Jesus.

Central Questions

2. Did you find anything odd or interesting or compelling about the message? (RQ3)
3. Have you ever had a thought that you needed to repent or change your heart? Have you ever had a sense of personal sin? Please tell about that. (RQ3)
4. Was there ever a sense that you desired to change your life and behaviors? Please explain. (RQ3)
5. What do you understand to be the Christian teachings about Jesus's death and what it accomplished? What did you think about this initially? Did that change? (RQ3)
6. How did you come to be convinced that this message was true? How do you respond to others who might say that the message is not true? (RQ3)

APPENDIX A: INTERVIEW QUESTIONS

7. Did the message have personal meaning for you? If so, can you describe that? (RQ3)
8. Have you been baptized? Why were you willing to do it? (RQ3)
9. You appear to say that you follow Jesus only, and do not follow other prophets or religions. If that is true, why do you follow Jesus only? (RQ3)
10. Since you have decided to follow Jesus, have you experienced any difficulties or obstacles? Please tell about that.
11. Who told you about Jesus? What language did they use? Did you ever have any difficulty in understanding because of the language? (RQ1)
12. How did other people explain the good news to you? (RQ1)
13. Have you told others about Jesus and your decision to follow him? What do you tell others in order for them to understand clearly about this message? (RQ1)

Concluding Questions

14. As you think about your life, can you identify what thing or things were most important in influencing you to make this decision to follow Jesus? (RQ2)
15. How do you identify yourself to others who follow Jesus? How do you identify yourself to others who do not follow Jesus?
16. Is there anything else about this decision to follow Isa that you would like to tell me about?

Appendix B
Cloth Illustrated with Bible Stories

Figure 5. Cloth Illustrated with Bible Stories

Bibliography

Adams, Eric, et al. "Seven Themes of Fruitfulness." *International Journal of Frontier Missiology* 26.2 (2009) 75–81.
Ali, Abdullah Yusuf. *The Meaning of the Holy Qur'an*. 10th ed. Beltsville, MD: Amana, 2001.
Babbie, Earl R. *The Practice of Social Research*. 10th ed. Belmont, CA: Thomson/Wadsworth, 2004.
Basso, Keith H. "'Stalking with Stories': Names, Places, and Moral Narratives Among the Western Apache." In *Text, Play, and Story: The Construction and Reconstruction of Self and Society*, edited by Edward M. Bruner and American Ethnological Society, 19–55. Proceedings of the American Ethnological Society 1983. Washington, DC: American Ethnological Society, 1984.
Beckford, James A. "Accounting for Conversion." *The British Journal of Sociology* 29.2 (1978) 249–62.
Bernard, H. Russell. *Research Methods in Anthropology: Qualitative and Quantitative Approaches*. 4th ed. Lanham, MD: AltaMira, 2006.
Bloomberg, Linda Dale, and Marie Volpe. *Completing Your Qualitative Dissertation: A Road Map from Beginning to End*. Third ed. Los Angeles: SAGE, 2016.
Bruckmayr, Philipp. "The Cham Muslims of Cambodia: From Forgotten Minority to Focal Point of Islamic Internationalism." *American Journal of Islamic Social Sciences* 23.3 (2006) 1–23.
Bultema, James. "Muslims Coming to Christ in Turkey." *International Journal of Frontier Missiology* 27.1 (2010) 27–31.
CartoGIS Services. "Cambodia Colour Provinces." College of Asia and the Pacific, The Australian National University. http://asiapacific.anu.edu.au/mapsonline/base-maps/cambodia-colour-provinces.
Cheong, John. "The Socio-Religious Identity and Life of the Malay Christians of Malaysia." PhD diss., Trinity International University, 2012.
Colgate, Jack. "Bible Storying and Oral Use of the Scriptures." In *From Seed to Fruit: Global Trends, Fruitful Practices, and Emerging Issues among Muslims*, edited by John Dudley Woodberry, 219–31. Pasadena, CA: William Carey Library, 2008.
———. "Relational Bible Storying and Scripture Use in Oral Muslim Contexts Part 1." *International Journal of Frontier Missiology* 25.3 (2008) 135–42.
Collins, William. "The Muslims of Cambodia." In *Ethnic Groups in Cambodia*, edited by Sokhom Hean, 1–110. Phnom Penh: Center for Advanced Study, 2009.
Danker, F. W., et al., eds. *A Greek-English Lexicon of the New Testament and Other Early Christian Literature*. 3rd ed. Chicago: University of Chicago Press, 2000.

BIBLIOGRAPHY

Dawson, Lorne L. "Cult Conversions: Controversy and Clarification." In *Religious Conversion Contemporary Practices and Controversies*, edited by Christopher Lamb and M. Darroll Bryant, 287–314. London: Cassell, 1999.

Department of Non-Buddhist Religion. "Statistical Chart of Non-Buddhist Religions Throughout Cambodia 2016." Ministry of Cults and Religion, Kingdom of Cambodia, February 8, 2017.

Durán, Abraham. "The Beauty of Jesus as an Evangelistic Factor." In *From the Straight Path to the Narrow Way: Journeys of Faith*, edited by David Greenlee, 265–76. Waynesboro, GA: Authentic Media, 2006.

Dye, T. Wayne. "Toward a Cross-Cultural Definition of Sin." *Missiology* 4.1 (1976) 27–41.

Eng, Kok-Thay. "From the Khmer Rouge to Hambali: Cham Identities in a Global Age." PhD diss., Rutgers University, 2013.

Engel, James F. "The Road to Conversion: The Latest Research Insights." *Evangelical Missions Quarterly* 26.2 (1990) 184–93.

Farah, Warrick. "Emerging Missiological Themes in MBB Conversion Factors." *International Journal of Frontier Missiology* 30.1 (2013) 13–20.

Flemming, Dean E. *Contextualization in the New Testament: Patterns for Theology and Mission*. Downers Grove, IL: InterVarsity, 2005.

Garrison, David. *A Wind in the House of Islam: How God Is Drawing Muslims Around the World to Faith in Jesus Christ*. Monument, CO: WIGTake, 2014.

Gaudeul, Jean-Marie. *Called from Islam to Christ: Why Muslims Become Christians*. Crowborough: Monarch, 1999.

Geertz, Clifford. "'From the Native's Point of View': On the Nature of Anthropological Understanding." In *Meaning in Anthropology*, edited by Keith H. Basso and Henry A. Selby, 221–37. School of American Research Advanced Seminar Series. Albuquerque: University of New Mexico Press, 1976.

Gilliland, Dean. "Contextualization." In *Evangelical Dictionary of World Missions*, edited by A. Scott Moreau et al., 225–28. Baker Reference Library. Grand Rapids: Baker Academic, 2000.

Glassé, Cyril. *The New Encyclopedia of Islam*. 4th ed. Lanham, MD: Rowman & Littlefield, 2013.

Goffman, Erving. *The Presentation of Self in Everyday Life*. Woodstock, NY: Overlook, 1973.

Gooren, Henri. "Towards a New Model of Conversion Careers: The Impact of Personality and Contingency Factors." *Exchange* 34.2 (2005) 149–66.

Gray, Andrea, and Leith Gray. "Paradigms and Praxis Part I Social Networks and Fruitfulness in Church Planting." *International Journal of Frontier Missiology* 26.1 (2009) 19–28.

Greenham, Anthony. "Muslim Conversions to Christ: An Investigation of Palestinian Converts Living in the Holy Land." PhD diss., Southeastern Baptist Theological Seminary, 2004.

———. "A Study of Palestinian Muslim Conversions to Christ." *St. Francis Magazine* 6.1 (2010) 116–75.

Greenlee, David. "Christian Conversion from Islam: Social, Cultural, Communication, and Supernatural Factors in the Process of Conversion and Faithful Church Participation." PhD diss., Trinity Evangelical Divinity School, 1996.

———. "Coming to Faith in Christ: Highlights from Recent Research." *Missionalia* 34.1 (2006) 51–68.

BIBLIOGRAPHY

Grimes, Barbara F. *Ethnologue, Volume 1.* 2 vols. 14th ed. Dallas: SIL International, 2000.

Harding, Susan Friend. *The Book of Jerry Falwell: Fundamentalist Language and Politics.* Princeton: Princeton University Press, 2000.

Hefner, Robert W. "World Building and the Rationality of Conversion." In *Conversion to Christianity: Historical and Anthropological Perspectives on a Great Transformation*, edited by Robert W. Hefner, 3–44. Berkeley: University of California Press, 1993.

Hibbert, Richard Yates. "Negotiating Identity: Extending and Applying Alan Tippett's Model of Conversion to Believers from Muslim and Hindu Backgrounds." *Missiology* 43.1 (2015) 59–72.

Hiebert, Paul. *Anthropological Reflections on Missiological Issues.* Grand Rapids: Baker, 1994.

———. *Transforming Worldviews: An Anthropological Understanding of How People Change.* Grand Rapids: Baker Academic, 2008.

———. "Worldview Transformation." In *From the Straight Path to the Narrow Way: Journeys of Faith*, edited by David Greenlee, 23–34. Waynesboro, GA: Authentic Media, 2006.

Higgins, Kevin, et al. "Myths and Misunderstandings about Insider Movements." In *Understanding Insider Movements: Disciples of Jesus within Diverse Religious Communities*, edited by Harley Talman and John Jay Travis, 41–53. Pasadena, CA: William Carey, 2015.

Hindmarsh, Bruce. "Religious Conversion as Narrative and Autobiography." In *The Oxford Handbook of Religious Conversion*, edited by Lewis R. Rambo and Charles E. Farhadian, 343–68. Oxford: Oxford University Press, 2014.

Hoskins, Daniel Gene. "Conversion Narratives in Context: Muslims Turning to Christ in Post-Soviet Central Asia." PhD diss., University of South Africa, 2014.

James, William. *The Varieties of Religious Experience.* New York: New American Library, 1958.

———. *The Varieties of Religious Experience: A Study in Human Nature.* Seven Treasures, 1902.

Jindra, Ines W. *A New Model of Religious Conversion: Beyond Network Theory and Social Constructivism.* Boston: Brill, 2014.

———. "How Religious Content Matters in Conversion Narratives to Various Religious Groups." *Sociology of Religion* 72.3 (2011) 275–302.

Joshua Project and Bethany World Prayer Center. "Cham, Western in Cambodia." https://joshuaproject.net/people_groups/15361/CB.

Khmer Standard Version Bible. Phnom Penh, Cambodia: United Bible Societies, 2005.

Kling, David W. "Conversion to Christianity." In *The Oxford Handbook of Religious Conversion*, edited by Lewis R. Rambo and Charles E. Farhadian, 598–631. Oxford: Oxford University Press, 2014.

Kraft, Charles H. *Christianity in Culture: A Study in Dynamic Biblical Theologizing in Cross-Cultural Perspective.* Maryknoll, NY: Orbis, 1979.

———. "Conversion in Group Settings." In *Handbook of Religious Conversion*, edited by H. Newton Malony and Samuel Southard, 259–75. Birmingham, AL: Religious Education, 1992.

———. "Cultural Concomitants of Higi Conversion: Early Period." *Missiology* 4.4 (1976) 431–53.

Krish, John, and Peter Sykes, dir. *Jesus.* The Genesis Project. Warner Bros., 1979.

BIBLIOGRAPHY

Kvale, Steinar, and Svend Brinkmann. *Interviews: Learning the Craft of Qualitative Research Interviewing*. 2nd ed. New York: Sage, 2009.

Lofland, John, and Norman Skonovd. "Conversion Motifs." *Journal for the Scientific Study of Religion* 20.4 (1981) 373–85.

Lofland, John, and Rodney Stark. "Becoming a World-Saver: A Theory of Conversion to a Deviant Perspective." *American Sociological Review* 30.6 (1965) 862–75.

Luhrmann, T. M. *When God Talks Back: Understanding the American Evangelical Relationship with God*. 1st ed. New York: Vintage, 2012.

Maranz, David. "The Role of the Scriptures in Muslims Coming to Faith in Jesus." In *From the Straight Path to the Narrow Way: Journeys of Faith*, edited by David Greenlee, 51–64. Waynesboro, GA: Authentic Media, 2006.

Maunati, Yekti, and Betti Rosita Sari. "Construction of Cham Identity in Cambodia." *Suvannabhumi* 6.1 (2014) 107–35.

Maurer, Andreas. "In Search of a New Life: Conversion Motives of Christians and Muslims." *Missionalia* 30.2 (2002) 288–303.

Maxwell, Joseph Alex. *Qualitative Research Design: An Interactive Approach*. 3rd ed. Thousand Oaks, CA: SAGE, 2013.

McKenzie-Pollock, Lorna. "Cambodian Families." In *Ethnicity and Family Therapy*, edited by Monica McGoldrick et al., 290–301. New York: Guilford, 2005.

Merriam, Sharan B. *Qualitative Research: A Guide to Design and Implementation*. San Francisco: Jossey-Bass, 2009.

Miller, Duane Alexander. "Living Among the Breakage: Contextual Theology-Making and Ex-Muslim Christians." PhD diss., University of Edinburgh, 2014.

Miller, Duane Alexander, and Patrick Johnstone. "Believers in Christ from a Muslim Background: A Global Census." *Interdisciplinary Journal of Research on Religion* 11 (2015) 1–19.

Monette, Duane R., et al. *Applied Social Research: Tool for the Human Services*. New York: Holt, Rinehart, and Winston, 1986.

Montgomery, Robert L. "Conversion and the Historic Spread of Religions." In *The Oxford Handbook of Religious Conversion*, edited by Lewis R. Rambo and Charles E. Farhadian, 164–89. Oxford: Oxford University Press, 2014.

Moreau, A. Scott, et al. *Introducing World Missions: A Biblical, Historical, and Practical Survey*. 2nd edition. Grand Rapids: Baker Academic, 2015.

Mouw, Richard J. "Why Christus Victor Is Not Enough: Each Atonement Theory Highlights a Truth About the Cross—but None More so Than Christ's Substitutionary Death." *Christianity Today* 56.5 (2012) 28–31.

National Institute of Statistics, Ministry of Planning. "Cambodia Inter-Censal Population Survey 2013." Phnom Penh, Cambodia, May 2014.

———. "Cambodia Inter-Censal Population Survey 2013 Final Report." Phnom Penh, Cambodia, November 2013.

———. "General Population Census of Cambodia 2008." Phnom Penh, Cambodia, January 2011.

Nickel, Gordon D. *Narratives of Tampering in the Earliest Commentaries on the Qurʿan*. Leiden: Brill, 2011.

Nock, Arthur Darby. *Conversion: The Old and the New in Religion from Alexander the Great to Augustine of Hippo*. London: Oxford university press, 1933.

Ott, Craig. "The Power of Biblical Metaphors for the Contextualized Communication of the Gospel." *Missiology* 42.4 (2014) 357–74.

Padwick, C. E. "Dream and Vision: Some Notes from a Diary." *International Review of Missions* 28.110 (1939) 205–16.

Peace, Richard. "Conflicting Understandings of Christian Conversion: A Missiological Challenge." *International Bulletin of Missionary Research* 28.1 (2004) 8.

———. *Conversion in the New Testament: Paul and the Twelve*. Grand Rapids: Eerdmans, 1999.

Pereiro, Alberto Pérez. "Historical Imagination, Diasporic Identity and Islamicity Among the Cham Muslims of Cambodia." PhD diss., Arizona State University, 2012.

Priest, Robert J. "'Experience-Near Theologizing' in Diverse Human Contexts." In *Globalizing Theology: Belief and Practice in an Era of World Christianity*, edited by Craig Ott and Harold Netland, 180–95. Grand Rapids: Baker Academic, 2006.

———. "'I Discovered My Sin!': Aguaruna Evangelical Conversion Narratives." In *The Anthropology of Religious Conversion*, edited by Andrew Buckser and Stephen D. Glazier, 95–108. Lanham, MD: Rowman & Littlefield, 2003.

———. "Missionary Elenctics: Conscience and Culture." *Missiology* 22.3 (1994) 291–315.

———. "Tell Me About a Time You Were Bad." *CIU Quarterly* (1994) 4–6.

Priest, Robert J., and Robert DeGeorge. "Doctoral Dissertations on Mission: Ten-Year Update, 2002 2011." *International Bulletin of Missionary Research* 37.4 (2013) S195.

Radford, David. *Religious Identity and Social Change: Explaining Christian Conversion in a Muslim World*. London: Routledge, 2015.

Rambo, Lewis R. "Conversion Studies, Pastoral Counseling, and Cultural Studies: Engaging and Embracing a New Paradigm." *Pastoral Psychology* 59.4 (2010) 433–45.

———. "The Psychology of Conversion." In *Handbook of Religious Conversion*, edited by H. Newton Malony and Samuel Southard, 159–77. Birmingham, AL: Religious Education, 1992.

———. *Understanding Religious Conversion*. New Haven: Yale University Press, 1993.

Rambo, Lewis R., and Lawrence A. Reh. "The Phenomenology of Conversion." In *Handbook of Religious Conversion*, edited by H. Newton Malony and Samuel Southard, 229–59. Birmingham, AL: Religious Education, 1992.

Richardson, James T. "The Active vs. Passive Convert: Paradigm Conflict in Conversion Recruitment Research." *Journal for the Scientific Study of Religion* 24.2 (1985) 163–79.

Richardson, James T., and Mary Stewart. "Conversion Process Models and the Jesus Movement." In *Conversion Careers: In and Out of the New Religions*, edited by James T. Richardson, 24–42. Beverly Hills: Sage, 1978.

Robbins, Joel. *Becoming Sinners: Christianity and Moral Torment in a Papua New Guinea Society*. Berkeley: University of California Press, 2004.

———. "The Globalization of Pentecostal and Charismatic Christianity." *Annual Review of Anthropology* 33 (2004) 117–43.

Ross, Russell H., ed. *Cambodia: A Country Study*. 4th ed. Washington, DC: Federal Research Division, 1989.

Setudeh-Nejad, S. "The Cham Muslims of Southeast Asia: A Historical Note." *Journal of Muslim Minority Affairs* 22.2 (2002) 451–55.

Skreslet, Stanley H. "Doctoral Dissertations on Mission: Ten-Year Update, 1992 2001." *International Bulletin of Missionary Research* 27.3 (2003) 97–133.

Smith, Gordon T. *Beginning Well: Christian Conversion and Authentic Transformation*. Downers Grove, IL: InterVarsity, 2001.

Snow, David A., and Cynthia L. Phillips. "Lofland-Stark Conversion Model: A Critical Reassessment." *Social Problems* 27 (April 1980) 430–47.

Snow, David A., and Richard Machalek. "The Convert as a Social Type." In *Sociological Theory*, edited by Randall Collins, 259–89. San Francisco: Jossey-Bass, 1983.

Sremac, S. "A New Model of Religious Conversion: Beyond Network Theory and Social." *Journal of Empirical Theology* 28.2 (2015) 265–66.

Starbuck, Edwin Diller. *The Psychology of Religion, an Empirical Study of the Growth of Religious Consciousness*. London, 1899. http://hdl.handle.net/2027/mdp.39015019174203.

Stark, Rodney, and Roger Finke. *Acts of Faith: Explaining the Human Side of Religion*. Berkeley: University of California Press, 2000.

Stott, John R. W. *Christian Mission in the Modern World*. Downers Grove, IL: InterVarsity Press, 2008.

Streib, Heinz. "Deconversion." In *The Oxford Handbook of Religious Conversion*, edited by Lewis R. Rambo and Charles E. Farhadian, 271–96. Oxford: Oxford University Press, 2014.

Stromberg, Peter G. "The Impression Point: Synthesis of Symbol and Self." *Ethos* 13.1 (1985) 56–74.

———. "The Role of Language in Religious Conversion." In *The Oxford Handbook of Religious Conversion*, edited by Lewis R. Rambo, 117–39. New York: Oxford University Press, 2014.

Tippett, Alan Richard. "Conversion as a Dynamic Process in Christian Mission." *Missiology* 5.2 (1977) 203–21.

Trankell, Ing-Britt, and Jan Ovesen. "Muslim Minorities in Cambodia." *NIASnytt* 4 (2004) 22–24.

Van Klinken, Adriaan S. "Men in the Remaking: Conversion Narratives and Born-Again Masculinity in Zambia." *Journal of Religion in Africa* 42.3 (2012) 215–39.

Walls, Andrew F. "Converts or Proselytes?: The Crisis Over Conversion in the Early Church." *International Bulletin of Missionary Research* 28.1 (2004) 2–6.

———. "The Gospel as Prisoner and Liberator of Culture." In *The Missionary Movement in Christian History: Studies in the Transmission of Faith*, 3–15. Maryknoll, NY: Orbis, 1996.

Wells, David F. *Turning to God: Biblical Conversion in the Modern World*. Exeter, UK: Paternoster, 1989.

Woodberry, J. Dudley. "Conversion in Islam." In *Handbook of Religious Conversion*, edited by H. Newton Malony and Samuel Southard, 22–40. Birmingham, AL: Religious Education, 1992.

———. "A Global Perspective on Muslims Coming to Faith in Christ." In *From the Straight Path to the Narrow Way: Journeys of Faith*, edited by David Greenlee, 11–22. Waynesboro, GA: Authentic Media, 2006.

Woodberry, J. Dudley, et al. "Why Muslims Follow Jesus: The Results of a Recent Survey of Converts from Islam." *Christianity Today* 51.10 (2007) 80–85.

Woodberry, J. Dudley, and Russell G. Shubin. "Muslims Tell . . . 'Why I Chose Jesus.'" *Mission Frontiers*, March 1, 2001. http://www.missionfrontiers.org/issue/article/muslims-tell...-why-i-chose-jesus.

Author Index

Adams, Eric, 57, 78, 79nn42–43
Ali, Abdullah Yusuf, 71n37
Allen, Don, 57, 78

Babbie, Earl R., 25, 34n30, 35n31
Basso, Keith H., 132–33
Beckford, James A., 43
Bernard, H. Russell, 26n3, 27, 28n11, 33n25
Bloomberg, Linda Dale, 33n28
Brinkmann, Svend, 26
Bruckmayr, Philipp, 8n25
Bultema, James, 1n2, 22, 119n31, 121, 123

CartoGIS Services, 31n21
Cheong, John, 29n17
Colgate, Jack, 16, 18n30, 45n12, 78
Collins, William, 5–7, 8n25, 95n6
Corwin, Gary R., 15

Danker, F. W., 157, 158n25
Dawson, Lorne L., 154
DeGeorge, Robert, 3n4
DeJong, Cornell R., 88n1
Department of Non-Buddhist Religion, Kingdom of Cambodia, 5n8, 8n27
Durán, Abraham, 118
Dye, T. Wayne, 145

Eng, Koh-Thay, 6n13, 7, 8n28
Engel, James F., 19n37

Farah, Warrick, 67

Finke, Roger, 13n9, 13n13
Fish, Bob, 57, 78
Flemming, Dean E., 49–50

Garrison, David, 1n1
Gaudeul, Jean-Marie, 1n2, 21, 93, 117–18, 124, 169
Geertz, Clifford, 54
Gilliland, Dean, 49
Glassé, Cyril, 50n19
Goffman, Erving, 159n29
Gooren, Henri, 155
Gray, Andrea and Leith, 77n40, 120, 121n35
Greenham, Anthony, 1n2, 22, 23n53, 32n23, 88n1, 93, 117–19, 121, 123, 152, 169
Greenlee, David, 1n2, 23–24, 65–67, 85, 98, 122, 170
Grimes, Barbara F., 6n12

Harding, Susan Friend, 19, 124
Hefner, Robert W., 14, 168n1
Hibbert, Richard Yates, 14, 106n10, 158n28
Hiebert, Paul, 12, 15–16, 48, 60
Higgins, Kevin, 4, 5n7
Hindmarsh, Bruce, 43n9
Hoskins, Daniel Gene, 1n2, 23, 67–68, 85, 118,

James, William, 1, 13n10, 14, 18, 43n6
Jameson, Richard, 4
Jindra, Ines W., 13–14, 116, 168–69
Johnstone, Patrick, 1n1, 4, 8n26, 22

AUTHOR INDEX

Joshua Project and Bethany World Prayer Center, 8n29

Kling, David W., 12, 158
Kraft, Charles H., 66–67, 138–39, 154
Krish, John, 47n13, 70n35
Kvale, Steinar, 26

Lofland, John, 13n9, 13n12, 43, 77n40, 120, 121n35, 146, 169
Luhrmann, T. M., 175–76

Machalek, Richard, 43
Maranz, David, 119
Marks, G., 20, 117, 119, 121–22, 152, 169
Maunati, Yekti, 6n14, 6n18, 7n21
Maurer, Andreas, 124n48, 125
Maxwell, Joseph Alex, 25–26, 27n9, 34n30
McGee, Gary B., 15
McKenzie-Pollock, Lorna, 11n31
Merriam, Sharan B., 28n12, 29n16, 33n26, 34n30
Miller, Duane Alexander, 1n1, 4, 8n26, 21–22, 120–21, 124–25
Monette, Duane R., 88n1
Montgomery, Robert L., 154
Moreau, A. Scott, 15, 48
Mouw, Richard J., 145

National Institute of Statistics, Kingdom of Cambodia, 5n10, 5n11
Nickel, Gordon D., 50n19
Nock, Arthur Darby, 12, 13n6

Ott, Craig, 16, 79, 145
Ovesen Jan, 6n14, 6n16, 57n24

Padwick, C. E., 122n43
Peace, Richard, 12n1, 157n24, 173
Pereiro, Alberto Pérez, 7
Phillips, Cynthia L., 77n40, 120, 121n35
Priest, Robert, 3n4, 15, 16n24, 17–19, 54, 117, 118n22, 132–33, 145

Radford, David, 23, 26, 28, 43–44, 124, 125n49
Rambo, Lewis R., 13–15, 26, 43n9, 66, 67n30, 158n28
Reh, Lawrence A., 26, 43n9
Richardson, James T., 14n18, 154–55, 158n28
Robbins, Joel, 1, 14, 18, 105, 106n9, 158, 168n1
Ross, Russell H., 11n31

Sari, Betti Rosita, 6n14, 6n18, 7n21
Setudeh-Nejad, S., 7
Shubin, Russell G., 20–21, 117–19, 121–23, 125, 152, 169
Skonovd, Norman, 43, 146
Skreslet, Stanley H., 3n4
Smith, Gordon T., 12, 13n11, 14n18, 139, 158n28
Snow, David A., 43, 77n40, 120, 121n35
Sremac, S., 169
Starbuck, Edwin Diller, 13n10
Stark, Rodney, 13n9, 13n12, 13n13, 77n40, 120, 121n35, 146, 169
Stewart, Mary, 14n18, 155, 158n28
Stott, John R. W., 3–4, 19, 116, 139
Streib, Heinz, 13n7, 155
Stromberg, Peter G., 18, 43n9, 132–33
Sullivan, Thomas J., 88n1
Sykes, Peter, 47n13, 70n35

Talman, Harley, 5
Tippett, Alan Richard, 14, 106n10, 154
Trankell, Ing-Britt, 6n14, 6n16, 57n24

Van Klinken, Adriaan S. 14n17, 158n27
Volpe, Marie, 33n28

Walls, Andrew F., 12, 49–50, 157n24
Wells, David F., 19
Woodberry, J. Dudley, x, 1n2, 2n3, 13n13, 20–21, 117–19, 121–23, 125, 152, 169

Interviewee Index

(including people they refer to)

Abdul, 42, 59, 153
Aisah, 45, 58, 140–41
Ali, 73, 96, 104, 135, 150, 152, 155
Alex, 70, 93
Aminah, 45, 83, 90, 153, 161, 163
Amir, 56, 58, 73, 76–77, 94, 97–99, 119, 122, 126, 136, 147, 157

Bill, 40
Borey, 38, 85, 90, 94, 112–14, 123, 126, 138, 151, 155

Chenda, 37, 55, 57, 74, 95–97, 131–34

Fatimah, 45, 75, 96–97, 151

Hamat, 38, 41, 58–59, 76, 114, 138, 143
Hassad, 39, 55, 73

Ibrahim, 51–52, 77, 89, 103, 125–26, 130
Imran, 37, 41, 48, 58, 64–65, 134–35, 142, 150
Isak, 37–38, 42, 45–46, 56, 59, 61, 64, 75, 80–82, 86, 92, 130, 140–42, 144, 150–51, 157–59

Kari, 38, 46, 57, 160
Kevin, 42, 46–47, 60
Kosal, 56, 75, 82, 91–92, 125, 151, 157

Malik, 41–42, 58, 60, 95
Maria, 74, 109–11, 134, 137, 139, 155
Mary, 37, 134

Matt, 91, 151, 153
Minat, 47, 56, 96, 100, 107–8, 142, 161–62

Nabeel, 55, 73, 96, 135
Najee, 42, 47, 143
Narin, 38, 46–47, 51, 60, 100, 106–7, 121, 130, 143–44, 146
Nida, 40, 57–58, 94, 132, 134, 142

Omar, 37–38, 46, 76, 96, 114, 131–34, 138

Pes, 40, 45, 52, 73, 156

Rady, 29n18, 99, 136
Rahman, 40, 81, 83, 103, 107
Razaa, 42, 44, 82–83, 108, 111–12, 114, 123, 147
Rony, 52–53, 89, 91, 94, 140

Sagy, 40, 53, 80, 91, 157
Sara, 48, 75–76, 80, 84–85, 103, 114, 120, 131, 133–34, 138, 142, 158, 163
Shaza, 42, 73, 106, 143–44, 161, 163–64
Sofia, 41, 55, 58, 77–78, 96, 100–101, 129–30, 155, 161–62
Sok, 83, 95, 136–37
Srey Mum, 38, 84, 89, 92, 105–6, 121, 126, 143, 160
Steven, 36–42, 45–46, 59, 62–64, 75, 81, 86, 103, 141, 144, 149–50
Sukry, 59, 65, 80, 129, 160–61

INTERVIEWEE INDEX

Suliman, 81, 83, 103–4, 149

Tahira, 39, 46, 48, 51, 90, 95, 152
Tewi, 47–48, 55, 94–95, 108–9, 142, 149, 153
Timothy, 37, 41, 58
Tinak, 71–72

Yasmin, 39, 75, 78, 101–2, 110, 119, 147
Yusuf, 100